1995

TEXTUAL CRITICISM

AND

MIDDLE ENGLISH TEXTS

TEXTUAL CRITICISM AND MIDDLE ENGLISH TEXTS

Tim William Machan

UNIVERSITY PRESS OF VIRGINIA

Charlottesville and London

THE UNIVERSITY PRESS OF VIRGINIA
Copyright © 1994 by the Rector and Visitors
of the University of Virginia
First Published 1994

Library of Congress Cataloging-in-Publication Data

Machan, Tim William.
Textual criticism and Middle English texts / Tim William Machan.
p. cm.
Includes bibliographical references and index.
ISBN 0–8139–1508–2
1. English literature—Middle English, 1100–1500—Criticism, Textual.
2. Manuscripts, English (Middle)—Editing.   I. Title.
PR275.T45M3   1994
820.9'001—dc20   94–5441
CIP

Printed in the United States of America

Publication of this book has been supported by a grant
from the National Endowment for the Humanities,
an independent federal agency

In memory of my father
William John Machan

CONTENTS

ACKNOWLEDGMENTS

Most of this book was written while I held a Fellowship for University Teachers from the National Endowment for the Humanities, to which at the outset I therefore want to express my gratitude. I also want to thank the Marquette University Committee on Research for two Summer Faculty Fellowships that facilitated preliminary research as well as the American Council of Learned Societies and the British Academy for travel grants that enabled me to present portions of my argument as conference papers.

I am glad, too, to mention several of the individuals who helped me in one way or another. Ralph Hanna III, Bradley T. Hughes, and A. J. Minnis all encouraged and supported this project, while Milton J. Bates and A. S. G. Edwards did not only this but read and improved the typescript in several ways. I am especially grateful to D. C. Greetham and Derek Pearsall for reading the entire manuscript and offering criticisms and comments that strengthened the book enormously. Russell J. Reising has been patient friend and perspicuous critic, bestowing personal support, reading every word of this book in draft, challenging and refining my thinking, and urging me to see that my arguments could benefit from the occasional hockey game. Patricia Batchelor was my always reliable and sometimes prescient research student whose assistance was invaluable in bringing the manuscript to completion. Edwin Block, Edward Duffy, Richard Taylor, and Holly Wilson saved me from both infelicities and inaccuracies in translations of foreign-language material, which, unless the notes suggest otherwise, are my own. At the University Press of Viriginia, Cathie Brettschneider has been an editor both personably good-humored and professionally efficient. None of these individuals are responsible for the book as it eventually turned out, and some may in fact disagree with some of my conclusions. But I am deeply grateful for all the help I received, for without it, as much as without the financial support of the N.E.H., I never could have finished what I began now nearly a decade ago.

More personally I want to thank my wife and my two small sons, who never wavered in their love and belief in me during a difficult project that ultimately became the burden of us all and who enabled me to see the world of people as well as the world of ideas. Such unquestioning and unqualified affection is rare, and while it is possible to write books without it, I do not think I would care to do so.

Some passages in this book have previously been published in articles. I would like to thank Boydell and Brewer for permission to include in chapter 2 material that originally appeared as part of "Middle English Text Production and Modern Textual Criticism" in *Crux and Controversy in Middle English Textual Criticism,* ed. A. J. Minnis and Charlotte Brewer (1992), pp. 1–18, and to include in chapter 4 parts of "Chaucer as Translator" from *The Medieval Translator: The Theory and Practice of Translation in the Middle Ages,* ed. Roger Ellis (1989), pp. 55–67. Portions of chapter 4 also appeared in "Textual Authority and the Works of Hoccleve, Lydgate, and Henryson," *Viator* 23 (1992): 281–99, and in "Robert Henryson and Father Aesop: Authority in the *Moral Fables,*" *Studies in the Age of Chaucer* 12 (1990): 193–214; I am happy to thank the publishers of these journals as well. Chapter 3 draws on "Kynaston's *Troilus,* Textual Criticism, and the Renaissance Reading of Chaucer," in *Exemplaria* 5.1 (1993): 161–183, copyright, Center for Medieval and Early Renaissance Studies, SUNY Binghamton. Finally, a few paragraphs of chapter 5 originally were printed in "Editing, Orality, and Late Middle English Texts," ed. A. N. Doane and Carol Braun Pasternack (1991), pp. 229–45, and I am grateful to the University of Wisconsin Press for permission to include this material.

The photograph on the jacket is from Aberystwyth, N.L.W. MS Hengwrt 154 f. 165, reproduced with the permission of the National Library of Wales.

Finally, I want to note here that line and page number references for Middle English works are keyed to the editions listed in the first part of the bibliography. I have followed the texts of these editions in all regards save abbreviations, which I have typically expanded, and diacritics, which I have sometimes eliminated for the convenience of the reader. When I have cited the critical apparatus of these editions, I also list them under their editors' names in the second part of the bibliography.

Yet the Here and Now, which brings both joy and terror, comes but rarely—does not come even when we call it. That's the way it is: life includes a lot of empty space. We are one-tenth living tissue, nine-tenths water; life is one-tenth Here and Now, nine-tenths a history lesson. For most of the time the Here and Now is neither now nor here.

—*Graham Swift*

Introduction

T HIS BOOK EMERGES from certain problems I confronted when editing the Old Norse poem *Vafþrúðnismál* and Latin, Old French, and Middle English versions of the *Consolation of Philosophy*. Initially, the problems seemed to be of a practical sort, such as which are the relevant authorities? how should the base manuscript be determined? how should it be edited? Should the edited text of *Vafþrúðnismál*, for instance, be printed straight across the page, as it appears in the Codex Regius, the manuscript that contains the oldest and most complete text of the poem? Or should it be divided into lines with caesuras, as has been general practice for over one hundred years in Old Norse and Old English studies? Or, to take a different kind of problem: In what ways can Chaucer's Latin and Old French sources be used to reconstruct the text of the *Boece* as he wrote it? Should the assumption that Chaucer typically translated correctly (or, for that matter, incorrectly) be implicit in editorial procedure? To what extent can the source texts be reconstructed on the basis of the *Boece*?

In attempting to answer such questions I discovered two complicating factors. First, these problems could not be solved in the ways other, apparently related problems can be. If I cannot read or date a manuscript hand, for example, I can consult paleographic manuals like Thompson's or Parkes's; and if I do not recognize or understand a configuration of graphs, I can refer to the *OED* or the *MED*. But there are few such reference works for editing medieval vernacular texts. There are practical manuals, such as Havet's, for scribal practice in Antique works; there is extensive theorizing, such as Greg's or McGann's, about Renaissance and modern works; and there are some studies, such as Gaskell's, Williams and Abbott's, and Greetham's, of general bibliographic principles. But for the Middle English period in particular, the period upon which this study concentrates, the secondary criticism in the mid-1980s seemed slim indeed, as it continues to be today: the extensive work of Kane, who has always insisted that he meant only to speak about *Piers Plowman* and not to offer a general editorial theory; the simplistic discussion of Moorman, which seemed completely inapplicable to the texts I was working on; and a handful of more general studies, by Pearsall, Greetham, Hudson, and Patterson, for example. A work like Foulet and Speer's *On Editing Old French Texts* was of some help to the extent that it conceived medieval *vernacular* compositions as distinctive textual phenomena. But while *On Editing* provides useful discussions of the history of editing and of scribal practice, it does not explore the topics that increasingly seemed to me to be of primary importance, and its focus, of course, excludes Middle English.

The second complicating factor in an attempt to answer the questions I raised above is that the problems are not, in fact, practical: They are theoretical. The apparently simple decision of how to lay out the text of *Vafþrúðnismál,* I have come to believe, is constructed by a host of interpretive perspectives on the significances and consequences of the audience of the edition, of the way the original poem was received, of the way modern readers interpret, of the character of historicity and its relevance to editing and interpretation, and of the purpose of any edition. And implicit in any attitude toward the relation between a translation and its sources are decisions about the character of a work, of literary authority, and of literary history.

Another motivation behind this study was my belief that the validity of the hermeneutic labels scholars use to classify and analyze literary phenomena depends on the explanatory breadth of the labels. Terms like *Renaissance, Restoration,* or *Victorian* are useful to the extent that they describe distinctive modes of literary production, transmission, and reception. *Middle English,* accordingly, traditionally designates the various and cumulative manifestations of the English language from about the year 1100 to about the year 1500. Linguistically, the term refers to a chronological period in the history of English, not when the language was structurally uniform and static, but when grammatical flux was such that varieties of the language were for the most part mutually intelligible; on the other hand, the structure of the language before and after this period would have prevented verbal communication between a fourteenth-century speaker, for example, and one from the ninth or seventeenth century. *Middle English* also, then, designates the literature written in the language during this period—a multitude of lyrics, romances, treatises, plays, chronicles, sermons, translations, and saints' lives. Both these references are unremarkable, but a third, perhaps less frequently acknowledged application also needs to be mentioned: *Middle English,* like any other hermeneutic label, should refer to *how* the language was used during this period, for it is not enough to recognize only that specific linguistic forms were utilized in specific works during a specific period. If a term like *Middle English* is to have broad cultural applicability, it should also account for which speakers were using which forms of the language in which social contexts and for which culturally conditioned reasons. The chronological limits of the Middle English period, significantly, depend as much on social and political events—such as the Norman Conquest and the expansion of the English outside of England—as on oral or written phenomena. To say that a text is in Middle English, therefore, is to impute to it not only a range of linguistic and literary forms but also a range of sociolinguistic contexts in which it meant, as well as a variety of cultural practices that it mediated. If these forms, contexts, and practices do not distinguish the works written between 1100 and 1500 from those written before or after this period, then the hermeneutic usefulness of a literary and cultural label like *Middle English* seems problematic.

Medieval works can certainly be edited without the editor formally addressing any of these issues; indeed, for the most part they have been so edited for many years. And edited texts of medieval works can be read without the critic being cognizant either of the editor's positions on these issues or of the material and interpretive consequences of these positions. But neither the editor's lack of discussion of such issues nor the critic's lack of interest in them alters their significance.

Briefly stated, this book explores the issues I have just sketched out and their relevance to editing and interpretation: It is an attempt to articulate the textual and cultural factors that characterize Middle English works as Middle English and to indicate the ways in which these factors are relevant to the textual criticism, editing, and concomitant interpretation of these works. This book is not, I want to stress, a manual of practical editorial problems and their solutions for medieval texts; nor should it be thought that implicit throughout this study lurks my belief about the correct or best way to approach medieval documents. Indeed, one of the clearest implications of this book is that the answer to the question How should this work be edited? is itself a question: For whom and for what purposes? This study is not, then, a solution to the editorial problems that initially motivated me; it is, rather, a consideration of the theoretical and practical issues relevant to any answer to any such problem. By no means do I wish, however, to be disingenuous about my emphasis, which is clearly historical. But this emphasis is less ideological or theoretical than simply inherent in the character of the material in which I am interested: the historical constitutions of Middle English works and the modern editing of them, an activity that is historicized both by its retrospective orientation and through its determination by past and contemporary cultural forces.

A historical inquiry like this must confront the fact that absolute historical phenomena, whether broadly cultural or narrowly textual, are very problematic epistemologically; and even if they were not, they would not be recoverable by modern methods. As I suggest in chapter 3, historical inquiry always proceeds as a negotiation between past historicized phenomena and modern historicized investigations. Yet while such negotiation may now be recognized as inescapable, I think it is also inescapable that a present of any chronological period, including the one we now inhabit, is in part constructed from that present's functionally stabilized conception of its past. For the absolute past on which the present of Victorian England was predicated, this kind of conception is clear enough. But it is equally clear that, though a poststructuralist age theorizes the past as contingent, it conducts all manner of practical affairs—from government, to education, to the writing of history or even literary theory—within a paradigm that situates, however temporarily, *a* past that serves, for all intents and purposes, as *the* past. That is, for such affairs to be conducted, negotiation must inevitably become practical rather than theoretical. Hence, I have no illusions about the preeminence or absolute accuracy of the past I reconstruct in this book: It is in every way contingent on a present of the late twentieth century. But, equally, I feel no compulsion to reiterate this fact throughout the book, since in seeing my reconstruction, with all its variations and inconsistencies, as *the* past for *this* present, I am proceeding as all historians must.

The works with which I am chiefly concerned are those written in English during the end of the period conventionally known as Middle English, between about 1300 and 1500. Chronological periods like this, of course, are always more convenient than absolute, since many of the literary, sociological, or cultural phenomena that typically define a period gradually come into being across a number of years. I occasionally draw, therefore, on works produced outside this time frame and also, since my approach is contextual, on works composed in other, contemporaneous languages. Moreover, the restriction of my study to the years 1300 to 1500 is not meant to imply that the issues in which I am interested were not relevant and productive in the shaping of works composed before or after this period; indeed, much of what I say about late Middle English literature could be extended, I believe, to works composed in the years 1100 to 1300. For the most part I restrict my concerns and judgments to the later period because the proliferation of individual Middle English works and the survival of multiple copies provide the better opportunity for defining and supporting hypotheses: Some—but not all—of the issues I raise are moot for early Middle English works because so many of them survive in only one copy.

Most of my discussion focuses on works generally designated belles lettres, though given my views on the hermeneutic significance of Middle English, this discussion is contextually rooted in linguistic, social, and cultural considerations. Even as I invoke belles lettres, moreover, I am aware that this category is scarcely clear-cut. In fact, for a variety of theoretical and practical reasons, its ambiguity is particularly apparent in the medieval period, when genres like biblical paraphrases and historical chronicles displayed the cultivated rhetorical strategies and effects modern readers typically associate with fiction, and when poetry, not prose, was a common medium for technical and scientific works. Works like saints' lives and the Wycliffite sermons, thus, seem to be generically excluded from modern conceptions of belletristic writing, even though in medieval terms such works have as a primary purpose the cultivation of literary effects. Yet belletristic works have been distinguished in practice from civil or ecclesiastical proclamations, for instance, since they are the ones that have been of greatest interest to most scholars of Middle English literature, the ones that have received the most editorial attention, and the ones that therefore can be said to constitute a tradition of sorts. In concentrating on such works, I am thus both providing examples that are likely to have the greatest critical and pedagogical familiarity and also responding to the clearest editorial tradition in Middle English studies. To extend my discussion to scientific works, philosophical treatises, and the like would result in a book that was vastly longer but not, I suspect, much different in its conclusions. As I have already proposed and as will be apparent in chapters 4 and 5, the cultural contexts of late Middle English writing may well subvert any medieval distinction between belletristic and nonbelletristic literature, though only another long study could affirm or disprove this proposition.

In order to avoid terminological confusion, I also want here to specify the meanings of certain terms upon which I rely throughout this study: *work, version, text,* and *document.* These terms have wide currency in both textual and interpretive studies, though in both disciplines their meanings and consequences are often highly contested. Since traditional textual criticism is the point from which my study departs, I use these terms in their most accepted bibliographical senses, which Peter L. Shillingsburg has clarified so well. These same senses, however, central as they are to textual criticism, are largely inherited from humanism and are therefore, I will argue, unresponsive to the characteristics of late Middle English writing. Indeed, my arguments result ultimately in a new set of textual-critical definitions for late-medieval vernacular literature. Rhetorically and theoretically I am thus in an awkward position: To respond to the instability of these concepts, I need a stable set of these same concepts. The pervasive influence of the textual-critical tradition as it has developed since the Renaissance makes the traditional senses the most logical choice. For similar reasons, I concentrate here far more on linguistic codes than on bibliographical ones. Even though the latter are distinctive and varied in the late Middle English period, my attention is particularly directed to the former because they have loomed largest in the tradition of textual criticism.

Shillingsburg defines a *work* as "the message or experience implied by the authoritative versions of a literary writing."[1] For editors and readers, a work "is represented more or less well and more or less completely by various physical forms, such as manuscripts, proofs, and books," but the work itself has neither "substantial existence" nor "one fixed form."[2] Conceived thus, the work is in effect the correct text, rather than any extratextual features or frameworks, that the textual critic attempts to recover. The meaning of "correct" is of course the crux of much current scholarly discussion, but for most critics the textual-critical work is determined by a historical creator or creators, and for all critics a work may be described by any of the conventional genres, such as lyric, sermon, or dream vision. There are thus fundamental differences between a textual-critical sense of the literary work and those of contemporary interpretive criticism, which variously regards the work as process, or cultural artifact, or mutual construction of writer and reader, or infinitely deferred ideal. It is necessary to keep these differences in mind at the outset, for in chapter 5 it will become apparent that Middle English notions of literary production overlap not with their modern counterparts but with contemporary views on interpretation.

A *version* "is one specific form of a work—the one the author intended at some particular point in time."[3] Like a work, a version has no substantial existence, and in fact the distinction between work and version is often a complicated one predicated on a variety of aesthetic and temporal criteria. Poems like Wordsworth's *Prelude* or Whitman's *Leaves of Grass* would generally be considered to survive in multiple versions, though the changes Henry James effected in some of his novels might well qualify the revisions as new works.

A *text,* in a bibliographic sense, is simply "the actual order of words and punctuation as contained in any one physical form, such as manuscript, proof, or book."[4] Like a work or version, a text is the product of an individual's (or individuals') creative efforts and is not equatable with a specific, substantial existence: The same text—the same sequence of words and punctuation—may appear in a variety of formats. Text is never here used as a synonym for "poem," or "sermon," or "work," though such usages are in fact widespread in literary criticism.

A *document* "consists of the physical material, paper and ink, bearing the configuration of signs that represent a text. Documents have material existence. Each new copy of a text, whether accurate or inaccurate, is a new document."[5]

Finally, I want to say something about the organization of this book.

The first three chapters are broadly historical and theoretical: They discuss the history and character of textual criticism in general, the status and development of Middle English textual criticism within this framework, and alternative ways of approaching textual criticism. Chapters 4 and 5 expand my idea of the discourse of late Middle English manuscripts by exploring and defining Middle English versions of the concepts author, work, and text. In these chapters I draw on an intentionally wide rage of primary materials from the fourteenth and fifteenth centuries. I make no claim to have been exhaustive, though I do intend my examples to be representative of the significant diversity of views and practices in the period. The concluding chapter draws together the implications of the previous five chapters in order to suggest the practical ramifications of a textual criticism specifically suited to the historical characteristics of Middle English literature.

This book, then, is a hybrid, talking primarily about Middle English literature—though from an unfamiliar perspective—but also saying much about interpretation and textual criticism in general. My most general intention is not to prescribe a hermeneutic framework or specific interpretations but to encourage among both textual and literary critics greater self-consciousness about the kinds and consequences of the decisions they make when approaching Middle English documents. To this end, the hybrid character of the book is inescapable: To isolate Middle English from the larger textual-critical tradition that has received and transmitted it obscures both the particularities of Middle English and the problematic assumptions of the tradition.

❦

CHAPTER ONE

Humanism and
Textual Criticism

T ODAY IT IS the edited text rather than the medieval manuscript
upon which most students and scholars typically base their understanding of medieval literature. In fact, the edited text has become such a
norm in medieval studies that criticism that draws directly on primary
documents is often regarded as a distinct branch of scholarship independent of the main trends of inquiry; "Manuscripts and Textual Studies,"
for instance, are presented as a classification separate from "Sources,
Analogues, and Literary Relations" in the annual bibliography published in *Studies in the Age of Chaucer*. While such a classification is
eminently useful and entirely understandable, it nonetheless system-
atizes our removal from the Middle Ages. Moreover, our dependence
on edited texts is broadly based, for in delimiting and conditioning
understanding of the artistry and character of individual works, these
texts in turn shape our sense of medieval literature and help to define
the medieval literary canon. Since so much of contemporary historical
understanding rests on literary remains, it can in fact be said without
exaggeration that many of our notions about the Middle Ages itself are
ultimately mediated by edited texts. For these reasons, the theoretical
assumptions that enable the transformation of physically and lexically
distinctive medieval manuscripts into modern printed editions, espe-

cially when unacknowledged, have profound and far-reaching consequences.

These assumptions are so widespread in textual criticism and editing in general that they can be difficult to identify and evaluate: They can seem to constitute a theoretical horizon beyond which criticism simply cannot be applied. One way to glimpse the character and extent of this horizon is through a comparison between a medieval manuscript and its modern edited counterpart. One might compare, for example, a specific modern edition of Chaucer's *Canterbury Tales* with their realizations in medieval manuscripts. At the most general level one would notice that though every copy of the modern edition is essentially the same (at least when they leave the printer), the fifty-odd relatively "complete" manuscripts of Chaucer's poem vary considerably in size, script, layout, and content. Some have tales, links, and lines lacking in others, and some diverge markedly in arrangement of the tales. While each copy of the modern edition, moreover, is limited to just those works judged to be by Chaucer and contains a title page that announces as much, the medieval *Canterbury Tales* may be bound with any number of other works.

More particularly, one might compare two documents—one medieval, one modern—both opened to the same page of arguably the same work, such as the conclusion of Chaucer's *Franklin's Tale* as it appears on f. 165r in Aberystwyth, National Library of Wales MS Hengwrt 154 (Hengwrt) and page 412 in Robert Pratt's students' edition of the *Canterbury Tales*.[1] In Pratt's text there is a small blank space between the explicit of the tale and the incipit of the next one, the *Physician's Tale*. There is no visual clue in the form of an arabic number or a distinctive change in type font to indicate that the almost seamless connection between the tales is in any way editorial. To be sure, the shift in the discreet marginal line-numbering might alert a reader to the implicit editorial decisions, but to the novice reader it would quite likely be only the running head that, if noticed, would draw attention to the fact that here the absence of an unambiguous connection between the *Franklin's Tale* and another tale was one of the indications of the unfinished state of the *Canterbury Tales*. Instead, the presentation of the text, replete with glosses at the margin and the foot of the page, conveys the impression of a finished whole at the same time it offers ways for the reader to surmount the interpretive barriers of the Middle English language.

If the text of the last page of the *Franklin's Tale* in Pratt's edition seems uniform, coherent, and inviting, that in the Hengwrt manuscript, which probably was completed shortly after Chaucer's death in 1400, is in several ways just the opposite. One immediately notices the physical features common to many medieval manuscripts: the absence of punctuation, the variability and potential obscurity of medieval handwriting in comparison with modern typography, and, for this leaf, the absence of a running head. One also notices the indications that this *Franklin's Tale* was very much a temporal phenomenon. A later rubricator and not the main scribe, for instance, added the explicit "Here endeth the ffrankeleyns tale."[2] And the tale is not seamlessly followed by the *Physician's Tale*. Rather, the scribe left approximately the bottom two-thirds of f. 165r blank as well as, initially, the whole next quire. He then copied all of the *Clerk's Tale* before returning to the *Second Nun's Tale* on f. 165v,[3] a procedure that has typically been interpreted as another reflection of the fragmentary condition in which Chaucer left the *Canterbury Tales:* Either the scribe did not initially know what was to follow the *Franklin's Tale* or, for whatever reason, he did not have access to the tale that he believed ought to appear next.[4]

In the space left on f. 165r, on at least four occasions, three different sixteenth-century individuals supplied information about the genealogy of the Banestar family who at that time owned the manuscript. We are told, that is, of the date, day of the week, time of day, year, and regnal year of the births of Richard, Elenor, Frauncis, Ellyzabeth, and Martha Banestar. The last entry appears sideways in the margin and was written so as to accommodate yet another temporal phenomenon—the loss of the corner of the leaf to the gnawing of rats. The author of this entry, who may well have been the mother of the five Banestar children, had also clearly read the other, earlier entries, for to the first she appends the comment "having one tothe at his byrth."

In the Hengwrt manuscript, then, the conclusion of the *Franklin's Tale* reflects both the unfinished character of the *Canterbury Tales* and the fact that the manuscript (and the tales themselves) was produced and existed in several discrete moments of time; the various hands and the gnawing of the rats force the reader to confront the contextuality of this *Franklin's Tale*. In the same vein, the genealogy juxtaposed with the Franklin's *demande d'amour* ("Which was the most fre, thynketh yow?") appears as a gently ironic comment on the relationship between love and life in the real world and in the Franklin's rarefied Armorik. Whether the irony is intentional or dramatic—whether the writers recognized the genealogy as in part a response to the tale—its existence depends on the reader's awareness that this text was produced diachronically. The physical character of the leaf thus emblematizes the reader's figurative distance from the tale Chaucer originally wrote and the consequent barriers this distance poses for interpretation. Pratt's *Franklin's Tale,* on the other hand, projects itself as the product of coherent, completed artistic creation; it renders a *Canterbury Tales* that appears as the construction of a single production moment, that, at least so far as copyright dictates, will retain that construction through time, and that overtly invites interpretive responses.

In enumerating these features, I am not implying that one text contains the authentic Chaucer and the other does not. Nor am I merely suggesting how radically different the documents are from one another. Rather, my interest is in the editorial assumptions that enable the transformation of one document and text combination into the other. To account for the physical and textual differences between the Hengwrt manuscript and Pratt's edition, one needs to recognize that an edition like Pratt's assumes that the ontology of the *Canterbury Tales* is lexical and idealist—lexical in the sense that words are privileged over their material manifestation and idealist in the sense that the essential intended work has priority over a text that might have appeared at a specific moment in a specific document. In turn, either this lexical and idealist ontology is presumed to be preeminent and identical for both medieval and modern writers and readers or, if differences are recognized, this ontology nonetheless governs conception of the work and its appearance in a modern edition. The physical presentation of the text in Pratt's edition, furthermore, assumes that the juxtaposition of the Middle English and the interpretive aids is unambiguous and unproblematic: The Middle English in the modern edition is intended to be understood as a realization of the actual work, conceptually and interpretively unaffected by the apparatus surrounding it. Chronologically, Pratt's edition assumes that the work manifested in manuscripts such as Hengwrt was terminated (if not completed) at the moment Chaucer died, that material added ten or a hundred years after his death is not part of the work itself. Concomitantly, there is in the modern edition the assumptions that a single individual—Chaucer—created and determined the work known as the *Canterbury Tales* and that manuscripts like Hengwrt are attempts, with greater or lesser degrees of success, to represent the words Chaucer intended. For this reason, the Banestar genealogy is presumed to be not part of the *Canterbury Tales*. Finally, Pratt's edition assumes, through its reproduction in multiple copies, that the material manifestation of the idealist and lexical work known as the *Canterbury Tales* is to be lexically and physically identical for all modern readers.

None of these assumptions, to be sure, are surprising in modern editions. It has typically been the modern editor's task to construct a printed and therefore stable, infinitely replicable text that is characteristically conducive to interpretation for an audience that accepts all of these qualities as the givens of an edited text. But with a very few exceptions—of which the *Canterbury Tales* was not one—the situation is precisely the opposite for vernacular works as they were produced and existed in the Middle Ages: Over time manuscript copies proliferated diversely, and individual copies underwent alteration without the stabilizing and provident influence of a modern editor. Thus, if the fact that two copies of Pratt's edition are lexically and physically identical is a function of the process through which books appear in the modern period, the fact that the Hengwrt and Ellesmere manuscripts are divergent in these ways is equally a function of the medieval process of production. These qualities—duplication or divergence—characterize the ways medieval and modern documents of a given work exist, and it would be as anachronistic and disorienting to find two identical Middle English manuscripts as it would be to see two divergent copies of Pratt's edition.

This example offers only a glimpse at the theoretical horizon that has come to define textual criticism and editing. It does not reveal how and why medieval documents and texts should be rendered in modern editions in this way, why some features are imitated, others transformed, and still others ignored. Since one of my objectives is to articulate those aspects of Middle English works that are not well respresented in modern editions, I shall explore these issues in further detail. The first three chapters of this book, thus, characterize the theoretical framework that has come to define textual criticism, demonstrate the place of Middle English in this framework, and suggest certain inadequacies in this framework and offer alternatives to them. Paradoxically, I will not begin my study of Middle English works with Middle English. This is so because the resolutions of the physical, chronological, and conceptual issues that underlie Pratt's edition in fact emerge from principles of authority, work, and text that are central to textual criticism in general and that inform editions of works from all historical periods. The editing of Middle English works is, in short, an accommodation to a larger editorial tradition that is itself the product of a variety of historical and ideological forces.

For the beginning of textual criticism one might well point to the time of the Alexandrian librarians Zenodotus and Aristophanes, who divided the Homeric poems into books and composed scholia for them. Indeed, throughout the Antique and low and high Middle Ages a variety of scholars prepared the collations, corrections, and commentaries that still in part define textual criticism. In the ninth century Lupus of Ferrières, for example, carefully corrected his copy of Cicero's *De oratore* and supplied its margins with variant readings.[5] But in later humanist scholarship several factors coalesced to give the Renaissance the label birthplace of textual criticism. While this designation may seem commonplace, the full implications of this origin for textual criticism have perhaps not been appreciated: Specifically humanist positions on textual criticism were safeguarded in such a way that even late in the twentieth century they remain synonymous with textual criticism itself.

One indication of the immanence of textual criticism in the humanist project is the fact that anything resembling modern textual criticism would have been impossible without a number of cultural factors that first emerged forcefully in the Renaissance. It was the humanists' appreciation of the Antique world, their now almost clichéd valorization of the self, and their self-proclaimed refined sense of historicity (which they denied to their predecessors in the Middle Ages) that motivated and enabled recognition of an original form of a text as the product of an individual and as distinct from subsequent developments of that text—as, in fact, the *correct* form of the text. Another significant factor in the humanist construction of textual criticism was the Renaissance view of language, which tended to be far more empirical than the speculative and philosophical medieval linguistics of the *modistae*. "Meaning," John D'Amico notes, "was connected to and dependent upon the integrity of the word, and the wrong word led to falsehood. In order properly to understand a text, one had to discover the actual words of the author; this usually meant extracting them from the corrupt manuscripts."[6] Indeed, the entire humanist project was language-centered, involving both mastery of Greek and Latin and, ultimately, codification of the vernaculars. The humanist emphasis on language as "the door to reality" thus rendered imperative the correct reproduction of the words of a text.[7]

In the early modern period, a similar need arose from the essentially ethical orientation of textual criticism, which served both theological and secular agendas. In R. J. Schoeck's characterization of Erasmus's thinking, for example, language is "the source of good order, civility, and understanding in human culture and society"; on the other hand, through "misuse of language, and all that this implies, have come lying, violence, and the destruction of civil order."[8] At stake in the recovery of an author's language, therefore, was not only the morality of the individual but also the preservation of society. In this vein the Reformation was especially conducive to textual criticism through its emphases on reliance upon the *word* of God, on the determination of authentic Christian teachings, on the production of sermons and treatises that validated Protestantism, on the need for individuals to take personal responsibility for their understanding of church history and instruction, and on the extension of the need for accurate texts into the vernaculars. The Bible in particular was a catalyst in the development of textual criticism, since one of the major points of contention between Catholicism and Protestantism was how to distinguish authentic writings from apocryphal ones; and biblical textual criticism, in turn, has proved central to the development of textual criticism in general.[9] On a secular level textual criticism enabled the recovery of those literary works and the values they illustrated to which the Renaissance regarded itself reborn. The "position of classical philology" in the Revival of Learning, Edward J. Kenney observes, "was originally and essentially ancillary; ancient authors were to be rescued and brought back into the effective service of humane studies."[10]

Yet another cultural factor that facilitated the Renaissance development of textual criticism was the advent of print, which both provided technology for textual criticism and helped to foster a psychology that required it. In creating the opportunity for collation against a standard text by scholars separated by geography and time, multiple production of essentially identical texts offered the means by which the work of one scholar could be checked and evaluated by another as well as the potential for the preservation of the collations accumulated over time.[11] Psychologically, as exposure to written works came increasingly to depend on physically and lexically identical copies, readers would have come to regard these qualities as inherent in the nature of literary works. Their expectations for written works would in turn have encouraged the processes by which such copies were made.

The textual criticism that resulted from these factors was indelibly informed by them, with the very course of its movement across Europe in fact reflecting the spread of humanism. The work of Italian scholars like Collucio Salutati (1331–1406), Niccolò Niccoli (1367–1437), and Lorenzo Valla (1407–1457) provides a terminus a quo for modern textual criticism. Like the Renaissance movement itself, then, textual criticism only gradually spread northward, next establishing itself in France with the work of Muret and becoming widespread in Germany first with the work of Erasmus and Beatus Rhenanus and in England, perhaps, not until the efforts of Richard Bentley late in the seventeenth century and afterwards. According to D'Amico: "In general, Northern humanists at the beginning of the sixteenth century had not incorporated in their work the Italians' concern for the establishment of accurate texts. In part this was attributable to the dominance of scholasticism in the Northern University system. . . . Logic and metaphysics, not philology, provided scholastics with the means of understanding a text. Thus Northern European pedagogy inhibited a commitment to textual study." [12]

As a humanist construct, textual criticism was not an acontextual praxis but a dialogue with the past and an ideological discourse. From the broadest perspective, textual criticism validated a view of the contemporary period as a rebirth of the cultural achievement of the Antique after a middle period that had lost sight of this achievement. More narrowly, the fact that the forces driving this view were cultural, theological, and philosophical—the fact that the entire humanist project was conceived as a moral undertaking—manifested itself in the moral overtones that characterized as degeneration the developments a text underwent through transmission.[13] The magnitude of what was at issue in textual criticism helps to explain the Renaissance preference, particularly outside of Italy, for *emendatio ope ingenii* or *coniecturae* (emendation by means of intellect) over *emendatio ope codicum* (emendation by means of books). Part of the explanation lies in the fact that understanding of paleography and manuscript transmission was often not sophisticated enough to facilitate determination of the relative authority of manuscripts and readings; manuscripts could be designated *vetus* (old) or *antiquus* (ancient) without qualification, and obscure manuscript hands could be called simply Lombardic.[14] But, more significantly, the critic's primary motivation was not the recovery of an absolute past but the active resurrection of a past that would validate the ideology of the present. Hence, while the "reasons for inconsistent attitudes toward manuscripts were several," in D'Amico's analysis, "perhaps the fundamental one mirrored humanist attitudes toward the past and its recoverability. Renaissance critics were not engaged in a scientific enterprise but in creative (even romantic) archaeology. While manuscripts were artifacts that revealed the past, their corrupt state also concealed it. Editors felt required to make an imaginative leap beyond them in order to extract valid readings."[15] The balance between the moral and the textual could be, of course, variously effected. In the fifteenth century, Domizio Calderni flat-out "invented a Roman writer, Marius Rusticus, from whom he claimed to derive disquieting information about the youth of Suetonius."[16] Similarly, Jacques Lefèvre d'Etaples (c. 1460–1536) gave such high priority to morality that in his edition and translation of St. Paul's epistles "he even altered the text in order to arrive at what he felt was doctrinally more acceptable." Erasmus, conversely, saw textual matters as "prepatory" and "ultimately complementary" to moral ones and therefore rigorously advocated careful and faithful attention to the readings of manuscripts.[17]

The ideological character of early textual criticism is also apparent from the institutions that created and sanctioned it—the system of patronage, the church, and the universities. Joseph Scaliger, for instance, worked under the aegis of a patron, while Erasmus was both an Augustinian canon and a priest; later English critics of the seventeenth century were characteristically in holy orders and often were placed high in the Church of England.[18] And still later a critic like Bentley depended on the university for his livelihood. Not surprisingly, such institutions encouraged the production of works that sustained them, just as scholastic theology both emerged from and sustained the church of the high Middle Ages.[19] This self-validation is clear in the strong regulatory character of much early textual criticism, which interests itself in categorical pronouncements about right and wrong readings and procedures. Similarly ideological is the restriction of this criticism to the traditional learned church commentators or those Antique writers whose tradition the Renaissance imagined itself to inherit. Of necessity the textual origins that early critics uncovered justified the critics and their institutions. If Salutati, for example, recognized that then-modern writers like Dante and Petrarch might be subject to the same sorts of manuscript corruption that the ancients suffered,[20] Beatus Rhenanus, one of the foremost humanist textual critics, is best known for his *Commentariolus* on Tacitus' *Germania,* his *Castigationes* to Tacitus' opera in general, his *Annotationes* to Pliny's *Naturalis historia,* and his similar work on Velleius Paterculus' *Historia Romana.*

There is nothing surprising in the fact that the humanists should have created self-validating institutions, practices, and discourses; surely any culture or social group does the same to the extent that it is able. Nor within the context of humanism is there anything troubling about the basic theoretical principles the humanists developed and the strong moral orientation that characterized their textual criticism. Their principles are in essence the assumptions I noted in my discussion of Pratt's edition of the *Canterbury Tales:* the equation of the authority of a text with an author, an idealist conception of the work, the privileging of the lexical over the nonlexical, and a problematic sense of historicity that both desires the historical construct of a work and disregards the historical context of an edition. What is surprising and what makes the creation of textual criticism by the humanists particularly relevant to Middle English literature is the fact that these principles, which were developed for specifically ideological reasons and applied to specific classical and biblical works, have been adopted consistently since the Renaissance for works and in contexts that shared little with Renaissance humanism and that were, at times, even overtly antithetical to it. In effect, critics have consistently taken the humanists at their word about the character of textual criticism and have not acknowledged the ideological underpinning of their project: They defined not a transcendent textual criticism but one that served various social and institutional needs. This is precisely the response, however, that the humanists invited, inasmuch as they safeguarded their principles through their views of ethics and aesthetics as transcendent truths. As a result, the history of textual criticism is a history remarkably free of fissures and ruptures; it is a history that has consistently silenced the opposition offered by an antithetical tradition like that of Middle English, one in which there have been methodological refinements but few alterations of basic theoretical assumptions. It is this history that accounts for the theoretical horizon of textual criticism—ultimately, how and why Middle English documents and texts are transformed into modern ones. In order to explore the theoretical horizon of textual criticism in more detail, I turn now to each of the basic humanist principles, which, like threads, have tied together the fabric of textual-critical history and determined its broad outlines.

A recent handbook of bibliography and textual studies articulates one of the basic tenets of modern textual criticism when it observes: "The point of textual criticism" is "to present an authoritative text based on a full study of the text's transmission through manuscript and print."[21] More particularly, the authoritative text has typically been equated with an authorial one—the text composed by the original author. Fredson Bowers, one of the most influential textual critics of the twentieth century, accordingly states, "The attempt to determine what the author wrote defines textual criticism."[22] This equation has recently experienced all manner of aesthetic and ideological attacks. Psychoanalytic critics, for example, speak of the creation of self as always textual, irrespective of historical period, while among New Historicists it has become commonplace to situate, often accusatorily, initial interest in an authorial text in the nineteenth century and its privileging of origins in linguistics, criticism, and mythology.[23] Such a view, however, is ultimately an index of the way the humanists safeguarded their textual criticism. Because the motivation behind principles inherited from them has been recuperated differently and because the procedures in which these principles have been manifested have often changed, it can appear that a given principle originated much later than the Renaissance. Interest in the authorial text is in fact not only datable to a specific period several centuries prior to the advent of philology but also is synonymous with the tradition of textual criticism.

Already in his *De fato,* for example, Salutati laments scribal corruptions of intrinsically superior authorial works due to ignorance and arbitrary alterations.[24] Similarly, for Francesco Robortello (1516–1567), in his *De arte sive ratione corrigendi antiquorum libros disputatio* (1557)—

arguably the first handbook in the field [25]—the goal of the "art" of textual criticism was that "old writers should be returned to their earlier splendor and refinement." [26] Accordingly, "if books written by the hand of ancient authors existed, we would labor less." [27] Two centuries later Johann Gotfried Eichhorn assumes throughout his monumental *Einleitung ins Alte Testament* that authors' texts lie behind the biblical writings and that the recovery of the earliest possible form of these texts is both desirable and possible. He devotes several pages to a discussion of mistakes in the autograph, for instance, and elsewhere observes: "In short, all the books of the Old Testament whose authors we know by name are marked with the stamp of the authenticity of their authors. And with the books whose authors are unknown, they always exhibit internal reasons for having to recognize the same as genuine." The writings of the Old Testament, moreover, "have lost much of their original form, through accidents and mistakes of the copyist." Criticism "must therefore discharge its office on them, if they are to be restored again to themselves, if not completely then in part." [28]

In his *Prolegomena ad Homerum,* F. A. Wolf (1759–1824) draws on Eichhorn's work on the Old Testament and so, not surprisingly, also articulates a belief in the preeminence of an author both as the creator of a work and as a reference point for editorial reconstruction.[29] The assumption that a Homeric text once existed was necessary for Wolf's then-revolutionary arguments about the subsequent transmission and alteration of this text: "I am led by the traces of an artistic framework and by other serious considerations to think that Homer was not the creator of all his—so to speak—bodies, but rather that this artistic structure was introduced by later ages." [30] Wolf did not believe that the Homeric poems could be reconstructed past the stage at which the Alexandrians had left them. What Homer had written nonetheless determined the course by which the poems developed and thus enabled exposition of the various stages of the poems' transmissions from author's pen to most recent manuscript—the history of scholarship that interested Wolf the most: "But to make clear the main rules by which the emendation of Homer is governed, it is necessary to investigate with the greatest application the changes in the transmitted text, by examining those sources and currents of them that either flowed forth in the past or are visible even today." [31]

From a perspective that includes Salutati, Robortello, Eichhorn, and

Wolf, the theories behind the nineteenth century's interest in textual origins seem scarcely unprecedented. Moreover, the achievement of Karl Lachmann (1793–1851), the best-known figure in nineteenth-century textual criticism, was in fact less theoretical than practical: the assignment of manuscripts to genetic groups on the basis of shared errors and the arrangement of these groups in a tree structure, the root of which is the lost archetype from which all authorities descend. Even in the realm of practice, few of Lachmann's procedures involving manuscript genealogy were original with him; his great achievement, Sebastian Timpanaro points out, was to synthesize a variety of current ideas, so that the phrase "Lachmannian Method" is "more symbolically than historically exact."[32] Lachmann's understanding of the authority of an author, in any case, was entirely consistent with that of his predecessors. His preface to *De rerum natura* begins, for instance, with a focus on a specific author and an assertion about the transmission of his poem from a single manuscript, the reconstruction of which is Lachmann's goal: "Over a thousand years ago, in a certain part of the kingdom of France, one ancient copy of the Lucretian poem existed, from which others, constituting a memorial record from those times forward, are descended." He goes on to discuss in detail the contents of this manuscript, its transmission, and then the history of the corrections to which it was subjected.[33] Similarly, in his edition of the New Testament, Lachmann observes, "And thus, before everything else, what the most trustful authors might have handed down is to be sought, then what might have come from the hand of a scribe is to be judged, and as a third step what common practice might have written—in which time, by which condition, and with which assistance—is to be explored."[34]

To be sure, Lachmann and other nineteenth-century critics left an indelible stamp on the character of textual criticism, but it was a stamp that confirmed rather than initiated an interest in textual origins and authorial texts. If the latter sometimes seems to be the case, it is in part because of technological improvements that may have made the recovery of an original text a greater possibility than it had been for Wolf or Bentley or Valla.[35] For example, progress in historical paleography led to advances in library cataloging and surer means of dating manuscripts so that certainty over textual transmission might well have seemed possible.[36] These methodological advancements, in turn, render the humanist principles and objectives of textual criticism consonant with procedures in other disciplines and thus enable modern critics to recuperate nineteenth-century textual criticism as a manifestation of cultural projects like "empiricism" or "positivism." In a much-quoted passage in his edition of the New Testament, for instance, Lachmann notes, "We can and must without interpretation demand from the authors what I have positioned in the first place, that which is called recension," [37] and thereby seems to articulate a principle parallel to those informing other disciplines at that time. For example, the German historian Leopold von Ranke inspired, however unintentionally, a school of historical realists dedicated to the objective recovery of the unadulterated past and devoted to his position not to judge the past but to show it "as it actually was." [38] And Darwin, however disingenuously, outlined in the opening words of *The Origin of the Species* a procedure embodying the ideals of the so-called nineteenth-century scientific method:

> When on board H.M.S. *Beagle* as naturalist I was much struck with certain facts in the distribution of the organic beings inhabiting South America, and in the geological relations of the present to the past inhabitants of that continent. . . . On my return home, it occurred to me, in 1837, that something might perhaps be made out on this question by patiently accumulating and reflecting on all sorts of facts which could possibly have any bearing on it. After five years' work I allowed myself to speculate on the subject.[39]

Genetic manuscript classification might also be understood as a reflection of the scientific empiricism of Lachmann's time. In particular, a parallel could be sketched between the Lachmannian method and the use of genealogy and tree diagrams in contemporary comparative linguistics. Just as linguists working before Sir William Jones's pioneering work on Sanskrit attempted to trace all known European languages to another known language—most often Hebrew—rather than to postulate a lost parent language, so textual critics of the seventeenth and eighteenth centuries often strove to derive all extant manuscripts of a work from another extant manuscript. But Lachmann, like Jones, championed the postulation of lost archetypes; the opening pages of his edition of *De rerum natura,* in fact, are devoted to a description of what Lachmann calls the "Archetypon" and include assertions about its size, pagination, layout, and handwriting. And in both disciplines, Timpanaro points out, "the desire for a stronger consideration of 'horizontal tradition' made itself felt at the same time." [40] To be sure, the wish to move down the tree to its root, original text was the fundamental motive in Lachmann's procedure, just as the desire to recover lost original languages like Proto-Germanic or Indo-European was fundamental to the work of the neogrammarians. In both cases, significantly, the tree was actually reversed, so that the root appeared at the top.

Procedures such as those of Ranke or Darwin or the neogrammarians can indeed form striking parallels with those of Lachmannian critics, who are often understood to be patient and nonjudgmental collectors of all the relevant textual facts before they begin the task of classification, which will, if properly exercised, lead inevitably to only one conclusion. But as the typically uncited continuation of Lachmann's observation about recension reveals, Lachmann did in fact grant a substantial place to interpretation as well: "On the other hand, interpretation—unless what the witnesses carry was understood and unless a judgment is made about the writer—cannot be freed from having a place. Again, emendation and determination of the origin of a book, because they extend to knowing the genius of a writer, just so utilize interpretation as a foundation. By which it may be that no part of this task can safely be separated from the others, except that one which ought to be first of all."[41] And if Lachmann's interest in the text that Lucretius himself wrote betrays the humanist origins of his textual-critical positions on authorship, so in fact does his interest in archetypes: The construction of an archetype was Scaliger's great achievement in his edition of Catullus. It also reflects a way of thinking that guided Scaliger's attempt to trace the development of Latin words from Greek ones in his *Coniectanea* on Varro, his reconstruction of an ancient calendar in *De emendatione temporum,* his efforts to define the lost language from which all European languages developed, and his work to demonstrate that the Phoenician alphabet was the origin of all the ancient alphabets.[42] An interest in archetypes might be traced back even earlier, to the days of Poliziano, who demonstrated that certain manuscripts were copies of others and therefore that their agreement in readings did not offer valid additional testimony about the character of the original work. And already in *De vulgari eloquentia* Dante describes the origin of all languages in the archetypal speech of Adam and also the ways by which they diversified and changed over time.

If the equation of authoritative text with author is a thread that ties together the textual criticism of scholars from Salutati through

Eichhorn to Lachmann, it also firmly binds these critics to Joseph Bédier (1864–1938), though this connection, too, has sometimes been lost. Bédier's work is often regarded as a radical break with the Lachmannian tradition, and to the extent that Bédier rejected Lachmann's method it of course is: He championed the editing of a single "best" manuscript, rather than the reconstruction of a hypothetical archetype, because he saw the overwhelming tendency toward bifid stemmata among Lachmannians as a reflection of the willful rather than scientific nature of the method. But his work on textual criticism represents far less of a rupture in the tradition of scholarship than does his work on the fabliau.[43] For the latter, he may indeed reject the primacy of the alleged original Indic tales because, as Hans Aarslef maintains, "the romantic scholarly tradition had folded the psychological and cultural dimensions into the speculative quest for origins, almost as if it was an Adamic pursuit of the ultimate archetype."[44] No such rejection occurs, however, in his textual-critical studies. Because Bédier's positions are not the fissure in editorial history they are commonly assumed to be, I want to characterize them in his own words in some detail.

Though his textual-critical work draws on psychologizing similar to that found in the fabliau study, it is the scientific *reliability* of the Lachmannian method, rather than its overall *goals,* that Bédier found most troubling, and throughout his work on *Lai de L'Ombre* he adheres to received notions of author and authority. He judges, for instance, that the reason that Lachmannian editors almost inevitably ended up with a bipartite stemma was inherent in the method: "This fatal result was imposed on them by the logic of the stated system."[45] Similarly, the reason Bédier doubted the Lachmannian method in the first place was that the occurrence of 105 bifid stemmata in the 110 instances he examined seemed to exceed the laws of scientific probability: "A bifid tree is nothing strange, but a thicket of bifid trees, a grove, a whole forest? *Silva portentosa.*"[46] It is the limitations of this scientific method and the insecurities of human psychology, for Bédier, that in the end prevent the recovery of the authorial text: "These obscure forces, confined within the depths of the subsconcious, have exerted their influence. Impatience at hearing once too often the grinding gears of an overly complicated mechanism, niceties of taste, the necessity of deciding for oneself wherever one finds as many competing readings as families—depending on the particular case, these all come into play either separately or concurrently."[47]

Bédier's landmark articles on the *Chanson de Roland* also reflect a strongly traditional view of authorship and authority in poetic works as well as a scientific distrust of the results of textual scholarship. In his discussion of violations of certain metrical and linguistic rules of Old French, for example, Bédier ironically notes: "It would appear that not all the twelfth-century versifiers surrounded Bartsch's law with the same veneration as our contemporary grammarians, and that consequently the author of the *Chanson de Roland*, he, too, could have occasionally allowed himself to break it." And he observes that it is a desire for "the true reading . . . that which the poet wrote by his own hand" that has exercised all editors of the *Roland*. [48] But the recovery of "the true reading" appears beyond the abilities of textual scholarship, the limitations of which the critic needs to recognize in the construction of a new method: "That in the matter of textual criticism, one should not make it a point of honor to have a response to everything, and that the great secret is, on the contrary, to know how to determine where our ability to know stops. To say these things is not at all—it is far from it—to advocate a lazy method." [49] There are 1,700 places in which the text of *Roland* is in doubt, and each of these 1,700 might have two or three possible solutions; to a large extent, Bédier contends, such irreducible diversity is inevitable in the nature of editing as it has been applied to *Roland*. [50]

Significantly, when Bédier's positions were challenged by Dom Henri Quentin, the critique was conducted on a practical level—through suggestion of an alternative system—and not on the assertion that Bédier's work offered an untenable theoretical reorientation of authority and authorship. Dom Quentin advanced a method that replaced shared error with simply shared reading as a basis for genetic classification: "Having committed himself to the 'common error' postulate, the distinguished critic [Bédier] found himself in such a difficult position that he was moved to reject any classification of manuscripts and to propose an editorial method for an edition which, in less skillful hands, could be very damaging to textual criticism." [51] In his response, Bédier still did not advance a challenge to received notions of authority, for his objection to Dom Quentin's theory is that it is inaccurate as a *scientific method*, and all such methods must be subservient to critical taste: "No conclusion derived from merely numerical calculations should be adduced unless and until the study of the entire text has convinced one that nothing in the domain of psychological, grammatical or literary probability contradicts this conclusion."[52] His way of critiquing the method, in point of fact, is "to examine minutely, piece by piece, the elements of that construction [i.e., the stemma] and the ways in which they are combined" and involves, in the best scientific fashion, duplication of Dom Quentin's analysis.[53] He demonstrates, moreover, that certain readings that would necessarily be rejected as unauthorial by Dom Quentin are in fact of such *aesthetic* quality that they must come from the pen of Jean Renart, the author of *Lai de l'Ombre:* "But it is scarcely conceivable that Jean Renart, at that decisive moment of dialogue between his heroes, could not find for himself the word so easy to find, which is the necessary, the unique word."[54]

Bédier particularly shows his belief that there once existed correct, superior authorial readings in the characteristic sarcasm he uses in demonstrating the authenticity of passages rendered inauthentic by Dom Quentin. For example: "One admires once more the scribe of manuscript z: how well he can divine the intentions of the author and assume for himself his manner!" "This reviser has felt that Jean Renart said these things in an intelligible fashion, to be sure, but an ambiguous one, something only roughed out. He intervenes: four words changed, and the situation is illuminated, and precisely with the light with which, for all appearances, Jean Renart, if he had completed his effort, would have illuminated it."[55] Far from eliminating the equation of authority with authorial text, Bédier in fact suggests that Jean Renart may have twice revised the poem so that the extant manuscripts of *Lai de l'Ombre* might reflect three different authorial versions. Moreover, in his 1913 edition of *Lai de l'Ombre,* after stressing that style constitutes the "individual physiognomy of a writer," Bédier argues for the existence of anagrammic signatures at the end of both the *Roman de l'Escoufle* and the *Roman de Guillaume de Dôle.* Together, the shared style and concealed signatures mark these poems as also from the pen of Jean Renart.[56]

The thrust of Bédier's textual-critical arguments, in other words, is not that there never was an original, authorial text, nor that if a reliable method could be found by which this text might be isolated it would not be the only editorial choice, but that the state of scholarship—or at least the scholarship of Lachmann and Dom Quentin—did not enable such a recovery. While it is true that an editor following Bédier's method would essentially attempt to be more faithful to the scribe than to the author, this would be so because that particular scribe would be presumed to offer the closest approximation to what the author had actually written.[57] Thus, Aarslef is surely right to say that, to Bédier, "the trusted tradition of technical scholarship had greatly overestimated its powers to reach ultimate origins by divining the true essence that existed in the beginning."[58] But for textual criticism it did not follow that the "true essence" never existed or that it was not inherently the more authoritative and valuable. The best-text method was simply that—a method intended to do the *best* one could, given the circumstances, to represent the original text. As he says of *Roland:*

> It struck me . . . that the Oxford manuscript is our only real and tangible asset; that in attempting to recover the language of the archetype manuscript, one left oneself open to lumping together features of French spoken by Louis the Fat with the those of that spoken by Hugh Capet; that, moreover, it's not sufficient to be able to ascertain two or three or ten of the features constituting our poet's usage, because such usage is not made up of two or three or even ten features, but of hundreds of them, and every last one needs to be integrated into a picture of the poet's language as a whole—something which is impossible in this case; in short that [the quest for the archetype] only succeeds in making the author of the *Chanson de Roland* speak the language of a grammarian—a very refined language to be sure, but exactly as such, a troubling language, one too refined to have ever been anywhere spoken.[59]

The equation of the authoritative text with the authorial one is but one of the threads that tie much textual criticism today to its origins in humanist ideology. Another characteristic feature that reflects the context of humanism—specifically, the humanist emphasis on language in conjunction (eventually) with the availability of mass reproduction of texts by means of the printing press—is an idealist conception of a work as primarily lexical. Robortello, for example, locates the essence of a "thing" in the "words" that describe it: "Those who emend old books perform a great utility for men: since, indeed, things are signified by words, it is of necessity that you often do not know the thing if the words are corrupted."[60] The equation of a work with its language is also apparent in the striking metaphor Salutati uses while lamenting the inaccuracy of even manuscripts of Petrarch and Boccaccio. Here, the fact that a work can "speak" inaccurately renders it potentially far more egregious than inaccurate mute objects: "Indeed, these copies [i.e., certain manuscripts] are traces and images of exemplars; in truth, what we have for copies depart to such an extent from the exemplars that they diverge more from them than statues customarily diverge from the men of whom they are likenesses. These, indeed, although they might have mouths, say nothing; in truth those—which is worse—often say things contradictory to their exemplars."[61] The critic's primary task, accordingly, is to enable the text to speak once more as its author intended it to. In the view of the sixteenth-century Florentine Pier Veltori, critics should study scribal habits and the spellings of the oldest manuscripts in order to determine the causes of error, and they should also master the whole of Latin vocabulary to enable themselves to recognize traces of unusual words. Anthony Grafton explains: "The critic who fulfilled all these requirements could restore a text to its original state, so that its author spoke again in 'the dialect which was used in [his] time . . . and not in one adjusted to the rules and custom of later men.'"[62]

In order to construct their interpretation of a text's genre, grammar, or usage, early textual critics typically assembled a variety of usage evidence; the arguments of Scaliger in particular offer daunting lists of corroborating passages from Greek and Roman writers. One of Valla's reasons for rejecting the authenticity of the *Donation of Constantine,* for instance, was the fact that its conclusion—"Given at Rome on the third of the kalends of April"—was generically inappropriate: "Nor will I here pass over the fact that 'given' is usually written on letters, but not on other documents, except among ignorant people."[63] The inauthenticity of the treatise is also indicated by inappropriate usages, such as the word *satrap* for high offices, which did not gain currency until several centuries after the *Donation* had allegedly been written: "What! How do you want to have satraps come in here? Numskull, blockhead! Do the Caesars speak thus; are Roman decrees usually drafted thus? Whoever heard of satraps being mentioned in the councils of the Romans?"[64] As Salutati had suggested, it is the very fact that the work speaks that reveals it to be false and therefore wicked: "For the present, however, let us talk to this sycophant [i.e., the forger] about barbarisms of speech; for by the stupidity of his language his monstrous impudence is made clear, and his lie."[65] The methodological achievements of the fifteenth and sixteenth centuries are also, significantly, primarily concerned with the lexical aspect of a work. Robortello, for example, takes into consideration the origin and date of the manuscripts he considers, cites typical Latin transliteration procedures for Greek as evidence for correct spellings, and itemizes eight types of conjecture; and Beatus Rhenanus bases emendations on paleographic confusion and incorrect word division. These are the same techniques, of course, that are used today.

The humanists' priority on language is also apparent, in a slightly different vein, in Erasmus's defense of his use of *inducit* for a passage in the first verse of Hebrews where St. Jerome had used *introducit*. He grants that the Greek noun corresponding to the verb in question can refer to "introductions. True enough, but erroneously in Latin; by others they are called institutions. For the fact that you understand in the same way what translates different places of Scripture neither troubles me nor supports its own cause."[66] The premium placed on correct language extended to the most pedantic points, such as Erasmus's distinction between *fuisse* and *esset,* or Valla's observation on the accentual differences between the active subjunctive of a verb and its passive indicative.[67] The idealist sensitivity to the *written* form of *language* irrespective of a particular documentary manifestation appears in early recognitions that a text's reading rests on an error in transcription or typesetting.[68]

As with the thread of the authoritative text, that of the idealist, lexical work ties together many of the critics between Renaissance humanism and the present. Eichhorn, for instance, devotes considerable attention to Hebrew and its dialects, ancient alphabets, and word division; and his arguments about individual books of the Old Testament often rest on linguistic proofs.[69] Wolf, similarly, desired to produce a text that not only linguistically *looked* the way its author would have wanted it to but also *read* the way an ancient would have read it: "My single primary intention was to correct the text of Homer by the standard of learned antiquity, and to display him in a text the wording, punctuation, and accentuation of which, remade from the recensions that were once considered best, might—if one may properly hope for so much—satisfy some Longinus or other ancient critic who knew how to use the materials of the Alexandrians with skill and tact."[70] For all of Lachmann's meticulous attention to the physical appearance of the archetypal manuscript of *De rerum natura,* it is the *reading,* shared or not, that characterizes his "method" both in general outlook and in particular principles. A manuscript reading for Lachmann is always more desirable than a conjectural emendation—"therefore, nothing [i.e., no reading] can be better attested than that in which all authorities everywhere agree"— and his edition of the New Testament contains lengthy discussions of orthography and synonyms.[71] It is in turn the alleged impossibility of identifying scientifically the only authorial readings that lies at the heart of Bédier's rejection of recension, while such identification, according to Louis Havet in an early modern handbook of textual criticism, is the focus of the critic's attention: "Since copyists make errors, our texts present us with difficulties, that is, presumptions of error. Criticism, if it is scientific, endeavors both to note these difficulties and to get them noticed, in order to prevent those who read the texts from being tricked by the copyists, and in order to forestall any misjudgment about aesthetics, morality, history, grammar, or versification."[72] Finally, W. W. Greg's famous theory of copy-text, which has come to define much contemporary textual criticism, prioritizes textual—particularly lexical— phenomena over everything else: It argues how to reconstruct the text of a work by relying on the earliest extant document for the accidentals (such as punctuation) and notes "that the choice between substantive readings belongs to the general theory of textual criticism."[73]

To be sure, I do not want to downplay the facts that not all the arguments of all these critics are consistent with one another and that some critics, particularly the earlier ones, say a great deal about nonlexical matters. Much of Valla's argument about the forged nature of the *Donation of Constantine* rests on historical evidence, while Scaliger frequently draws heavily on ancient laws and customs. Robortello stresses that the aspiring critic should study the ancient grammarians, "who observe the old rule of speaking" and who consequently have "a conception of all antiquity." It is historicity, in Robortello's view, that must motivate any change an editor effects: "Now in truth, emendations which are correct are confirmed by old books in three ways: by a conception of antiquity, by a conception of ancient writing, and by a conception of ancient expressions and words."[74]

In a similar vein, Bentley made his first mark in the textual-critical world by using quotations from a variety of authors to show the historical anachronism—and thus the spuriousness—of the allegedly sixth-century B.C. letters of Phalaris.[75] The first sentences of Eichhorn's staggeringly thorough and wide-ranging *Einleitung* declare his interest in nonlexical matters:

The bare theological use, which is commonly made of the writings of the Old Testament, has hitherto, more than one might think, hindered the appreciation of the merit of these works of gray antiquity. One sought therein nothing other than the ideas of religion and was blind to their remaining contents; one read them without a sense for antiquity and its speech, not much different than a work of the contemporary period; and according to the difference in intellectual powers, one must have felt in them the greatest unevenness of success.[76]

A broadly cultural approach characterizes Wolf's work on the Homeric poems as well, which seeks to encourage historical sensibilities in the reader: "For the method of those who read Homer and Callimachus and Virgil and Nonnus and Milton in one and the same spirit, and do not strive to weigh in reading and work out what each author's age allows, has not yet entirely been done away with."[77]

For all these critics, however, the literary work remains essentially idealist and lexical. The other issues suggest what the work can reveal about the past or how the *text* of the work might be constructed. But none of these critics—including Eichhorn, Lachmann, and Bédier, the three most distrustful of conjectural emendation—define the work even in part on the basis of a particular physical realization or include nonlexical qualities in its editorial construction.

Of the threads of humanist ideology that tie together the history of textual criticism, the moral thread, given the decline of the church's influence, is perhaps the most anachronistic. As I suggested earlier, the philosophical and religious issues that early textual criticism mediated within the institutions that sustained it rendered it inescapably ideological. These same issues and institutions, in turn, guaranteed that the ideology was characterized by a moral stance. At stake in Calderni's invention of Marius Rusticus was the conception of the ancient literary tradition to which the contemporary world aspired, and the issue involved in d'Etaples's alteration of the Pauline epistles was nothing less than the word of God—the logos that defined and governed life. Valla's exposure of the *Donation of Constantine* undermined papal power and thus had political as well as religious significance. Early practitioners' ideological morality (to risk a tautology) helps to account for the tone of righteous indignation that pervades the work of critics like Valla, Poliziano, and Scaliger and also accounts for the moral resonance of some of the basic vocabulary of textual criticism. Salutati, for example, speaks of manuscripts as being either *faithfully written* or *degenerating:* "There already is, indeed, scarcely a single codex faithfully copied from the little books of Petrarch and Boccaccio which does not degenerate very much from the exemplars; they are indeed not copies but likenesses of copies."[78] Similarly, in a letter defending alleged faults in his Latinity in *De elegantia lingue latine,* Valla turns the double-edged vocabulary of his opponents back onto them: "Therefore, so that these ones who slander me may understand themselves to be unjust and rash and snarling, when they call me snarling and rash, I say . . ."[79] And Robortello, in a passage I have already cited, notes that books themselves become unknowable if their vocabulary is corrupted (*corrupta*). For the humanists, the double emphasis on the lexical and the moral was mutually reinforcing because linguistic competence was simultaneously one of the requisites and alleged reflections of the moral, cultured gentleman. This strong moral orientation, moreover, partially explains textual criticism's characteristic imperative not simply to examine texts and documents but to discriminate *right* texts and readings from *wrong* ones.

Just as the equation of author with authority and the privileging of the verbal text have remained constant from the work of Salutati to Greg, so too have the moral implications of much textual criticism. But, like these other aspects, the motivation behind the morality imputed to textual recovery has been recuperated differently, so that its character may appear disjunctive. For Eichhorn, an ability to recognize the fundamental historical character and value of the Old Testament is preeminent, and so his contemporaries' poor sense of historicity is a fundamental flaw that easily leads them into "error": "These essential concerns and points of view, without which one can fall into error so easily in many parts of the Old Testament, I had already grasped early on."[80] In Lachmann's discussions, however, the moral vocabulary of textual criticism serves neither humanism nor a broadly philological interest in history but nineteenth-century scientific empiricism. To Lachmann, when manuscripts "sin" they must be called back to "truth": "For what has been written is understood in two ways—by examining witnesses and by calling witnesses back to truth when they sin: thus gradually ought [a text] be changed from writings to writer."[81] Since the nineteenth century, indeed, the moral strand of textual criticism has largely served the imperative of scientific accuracy and objectivity. Havet, as I have noted earlier, envisages textual criticism as a sort of interpretive watchdog: He maintains that by detecting the errors perpetrated by copyists, scientific textual criticism serves the good of literary critics by saving them from the tricks of copyists and by providing an accurate basis for their discussions of style, history, grammar, and the like. Later in his *Manual* he stresses the need for the critic to be honest and non-judgmental with both his audience and his evidence: "A careful editor should note equally all evidences of error. His duty is to shed an equal light on every such evidence of error so that, in his turn, the reader may be his own judge as to the nature of the error. Hypotheses of error are conclusions; evidences of error are points of departure."[82]

It is this same morality of science that characterizes Greg's *The Calculus of Variants* and Paul Maas's *Textkritik* and underlies cautions by Bowers and others that careful bibliography is a *prerequisite* to valid (yet still subjective) literary criticism.[83] Within this tradition, textual criticism is thus understood to have an integrity that protects critics from the blandishments of aesthetics and keeps them on the righteous road of textual recovery. Or, in the words of G. Thomas Tanselle, what "the scholarly editor attempts . . . is to remove from the discourse those features for which the initiator was not responsible. The result is not necessarily what the editor himself prefers but what he believes to be the author's contribution to a given discourse."[84] The morality of scientific accuracy, like any morality, can even be self-protecting and self-generating, as D. C. Greetham suggests after describing an "editorial flow-chart demonstrating the actual process whereby a normalised form is created with reference to the documentary evidence": "I would emphasize that the system has sufficient safeguards . . . to prevent a too-licentious editorial enthusiasm. I have to admit, however, that once editors have got a whiff of normalisation, they are often tempted to take off with abandon, casting off all constraints, so heady is the power given! It is then that the structured format of the flow-chart becomes most chastening."[85]

What all these threads fabricate, finally, is a discursive tradition that accepts its objectives, its principles, and, above all, itself as givens. From the early fifteenth century discussion has been characterized by attempts to fashion broadly, if not universally, applicable systems of textual criticism. In that period, moreover, critics tended to present and defend their procedures on the basis of their consistency with the arguments of Poliziano (for the Italians) or Muret (for the French). For the most part these arguments appear scattered through letters, introductions, and explanatory notes, but when Robortello's *De arte sive ratione corrigendi*

appeared in 1557, it, too, spoke in absolutes about the nature of manuscripts, their transmission, and editing. The conviction and motivation
underlying this systemization seem clear enough: If the Renaissance
was to define itself in terms of the Antique world, textual stabilization
facilitated self-definition; the humanists *were* concerned with a relatively homogeneous group of classical works to all of which, it would
seem logical, the same principles and procedures might apply; and the
ideological quality of humanist textual criticism meant that the issues
involved in editing or interpreting any given work went far beyond that
work by itself to the work as it intersected a multitude of ideas and
institutions. These same motivations and convictions underlie another
aspect of humanist textual criticism: its ambivalent sense of historicity.
On the one hand, scholars like Scaliger and Valla displayed an extraordinary knowledge of ancient works, customs, and laws that they
brought to bear on their textual-critical efforts to recover the work as
it had been written. On the other, the historicity of their own labors
seems to have been largely disregarded, perhaps under the supposition
that if the present is reborn to the values and aesthetics of the Antique,
these values and aesthetics are in effect universal.

Because the origins of textual criticism have been dehistoricized and
the humanist principles regarded as transcendent, the systemization and
historical ambivalence of early textual criticism have also been accepted.
Accordingly, the textual criticism that later scholars inherited and transmitted has been defined in systemizing, totalizing ways, even though
the cultural milieu that had initiated and justified these attitudes has
long since passed away. If over time certain procedures have been contested—such as close adherence to testified readings as opposed to conjecture, recension as opposed to best-text editing—the systemization,
the tendency to make totalizing pronouncements about the nature of
texts and their editing, has remained constant. For example, in the late
eighteenth century Eichhorn, even though he contended that with respect to the Old Testament "criticism still stands in its first years of
childhood," asserted: "The critical history of the text of all hitherto
critically edited authors demonstrates that in the beginning of their
critical treatment far too much freedom has been allowed to conjectural
criticism."[86] Lachmann also remonstrated against those who failed to
recognize the value of the system of recension and instead delighted
themelves in their own conjectural reconstructions.[87] In turn, Lach-

mann's "method" came under attack from Bédier, whose method was challenged by Dom Quentin's method.

More recently, the tendency to clarify, defend, and broaden the applicability of received opinions—to place system before the text, whatever its genre, chronology, or origin—has been particularly apparent. Various apologiae continue to appear on behalf of Lachmannian recension.[88] Even more striking in this regard, perhaps, are the numerous defenses of Greg's theory of copy-text, which as a theory, it should be recalled, is a theory about practical procedures—how to recover both authorial accidentals and substantives—and not one that addresses any of the narrowly "theoretical" assumptions of textual criticism.[89] At the same time, many of these apologiae adopt the righteous indignation that was common in textual criticism (though for ideological reasons) in its humanists beginnings. By taking the humanists at their word about the character of textual criticism, scholars have been complicit in the construction of a fissureless editorial history, thereby apparently validating humanist views. The interpretation of Bédier's work as a rupture of the tradition in fact only further serves to consolidate potential discontinuities: Since his work can be so easily accommodated, figuring his positions as the Other preempts truly antithetical challenges.

This tendency to systemization makes even more prominent the ambivalent sense of historicity that informed humanist textual criticism and is still operative today. Though the primary objective of most critics seems to remain the recovery of the "original" work, the character of an original is often presumed to be a literary constant irrespective of time and space. It was Greg himself, in his landmark paper on copy-text, who maintained that "the underlying principles of textual criticism are, of course, the same in the case of works transmitted in manuscripts and in print,"[90] and the totalizing notion that a system can be created that will apply to all literary works—that single definitions will apply transhistorically to authors, works, and texts—is inherent in a number of recent studies.[91] Outside the ideology of humanism, however, there is a striking lack of commensurability between the avowed goal of recovering a historicized object and the assertion that all such objects are fundamentally the same and can be recovered in fundamentally the same ways.

In many ways, then, the work of Greg, Bowers, Tanselle, and others in the Anglo-American tradition of editing—including Pratt, editor

of Chaucer's *Canterbury Tales*—represents a perhaps inevitable consequence of humanist-derived textual criticism, a criticism that consolidates itself against opposing views by acknowledging neither its own
origins nor its theoretical underpinnings and consequences. Today, this
tradition still represents the textual-critical status quo to which Middle
English (as I shall consider in the next chapter) has been accommodated and against which genuine theoretical challenges (as chapter 3
will suggest) have recently been articulated. That humanist principles
should endure against entire traditions and be exposed to truly antithetical paradigms only within the last twenty years or so further testifies to
the tenacity and resilience of humanist notions of textual criticism. Indeed, the persistence through history of the same basic textual-critical
principles implies the pervasive implicit acceptance of these principles
as givens, regardless of their applicability to particular historical works.
Even when these principles have been apparently recuperated in subsequent epochs—such as in the coalescence of the humanist interest
in authorship with nineteenth-century interest in origins—they have
not been divested of their original significances and effects. To the extent that historical inquiry is predicated on edited texts, the humanist
paradigm has remained a determinative influence on the identification
(even production) of historical records and history itself—in essence, an
a priori prime mover of textual material that itself then can be second-
arily and variously recuperated. Traditional textual-critical principles,
in other words, may not always have been interpreted in the same way,
but they have always predetermined textual criticism and the editions
it has produced in a fashion that is above all consistent with humanism, even when what was done with the editions so produced was not.
Since I have already suggested something of this durability through
broad-based cultural, political, and literary transformations, by way of
a conclusion I want to consider one brief historical period: the decades
surrounding World War I.

During this period the major movements in many intellectual arenas
were what could loosely be called "relativistic," emphasizing the conditional and contextual nature of method and theory. The inspiration
of these developments might well have been physics, where Einstein's
theory of relativity, however misunderstood and misapplied by non-
physicists, ruptured the absolute certainty of the Newtonian universe.
In mathematics, for instance, non-Euclidian geometry was explored,
with Henri Poincaré observing in 1929, "One geometry cannot be more

true than another, it can only be more convenient." In philosophy, C. I. Lewis suggested in 1932, "There are no 'laws of logic' which can be attributed to the universe or to human reason in the traditional fashion."[92] The Legal Realism movement stressed the personal and social background of judges and legislators rather than bare legal precedent as the central determining factor in judicial decisions, while the anthropologist Margaret Mead examined cultural relativism. In linguistics, Edward Sapir and Benjamin Lee Whorf initiated their work on the way language conditions worldview, and in historical studies the Historical Relativists were ascendent. In 1921 the noted American historian Carl Becker, for example, observed: "The mere 'fact,' if you allow the wretched creature to open its mouth, will say only one thing: 'I am, therefore I am right.'"[93] In the various fine arts as well a kind of relativism informed the experiments with perspective by James Joyce, William Faulkner, Pablo Picasso, and Salvator Dali. The situation in interpretive literary studies, where formalism and practical criticism dominated in the 1920s and 1930s, is less clear, though it could be maintained that in severing texts from the physical and cultural contexts that produced them scholars were de facto elevating the importance of their own perspectives.

During this same period, however, textual criticism continued to adhere to notions of authority and an idealist, lexical work that had originated among the humanists. A comparison of dates here is illuminating. In 1921 Edward Sapir published *Language,* in 1928 Whorf first met Sapir,[94] and in 1930 Margaret Mead published *Growing Up in New Guinea.* Each event had significant consequences in the ongoing relativistic assessment of phenomena, and each thus contributed to the further rupturing in Western society of the prewar ethos. On the other hand, the important textual-critical works that appeared in the same decade— works still influential today—involved methods that were largely reflections of putatively objective nineteenth-century scientific empiricism and theories that originated with the humanists. Thus, Dom Quentin's *Essais de critique textuelle,* in which he advanced his arguments against Lachmannian recension and for the principle of shared variants, appeared in 1926; 1927 witnessed the publication of Greg's *The Calculus of Variants* and Maas's *Textkritik,* both of which prescribe, in dispassionate and rigorous (and in Greg's case mathematical) analysis, methods for recovering genuine authorial texts.

My point, of course, is not to accuse textual critics of having sat out a necessary cultural revolution. Indeed, in some disciplines the intellectual pendulum has swung from relativity to objectivity and back yet again at least once since the 1920s. Rather, by this example I mean to underscore that the extraordinary resilience of the central principles of traditional textual criticism confirms the forces that created it: It was made by the humanists to transcend time, and despite the demise of many of the institutions and ideas that sustained humanism, this claim for transcendence, along with all the other original theoretical principles, has subsequently and repeatedly been accepted. The theoretical horizon of textual criticism, like all such horizons, is thereby both elusive and ubiquitous.

CHAPTER TWO

❦

Accommodating
Middle English

Textual criticism of Middle English works developed within the humanist paradigm. Middle English textual criticism has been fabricated, consequently, by the same threads that tie together textual criticism in general: the equation of the authoritative text with an authorial one, the valorization of an idealist, lexical conception of the work, a moral orientation, and an ambivalent sense of historicity. What problematizes and distinguishes textual criticism of Middle English works in particular is the fact that as works produced in the vernacular during the *medium aevum,* they represent the very traditions from which the humanists most wanted to dissociate themselves. The ideology of the Renaissance depended both on a resumptive embrace of Antique ideals and on the definition (and subsequent rejection) of works produced during the "middle age" as those that lacked the literary, aesthetic, and moral values of classical works. Thus, while traditional textual criticism has provided an inescapably humanist framework for editing Middle English materials, that same framework expressly excludes Middle English. To be edited at all, Middle English works have had to be accommodating and also accommodated to these incompatible forces.

One indicator of the awkward and precarious position of Middle English works in textual-critical studies is the lack of attention devoted to the theory and practice of editing of specifically these works. Comments on classical and biblical works appear in scattered letters and prefaces early in the fifteenth century, and 1557 marked the appearance of the first manual, Robortello's *De arte sive ratione corrigendi antiquorum libros disputatio,* whose title unambiguously declares its focus. In the wake of Robertello's *De arte* came a proliferation of other manuals devoted to textual criticism of Antique works, and such manuals continue to appear.[1]

By comparison, discussion of textual criticism of Middle English works has typically been restricted to introductions to editions and, only recently, to an increasing number of scholarly articles. At present, as I noted in the Introduction, Charles Moorman's study is the only book-length examination of specifically Middle English works. This absence of critical discussion reflects of course the totalizing orientation of humanist textual criticism: the presumption that one set of principles and methods is applicable to all works, irrespective of provenance and date, and, consequently, tacit recognition that a discussion of textual critical issues for Antique works precluded the need for such discussion of other works. Alternatively, even if this orientation had been rejected in the early modern period and some attempt made to address the specifically Middle English characteristics of the works, their failure to meet the humanists' literary standards—their manifestation of the literary qualities and values of the medieval period—would have cast them even farther into oblivion. Either perspective would silence the potential opposition to humanist principles that a Middle English tradition offered.

While all vernacular literatures were at some point recuperated in similarly problematic fashions, Middle English textual-critical studies have lagged behind those of medieval Italian, German, and French. Already in the fourteenth century, for example, Salutati was concerned about the difficulty of obtaining accurate copies of the works of Dante, Boccaccio, and Petrarch.[2] Further, Lachmann, one of the landmark figures of classical textual criticism, first enunciated his general editorial principles in his work on Middle High German poetry.[3] In responding to Lachmann at the beginning of this century, Bédier revolutionized the procedures for editing Old French poetry, and textual criticism of Old French literature continues to be more sophisticated and more attentive to the peculiar demands of vernacular works than that of Middle English.[4]

In the early modern period the conflicting and problematic demands of humanist textual criticism for the editing of Middle English literature were most generally manifested in what A. S. G. Edwards has called "the history of two contending claims": "On the one hand, the perceived need to make Middle English texts accessible to audiences with little or no knowledge of their grammar, orthography or syntax and, on the other, the need to retrieve and preserve the text."[5] Editions replete with reader aids encouraged recognition of the modernity of the works by facilitating contemporary reading of them, while diplomatic editions presented the Middle English text, in all its quaintness and obscurity, as an emblem of the cultural change separating the modern era from the *medium aevum.* These two critical extremes are the perimeters within which the humanist paradigm has broadly shaped the development of Middle English textual criticism.

The desire to facilitate contemporary reading is easily traced in early treatments of Chaucer. As Edwards points out, the glossary in Speght's 1598 edition of the *Works* was "the first significant indication of a response to the growing sense of linguistic distance separating Chaucer from a contemporary audience."[6] Consequently, the glossary can be seen as an effort to make the work as intelligible as possible to a large audience of nonantiquarians who otherwise would not have beeen able to read the Middle English language. The various adaptations and modernizations completed in the early modern period manifest even more clearly this urge to popularize Chaucer. In the years 1558–1625 thirteen plays based on Chaucer's works were composed,[7] and in 1630 a Chaucer adaptation entitled *The Tinker of Turvey* was published, which offers six tales told on a barge trip down the Thames from Billingsgate to Gravesend.[8] Sometime around 1630 the first of the Renaissance modernizations of Chaucer—the initial three books of the *Troilus,* most likely from the pen of Jonathon Sidnam—was written, though it was never published.[9] Five years later a modernization of a different sort was published: Sir Francis Kynaston's *Amorum Troili et Creseidae Libri duo priores Anglico-Latini,* which contains the first two books of the *Troilus* and a facing-page translation into Latin. Here, the poem was being modernized for a sophisticated, cultured audience of humanist intellectuals: To modernize for such a group meant to return to the language of the Antique. The early strand of modernization, however, is most widely known in the *Fables* of Dryden, which appeared in 1700, and in Pope's various translations.

The desire for the other extreme Edwards identifies informs Caxton's remarks in the preface to his second edition of the *Canterbury Tales,* published about 1484. There Caxton, in a rhetorical posture that both defines the volume's audience and portends Renaissance interest in vernacular authorship, alleges his efforts to present the original text as accurately as possible. He maintains that a "gentylman" visited him and said that Caxton's first edition "was not accordyng in many places vnto the book that Gefferey chaucer had made"; this "gentylman" offered Caxton his father's manuscript, which was "very trewe," and Caxton asserts that production of the second edition was based on this more authorial text.[10] A similar interest in Chaucer's actual words informs Speght's 1598 edition, which was revised in 1602 and reissued in 1687. While the glossary included in these editions—the first to contain this lexical aid—does popularize Chaucer's works to some extent, it also imputes primacy to Chaucer's own language, which the contemporary reader is obliged to understand; like any glossary, Speght's efforts thus simultaneously encourage a sense of modernity and stand as an index of the original work's alterity. In yet another later edition of the *Canterbury Tales* (1775), Thomas Tyrwhitt demonstrates his interest in textual fidelity by maintaining that he based the text on manuscripts themselves.

In these and other cases, editorial procedure mirrored the practice (much condemned by Bentley) of basing new editions on *vulgata* rather than directly on the manuscripts. In effect, an announcement that the editor had scrupulously consulted and accurately reported the manuscripts might well be seen as an advertising sine qua non of such editions, regardless of how the actual text had been prepared. In point of fact, Caxton, for example, used the first edition, not another manuscript, for the base text of his second edition of the *Canterbury Tales,* and, though he did rearrange the order of the tales, most of the changes between the first and second editions are incidental and sporadic.[11] Similarly, Tyrwhitt, despite his alleged reliance on manuscripts and despite his antipathy for Speght's efforts, used Speght's 1602 revision to prepare the printer's copy of his edition.[12] John Pinkerton, in his 1786 edition of *Ancient Scotish Poems,* likewise noted that "the reader may depend upon finding thro-out a *literal* transcript of the MS . . . as far as human fallibility would permit." "Human fallibility," Edwards comments, "would permit quite a lot. Pinkerton silently regularises thorn and yogh, adds punctuation, and changes capitalisation, as well as making a number of transcriptional errors."[13]

Such an ambivalent attitude toward manuscripts, however, also informs classical textual criticism of the period and emerges from the humanists' conception of the work: Above all, the work is thought to be lexical, exclusive of its manifestations in particular documents and of other extratextual phenomena, but at the same time the texts of all these documents are regarded as only reflections—and typically as inadequate ones—of an idealist work. Similarly consonant with humanist textual criticism is the moral character of the very enterprise of early editing of vernacular works. In the preface to his edition of Chaucer's *Boece,* for example, Caxton voices the opinion that the translation merits printing because of its morality: "Atte requeste of a singuler frende 7 gossib of myne I william Caxton haue done my debuoir 7 payne tenprynte it [the *Boece*] in fourme as is here afore made / In hopyng that it shal prouffite moche peple to the wele 7 helth of their soules / 7 for to lerne to haue and kepe the better pacience in aduersitees."[14] Caxton similarly claims to present Malory's *Works* "to the entente that noble men may see and lerne the noble actes of chiualrye / the Jentyl and vertuous dedes that somme knyghtes vsed in tho dayes / by whyche they came to honour / and how they that were vycious were punysshed and ofte put to shame and rebuke."[15]

The humanist equation of the authoritative text with the authorial one is also apparent in early Middle English textual criticism. In fact, few (if any) Middle English writers save Chaucer would qualify as authors according to the humanists' aesthetic and cultural criteria, but without this equation textual criticism as the humanists defined it could not take place. The equation could function merely as a principle that enabled editing—as in Robert Crowley's 1550 edition of *Piers Plowman*—but in the extreme case of Chaucer the attempt seems to have been to present him as much as possible in the guise of an Antique *auctor.* Thus, Speght's 1598 edition of Chaucer's *Works* outlines and instigates an elaborate series of tasks necessary for the best understanding and presentation of Chaucer's oeuvre; these tasks include collecting Chaucer's life, correcting his text, explaining old words, declaring the cited authors, and adding what had not been printed before. This is precisely the humanist response to ancient literature, and it thus constitutes a pretext that conditions responses to a vernacular poet who himself aspired to auctorial status. In the same vein, John Urry's 1721 edition of Chaucer's *Works,* complete with a frontispiece of Chaucer and with an extensive critical apparatus on the model initiated by Speght, renders Chaucer's texts in appearance very much the equal of contemporary presentations of the texts of Homer or Vergil. Concomitantly, Chaucer's text is valorized in the same way the humanists valorized those of the ancients. For example, Timothy Thomas, who helped to complete the edition after Urry's death, observes that Urry's "chief business was to make the Text more correct and compleat than before." Chaucer is recuperated as an auctor not only in the sense that the texts of his works are presumed to be his responsibility alone but also in the sense that his artistic superiority is regarded as unarguable. Urry believed that Chaucer's meter was "exact" and so "he proposed in this Edition to restore him [Chaucer] (to use his own Expression) *to his feet again,* which he thought might be performed by a careful Collation of the best printed Editions and good MSS." Not surprisingly, Middle English editors themselves parallel their counterparts in classical studies, for they, too, according to Thomas, must be learned scholars with acute senses of historicity: "The Undertaker must be master of all that sort of Learning and Knowledge which was peculiar to that Age." [16]

A rather striking emblem of the problematic environment in which early editions of Middle English works were produced is Kynaston's *Amorum Troili et Creseidae Libri duo priores Anglico-Latini* (1635). The volume opens with a preface to the reader that discusses Kynaston's objectives in the translation, and there follows a sequence of fifteen poems, each affirming the value of Kynaston's translation. These are in English or Latin and in several instances were composed by Kynaston's acquaintances from Oxford. Book 1 is prefaced by a dedication to Patrick Young, royal librarian, and book 2 by one to John Rous, librarian of the Bodleian. Every verso of each page of text presents three Latin stanzas in italic font, while every recto contains the corresponding English stanzas in black letter.

The conception of Chaucer as a great auctor of great works emerges in the preface, introductory poems, and dedication of *Amorum Troili et Creseidae,* which everywhere speak of Chaucer in reverential tones. Kynaston commences his preface to the reader, thus, by foregrounding the superlative worth of Chaucer—"so great, dear reader, is the esteem and reputation of our venerable and ancient poet among all." [17] The recovery of his work through textual criticism is judged an undertaking that will benefit the whole of English culture and is thus essentially moral, as Edward Foulis suggests in his comments on the difficulty of Chaucer's language for seventeenth-century readers:

> Here is no fault, but ours: through vs
> True Poetry growes barbarous:
> While aged Language must be thought
> (Because 'twas good long since) now naught.[18]

The humanist conception of a work as lexical and idealist also informs Kynaston's translation of *Troilus and Criseyde,* but it is in this conception that the accommodation of Middle English literature to humanist textual criticism becomes most apparent and most awkward. On the one hand, Chaucer's actual words mark him as the founder of English poetry—the English Homer or Vergil—and are therefore of importance. In the preface, for instance, Kynaston invokes what was then an already well established tradition by imaging Chaucer as England's premier poet: "*Our* Chaucer, the ornament of *this* island and distinguished glory of poetry" (my italics).[19] In fact, as Dudley Digges indicates, Chaucer's preeminence as a poet, like Homer's or Vergil's, should extend beyond England to the world at large: "The fame of such a name ought / to lie before the world, not just an island."[20] But on the other hand, the Renaissance need to distance itself from a *medium aevum* is manifested in repeated claims that Chaucer's language is antiquated and nearly incomprehensible. For example, in the preface Kynaston observes that Chaucer is "not only growing old, diminishing in value beneath the obsolete and already scorned clothing of the ancient English idiom, but—how sad!—wholly wasting away and nearly dead."[21] In the dedication of book 1, similarly, in stating that one of his intentions in the translation was to restore the *Troilus* to intelligibility, Kynaston stresses—if not exaggerates—the obscurities of Chaucer's language: "First, I desired the preservation from ruin and oblivion of this gem of poems, which was nearly lost and scarcely understood by us (at least as the favorite of none) because of ignorance of the obsolete words in it which have fallen into disuse."[22] Yet again, in one of the introductory poems Guilford Barker observes:

> Like travellors, we had bin out so long,
> Our Natiue was become an vnknowne tongue,

> And homebred *Chaucer* vnto vs was such,
> As if he had bin written in High Dutch.[23]

Amorum Troili et Creseidae thus articulates a dilemma: Chaucer's preeminence as a poet who rivals the ancient Latin *auctores* and the obsolescence of his Middle English language. One possible solution, which Kynaston had considered it easy to effect, would have been "to change obsolete words scattered here and there throughout this entire poem into new ones, and to restore all the diction and worn-out sayings into purer words—those which obtain today—and to adjust them not only in language but also in meter towards the comprehension of the present age." He considered the various French modernizations of the *Roman de la Rose* as adequate precedent for such an approach. However, Chaucer's preeminence as a poet—a necessity in humanist conceptions of textual criticism—meant that a modernization of the *Troilus* would surely damage the quality of the poem: "But I should have thought myself to have committed an inexpiable sin on the spirit of Chaucer if I should have changed the slightest iota in his writings, which deserve to be sacred and untouched into eternity."[24]

Kynaston's actual solution, in line with the humanists' ambivalent sense of historicity, was of course to print the two texts together as simultaneously distinct and synonymous. In printing an English version in outdated black letter type, he responds to what Edwards calls "the need to retrieve and preserve the text" by offering the reader Chaucer's words in a format that stresses their antiquity. The facing translation, however, evinces what Edwards considers the claim of accessibility, since it retains the essence of the work by transmuting it into the permanent, codified, and prestigious medium of Latin and setting it in contemporary italic type. "It seems most well-considered to me," he observes in his Preface to the reader, "to give him a new language, and to adorn him with a renewed species of rhythm and song; and to secure him with the lasting support of Roman eloquence, and to render him again stable and immobile through all ages (however many we have left)."[25] This transmutation, John Corbet points out in a prefatory poem, will strengthen Chaucer's reputation outside of England:

> O knight, in your efforts lives
> Chaucer: known to the Britons
> formerly, he remains an inhabitant of the world.[26]

If the humanist lexical conception of a work was strong enough for
Kynaston to include the Middle English text, the idealist conception is
nonetheless strong enough to lead several of the contributing poets to
equate Amorum Troili et Creseidae with *Troilus and Criseyde,* as in "And,
though we know't done in our age by you, / May doubt which is the
Coppy of the two" or in

> Thus time can silence *Chaucers* tongue,
> But not his witte, which now among
> The Latines hath a lowder sound;
> And what we lost, the World hath found.
> Thus the Translation will become
> Th'Originall, while that growes dumbe:
> And this will crowne these labours: None
> Sees *Chaucer* but in *Kinaston.* [27]

Amorum Troili et Creseidae demonstrates the practical and theoretical difficulties that humanist textual criticism occasioned for Middle
English literature. The undertaking depends on imputing the status
of auctor to Chaucer. But if this procedure worked well enough for
a poet who himself had aspirations in this direction and whose contemporaries almost immediately judged to be qualitatively superior to
other English writers, it could scarcely be extended to the hundreds
of anonymous works that by humanist standards were rough in style
and content as well as language. In 1795, for example, Joseph Ritson
observed, "The creative imagination and poetical fancy which distinguish Chaucer, who, considering the general barbarism of his age and
country, may be regarded as a prodigy, admit, it must be acknowledged, of no competition." [28] Even Bishop Percy, one of the staunchest
defenders of medieval poetry before the modern period, felt the need
to apologize for the literary qualities of his *Reliques* and to offer as substitutes their "pleasing simplicity" and quaintness: "In a polished age,
like the present, I am sensible that many of these reliques of antiquity
will require great allowances to be made for them. Yet have they, for
the most part, a pleasing simplicity, and many artless graces, which in
the opinion of no mean critics have been thought to compensate for the
want of higher beauties, and, if they do not dazzle the imagination,
are frequently found to interest the heart." [29] While Kynaston's two-text
format does manage to realize the humanist conception of a work as

lexical and idealist, it seems an impractical solution for works of the sort I just noted; the very peculiarity of the format, moreover, foregrounds the awkwardness of the accommodation of Middle English literature to the demands of textual criticism. Though the book as a whole—as a semiotic object—both reflects and resolves the competing intellectual forces of the period through a linguistic ambivalence that presents the Latin and English versions as simultaneously distinct and synonymous, it also emblematizes the incompatibility of these forces.[30]

Furthermore, the specificity that is possible in tracing early treatments of Chaucer is perhaps misleading about the state of Middle English editing at this time, for he is one of a very few Middle English figures to receive explicit textual-critical discussion before the end of the nineteenth century.[31] The reason for this lack of attention, again, is clear. If Middle English textual criticism was informed by the principles of textual criticism in general, then one of the informing principles was that works of the Middle Ages were inherently and variously inferior to those of the Antique or the Renaissance. Hence, there could be little artistic or moral reason to devote a great deal of attention to the editorial theory and practice of these works. By comparison, even Old English, at least in the sixteenth century, received more critical attention than Middle English: As evinced in the many connections between Church reform and early Anglo-Saxon scholarship, the latter had the advantage of being perceived as offering grist for the Reformation's mill.[32]

The Reformation may have had just the opposite effect on much Middle English literature, however, since the 1550s and 1560s represent a highwater mark of editorial activity for Middle English works, after which there was much less interest until at least the middle of the nineteenth century. Numerous editions of various works attributed to Chaucer, Gower, Lydgate, and Rolle were produced in the fifteenth and early sixteenth centuries, though beginning with the decade of the 1530s it is the work of Chaucer alone that stayed in print: Berthelette's 1532 edition of the *Confessio* was reissued in 1554, but the poem was not published again until Alexander Chalmers reprinted Berthelette's edition in his *Works of the English Poets* in 1810; works attributed to Rolle—all of them spurious—also experienced a printing hiatus between the early sixteenth century and the modern period, while during the seventeenth and eighteenth centuries only a handful of Lydgate's compositions were printed, most of which were translations or, significantly, "Chaucerian" works like the *Siege of Thebes* and the *Complaint of the Black Knight;* and after Owen Rogers's edition of 1560 even the *B* text of *Piers Plowman*, at least parts of which should have appealed to the reformers, was not printed until 1842.[33] Malory's *Morte*, similarly, was printed in 1634 but not reissued thereafter until 1816. Moreover, there are only a handful of precursors to modern scholarly editions in the eighteenth century, such as the 1710 edition of Gavin Douglas's *Eneydos*, which contains a glossary of Scots words and a Life of the poet, or Thomas Hearne's 1724 edition of Robert of Gloucester's *Chronicle*.[34] These, like the later editions of Bishop Thomas Percy, arose from antiquarian interest—manifested in Edwards's claim of retrieval and preservation—though as Ritson enjoyed pointing out, Percy in particular could be quite willing to interpolate his own additions and corrections. Of the corpus of late Middle English literature, in fact, only the metrical romances and ballads were consistently printed in the seventeenth and eighteenth centuries, and interest in even these works was qualified. As Bishop Percy's attitude toward the artistic qualities of his *Reliques* suggests, romances and ballads were valued not for any intrinsic literary or cultural merits but for the quaintness and sense of primitivism that were thought to inform them.[35]

Though the nineteenth century witnessed a burst of interest in medieval literature in the form of popular medievalism, such interest did little to alter the inherited attitudes toward the editing of Middle English works. In textual-critical matters, the imaginative historical and textual reconstructions of a Scott, Bulwer-Lytton, or Morris scarcely effected greater historical sensibility. Rather, it was the advent of the neogrammarians that determined that the diplomatic side of Edwards's formulation would predominate, since their interest in linguistic forms emphasized historically attested lexicon and syntax. In turn, this interest, which defined and restricted the audience for Middle English, provided a way to produce editions within the paradoxes of humanist textual criticism: Philology depended on a lexical, idealist notion of the work without making the pretense of imputing artistic superiority. When Middle English editions began to proliferate in the latter part of the nineteenth century, it was under the aegis of the Early English Text Society, which was largely motivated by philological reasons and by the desire to provide serviceable—that is, lexically exact—texts for what became the *Oxford English Dictionary*. It accordingly produced ultraconservative editions, and in many cases these editions remain standard, if only because they are the only ones available. Though initial reading for the *OED* has long since been completed, the almost religious devotion to the appearance of a manuscript's text is sometimes still adopted. Following a principle first enunciated in Mabel Day's 1952 edition of the *Ancrene Riwle*, for example, the various EETS editions preserve manuscript wording, punctuation, and capitalization. While this principle is echoed in all subsequent editions, the rationale behind it is never given. In J. R. R. Tolkien's edition of the *Ancrene Wisse*, furthermore, even manuscript lineation is maintained, again without any expressed justification other than the fact that it was possible to do so.

As an editorial method, consequently, this focus on lexically exact texts remains extremely influential. It is a procedure that emerged, however, not from articulated theoretical concerns but from the cultural context of Middle English literature subsequent to the Renaissance and from a valorization of the lexical aspect of a work that was inherited from humanist textual criticism and consonant with the objectives of philology. It is difficult to overstate the impact this conjunction of humanist textual criticism and philological imperatives has had on modern conceptions of Middle English literature and its editing: It was this accommodation that in a sense created the canon of Middle English. As I noted earlier, only in the nineteenth century did the works of Gower, Langland, and Malory reappear in accessible, printed formats, along with many writers and works—including most of Hoccleve's poetry, *Pearl, Sir Gawain and the Green Knight,* the alliterative *Morte,* and numerous other romances, lyrics, and treatises—that had never been printed before that time.[36]

It is not in fact until the monumental work of John Matthews Manly and Edith Rickert on the *Canterbury Tales* that Middle English studies can be said to have received the degree of attention that Lachmann had devoted to Middle High German and Bédier to Old French. Their recensionist method is avowedly lexical, idealist, and, in their "complete collation of all the MSS" and in their printing of "all the variants,"[37] empirical. Like Bédier, Manly and Rickert rely on the laws of probability in their argument, though the theoretical framework of their discussion is far less well articulated than his.[38] Their Introduction, indeed, is devoted to method, both of recording and presenting the data as well as classifying it. They silently extend the concerns of classical textual criti-

cism to Chaucer in, for example, their consideration of "author's variants,"[39] and they nowhere explain just how they adjudicated between
variants and arrived at the text they printed. Such silences, in perhaps
the most ambitious edition of a Middle English work ever attempted,
speak volumes about the theoretical poverty of Middle English editing.

Chaucer studies in particular, perhaps, enabled such silences, for as I
suggested above, Chaucer has consistently received special attention as
the English claimant to the place held by Homer and Vergil in Antique
literature: the founder of a literary tradition. The time frame of the
bulk of Manly and Rickert's work, the 1930s, constitutes another important point of reference for assessing the fortunes of Middle English
textual criticism since then and for evaluating the ways in which Middle
English literature has continued to be accommodated to the imperatives
of humanism and philology. This period led, of course, to the flower-
ing of practical criticism in England, and in America of its counterpart, the New Criticism. Though initially received with hostility and
never monolithic in character, the New Criticism as a general theoretical force has infused all subsequent literary studies, including, at least
indirectly, those of the medieval period. Its practitioners were reacting
in part against the certitudes of philology, but they were also motivated
by social and political forces: In the face of increasing industrialization,
the New Critics sought to elevate the status of the artistic verbal object.
As Terry Eagleton observes, "The poetic response, unlike the scientific,
respected the sensuous integrity of its object: it was not a matter of
rational cognition but an affective affair which linked us to the 'world's
body' in an essentially religious bond. Through art, an alienated world
could be restored to us in all its rich variousness. Poetry, as an essentially contemplative mode, would spur us not to change the world but to
reverence it for what it was, teach us to approach it with a disinterested
humility."[40] By severing texts from their social and cultural contexts,
influential critics like F. R. Leavis and T. S. Eliot substituted aesthetics
for the morality that had lain at the root of literary studies in the "ethical poetic" of the Middle Ages and, later, in the ethical imperatives of
humanism.[41]

The extensive pedagogical, practical, and theoretical influence of the
New Criticism is only now becoming clear.[42] It has molded the very
conception of a literary canon—whether a Great Tradition or a chain
of anxiety or an anticanon—as well as the contents of that canon, and it

has informed ideas about how and why literature should be studied. Its interest in organic unity and its ambivalence about historicity, furthermore, had direct consequences for textual criticism. Within its interpretive framework the labors of textual critics of any historical period could only be pedestrian: They provided the texts necessary for serious and sensitive scholars to do serious and sensitive work. Having rejected the scientific method, cultural contexts, and romantic conceptions of literary beginnings, the New Critics argued that the transcendent verbal icon by nature simply *is,* and so any inquiries about its origin or development are nonquestions. Indeed, when the New Critics themselves glanced at textual criticism, the attention they manifested was often in essence indifference or ignorance. In their widely read *Theory of Literature,* for example, René Wellek and Austin Warren observe, "One must distinguish rather sharply between the problems which arise in editing classical or medieval manuscripts on the one hand and, on the other, printed matter." But as promising and apparently unproblematic as this observation is, it is belied by the unquestioned coupling of classical and medieval texts, by the concomitant apparent grouping of Latin and the vernacular in the Middle Ages, and by the fact that the problems Wellek and Warren see are limited to physical appearance and classification. They do not consider, for example, whether any problems might be attendant upon historically determined conceptions of author, text, and the function of literature or whether any other textual-critical features might distinguish literature of one provenance and time period from that of another. In suggesting that for *Piers Plowman* and the *Canterbury Tales* there probably never "existed an authorized recension or archetype analogous to the definitive edition of a modern work," they apparently intend only that the "authors" never "authorized" a text, not that the very notion of "authoritative" may have been different in the Middle Ages.[43] These latter positions, along with the New Critical ambivalence about historicity, are entirely consonant with humanist textual criticism: In noting the absence of an "authorized recension," Wellek and Warren implicitly identify the authoritative text with the authorial one, while their notion of the work—the "well wrought urn" of Cleanth Brooks—is pervasively lexical and idealistic. The characteristic contribution of New Criticism to literary study, indeed, is the development of skills for reading texts.

The irony here is that within the New Criticism there was thus a necessity both to honor the text under scrutiny and to be indifferent about how it was compiled. Editors have continued to edit, of course, but the critical milieu seems to have increasingly marginalized their efforts and theories. Indeed, as I suggested at the conclusion of chapter 1, the totalizing, universalizing quality inherent in traditional textual criticism has kept it theoretically constant and thus, in the modern era, increasingly divergent from interpretive studies. A comparison of publication dates again compellingly reveals this divergence. F. R. Leavis's *The Great Tradition* and Wellek and Warren's *Theory of Literature* both appeared in 1948, the same year in which the inaugural issue of *Studies in Bibliography* under the editorship of Fredson Bowers appeared, with the very first article being an example of empirical, descriptive bibliography: "The Manuscript of Jefferson's Unpublished Errata List for Abbé Morellet's Translation of the *Notes on Virginia*."[44] Next year Greg read his famous paper "The Rationale of Copy-Text" before the English Institute. In this almost schizophrenic theoretical environment, perhaps not surprisingly, textual critics sometimes adopted an almost schizophrenic procedure, as Patterson has seen in the Kane-Donaldson *B* text of *Piers Plowman*:

> The editors' empirical desire to make their data available . . . is in sharp contrast to their unwillingness to provide cross-references that would make the data available in individual instances. The result is a visual text curiously at odds with itself. On the one hand, the plethora of brackets and the thick band of variants at the foot of the page continually remind the reader that he is dealing with an *edited* text. . . . On the other hand, the data on which the text is based are resolutely hidden away in an introduction that is arranged not as a scientific exposition but as an elegantly written narrative.[45]

The various successors to the New Criticism, deconstruction for example, have perhaps only furthered its attitudes toward textual criticism, for if these more recent movements decry the tyranny of the text and praise the autonomy of the reader, they necessarily push the historical genesis of a text or an edition farther into the interpretive background.[46] Thus, in David F. Hult's view of medieval literature in particular, "the debates which raged earlier in this century over text editing methodologies have simmered down to a tacit 'consensus' that seems scarcely more than an indifference to method and, occasionally, to theoretical consistency."[47]

The New Critical elevation of the verbal icon left textual critics in an awkward position. For a work to transcend time, as the New Critical and (earlier) romantic and (ultimately) humanist doctrines require, it cannot very well have an indeterminate form: It is the fixity of the work that enables readers geographically and chronologically separated to respond to it with potentially equal sensitivity.

The problem for the New Critics of more recent literature, Hershel Parker has argued, was that they were confronted by a plethora of facts that belied the transhistorical permanence and organic unity of the work.[48] For numerous nineteenth- and twentieth-century novels, for instance, there exist holographs, corrected proofs, letters, and several editions produced within the author's lifetime that provide evidence about the genesis of the work and that may reveal that the verbal icon is cracked and chipped. To use two of Parker's examples, in a novel like Mark Twain's *Pudd'nhead Wilson* there is evidence that the work was written and revised in such a way that no single authorial intention can be said to operate in it; and in a novel like Stephen Crane's *The Red Badge of Courage* there is evidence that a youthful Crane substantively and inconsistently altered his composition upon the suggestions of his editor.[49] To these examples one might add *Ulysses,* for which Joyce evidently never reached a final lexical intention.[50] In order to see organic and transcendent unity in texts like these, whose genesis reveals disunity and error, elevation of the verbal icon was a necessity: If one proclaims the text free of historical constraints and proceeds to treat it so, the text is of course de facto transcendent. Thus, the New Critical emphasis on the text required the pronouncement that all historically determined (and determining) evidence—including evidence about the author and the genesis of the work—was irrelevant, and Wimsatt and Beardsley in fact killed off the author long before Barthes got around to reporting the death. It was these same emphases that enabled textual critics, with the further sanctions of humanist principles and Greg's rationale, to valorize the lexical content—the substance of words and the accidence of spelling or punctuation—over any other potential aspect of the work.

From this perspective, the kinds of scholarly editions that still dominate the literary landscape of any historical period appear very logical, even inevitable. These are editions whose text is eclectically constructed from both conjecture and the various extant authorities and that present the text clear and by itself, sequestering lexical differences in a schematic record of variants and discussion of disputed readings in textual notes, both of which are typically printed after the text. The text itself is thus both isolated from the material and lexical diversity out of which it was constructed and foregrounded as a free-standing, completed literary artifact. Even more is this the case in popular editions, where the text may be accompanied by only a brief introduction but no record or acknowledgment of the perhaps divergent materials from which it was produced. Such eclectic, clear-text editions, both scholarly and popular, are in fact the material actualizations of the theoretical impulses that led to the development of traditional Anglo-American textual criticism. As such, they also validate these impulses, prefiguring readers' senses of literature, individual literary works, and literary criticism in ways that must be fundamentally (if tacitly) consistent with the attitudes that shaped the editions and that thereby invite other, similar editions that in turn continue to delimit readers' responses.

For textual critics of medieval literature in particular, the problems created by the New Criticism were of a vastly different sort from those facing critics of more recent historical periods. While there are plenty of medieval compositions and texts from which one could construct the requisite verbal icons, they are preserved in ways that are not immediately responsive to modern interpretation and that would seem to preclude the possibility of organic unity: Authors typically did not sign their names; texts of very few manuscripts are consistent in even the superficialities of orthography, punctuation, and physical appearance that are essential for the verbal icon; and copies of the same work can differ substantively from one another, much more so than reprints or even revisions of modern novels do. Moreover, medievalists lack the evidence about the genesis of works that might indicate unity or incompleteness but that the New Critics nonetheless declared irrelevant; we do not have, for instance, proof sheets of *Pearl* or a letter from Chaucer to Gower about whether the *Troilus* exists in several distinct versions.

The ramifications for editing of these textual and cultural determinants of medieval works have never been addressed in any explicitly theoretical way. Indeed, in a New Critical climate, the inconsonance between the cultural factors that shaped vernacular medieval literature and the central assumptions of postromantic thought, if fully explored in editing and interpretation, would have placed medieval literature even farther toward the margins of the literary canon. Thus, the model of editing inherited and accommodated from the humanists has remained viable because it is a way of bridging the cultural chasms of humanism and romanticism—a way, that is, of treating, presenting, and interpreting medieval works as much as possible like modern ones. Due to the differing ways in which medieval and modern works are preserved, however, medievalists have diverged in at least one significant way from critics of modern literature. Recent authors could be insouciantly killed off, partly because their verbal icons were already, more or less, determined; there was, after all, a *Pudd'nhead Wilson* with Mark Twain's name on the title page that was published within Twain's lifetime. On the other hand, and as chapter 4 will argue in detail, medieval vernacular authors, in order to accommodate the aesthetic demands of romanticism and the textual-critical demands of humanism, had to be *created* as an editorial and interpretive rationale: The supposition that an author's final intentions and an authoritative text lay in the distant but recoverable textual past has been the principle that has enabled textual critics to construct the medieval verbal icon.[51] The anonymity of most Middle English works has in fact been conducive in this regard because it precludes the possibility of succumbing to the intentional fallacy without affecting the requirements of textual criticism.

Within this theoretical framework, it will be appropriate to consider in greater detail the historical significance of the work of George Kane, who has brilliantly exposed the problems of recension and has done a great deal to demonstrate the complementary natures of textual and interpretive studies.[52] Although Kane himself has insisted all along that he meant to speak only about his predicaments while editing *Piers Plowman* and not to offer a general editorial theory,[53] his work remains among the few—and certainly the best known and most influential—explicitly theoretical discussions of the editing of Middle English works. The influence of Kane's efforts lies only partly, however, in the fact that his sometimes controversial methods have been imitated by subsequent scholars. As with many theorists in the course of textual criticism since the time of Lachmann, Kane's stress is on method rather than theoretical motivation, and the controversy that Kane himself helped to focus on his eclectic method has made the question of *how* one recovers authorial intention, rather than *what* constitutes authorial intention, the most prominent issue in editorial discussions of Middle English literature. In bypassing the question of the historical and cultural value of Langland's particular lexical constructs (presuming they can be recovered) amidst the variation of the *Piers* manuscripts, Kane embraces and in fact requires the humanist equation of the authoritative text with the authorial, as well as the humanist valorization of an idealist, lexical understanding of the work. Kane therefore shares with Manly and Rickert the same central assumption shared by Bédier and Lachmann, as well as by many critics from Valla to Bowers. This is the ahistorical assumption that one conception of author, work, and text has been constant throughout all literary periods and provenances and that this conception, in turn, must be reflected in editorial procedure. More particularly, Kane assumes that in the fourteenth and fifteenth centuries Langland's words had the same cultural and aesthetic status as Wordsworth's or Faulkner's, for instance, have today or as Cicero's had in the fifteenth century. In this regard, it is significant that though Kane rejects the value of recension and Greg's calculus for analyzing the *Piers* manuscripts, he implicitly accepts the goal of both approaches.[54]

But the controversy that Kane's eclectic approach occasioned is thus surprising, for, given the New Critical doctrines and the dictates of humanist textual criticism, his editorial formulation was a historical inevitability—an editorial imperative. As Patterson points out, the *Piers* editions straddle a line between scientific empiricism and romantic aesthetics, so that while Kane reluctantly must refrain from conjecturing an "obvious" and more metrically correct reading on the grounds that he cannot empirically account for its corruption,[55] he also depends on an acontextual belief—a belief that is consonant with both New Critical aesthetics and humanist textual criticism—in the "major" themes of the "great" works of art of "major" vernacular writers. In his discussion of the evidence for William Langland's authorship of *Piers Plowman,* for example, Kane notes, "We . . . are concerned with three poems each a great work of art, and with a situation where creative abilities of a major order were applied to a major theme";[56] in the opinion of Kane and Donaldson, the *A* version "has no literary qualities which would justify considering it the work of anyone but a major poet";[57] it is the poet's "greatness" as a rationale for the distinctiveness and exclusive validity of Langland's text that Kane in part relies upon in his review of the *Z* version by Rigg and Brewer and again in general restatements of his positions.[58] Moreover, though the medieval distinction of *scriptor* from *auctor* was largely a quantitative one dependent on the extent of an individual's original contribution to the text he was transmitting, for Kane the distinction between scribal and authorial *usus scribendi* is qualitative. He judges a reading inauthentic, for instance, because "a passage where such lack of insight into the form and meaning of the poem is exhibited cannot be ascribed to the author."[59] In their edition of the *B* version Kane and Donaldson similarly observe:

> To determine originality from the criterion of the relative or absolute appropriateness of readings to the poet's style is the obverse of identifying a scribal quality in them. Just as scribal variants tend to flat statement or crude overemphasis, diffuseness in denotation and loss of connotation, dilution of meaning and absence of tension, in general a bald, colourless and prosy expression, so the style of the poet is vigorous, nervous, flexible, and relatively compressed, made distinctive by characteristic mannerisms and figures.[60]

The individuality, ambiguity, and compression of the great poet's style are precisely the qualities characteristic of the Metaphysical poets so often praised by the New Critics.

The historical applicability of these characteristics is rendered problematic, however, by the fact that within the medieval period and well into the humanist epoch that created textual criticism, literature recognized as great had for the most part been written by classical and patristic *auctores*. Furthermore, even within the vernacular corpus Lydgate, now so much in disfavor, would surely have been considered a greater stylist in the fifteenth century than Langland. It is in fact precisely on the issue of style that the aesthetic basis of Kane's editorial formulations becomes most apparent. In disparaging Derek Pearsall's belief that scribes were capable of a "high level of intellectual and even critical engagement," for instance, Kane observes: "Its height is relative to the level of the base. A scribe copying Lydgate might well seem to soar by variation."[61] Other aesthetic assumptions expose another New Critical principle that informs the Kane-Donaldson theories: "In the absence of other considerations a *natural* presumption that a poem under revision will *grow* in content, scope and meaning, rather than diminish, must make this [the *A* version] seem the earliest form of *Piers Plowman*" (emphasis added).[62] But the naturalness of this presumption of growth is rendered suspect by examination of the revisions and collaborations of even modern writers as diverse as Wordsworth, Whitman, James, Mark Twain, and Mailer.[63]

Similarly New Critical in orientation is Kane and Donaldson's insistence that each variant in the *Piers* manuscripts be treated on an individual basis. In divorcing readings from their manuscript contexts and the manuscripts, in turn, from the social environments that produced them and in which they meant, Kane and Donaldson adopt a procedure reminiscent of the New Critical separation of literary texts from cultural contexts. At the same time, however, they thereby accommodate the humanist demands for a lexical, idealist conception of the work: The "homogeneity of the tradition is our general authorization for editing a *B* version; but more particularly it implies that no manuscript is sacrosanct; no manuscript is demonstrably 'closer to' or 'more remote from' the original except with regard to the particular reading."[64] This separation of *Piers Plowman* from its cultural and literary contexts, which also recalls the ambivalent sense of historicity predominant in humanist textual criticism, is apparent elsewhere in Kane and Donaldson's theorizing. Though Kane maintains that *Piers* "was especially subject to variation as a living text with a content of direct concern to its scribes"[65]—though the records of variants for both the *A* and *B* versions reflect a very vital work indeed—Kane and Donaldson consistently downplay any significance of individual manuscripts, do not factor this extensive variation into their conception of what *Piers Plowman* was in the Middle Ages, only sporadically take into account the date of manuscripts, and nowhere explain in what cultural or narrowly practical context the sort of extensive convergent variation and cross-contamination on which they sometimes rely would be possible.[66] This latter point becomes especially problematic in light of Doyle and Parkes's subsequent work on the predominance of independent craftsmen (rather than large-scale atelier) in late Middle English book production.[67] When Kane observes that a particular combination of manuscripts from "the point of view of content and meaning . . . is forced and *inorganic*" (emphasis added),[68] the adjectives he uses reflect the theoretical orientation of much of his thinking.

I have dwelled at such length on the ideas of Kane because they remain the best-articulated theoretical position in Middle English textual criticism. Equally, they are fundamentally New Critical in character and consistent with the tradition of textual criticism begun by the humanists. It is this tradition, indeed, that Kane implicitly sees himself protecting and furthering, thereby reflecting two other qualities of traditional textual criticism—self-conscious totalizing that silences opposition and a moral valence recuperated as scientific empiricism. He observes, for example, that "knowledgeable editors use" the term "sophistication" cautiously.[69] Elsewhere, in a vein reminscent of Poliziano's or Scaliger's indignation, he asserts that Rigg and Brewer's belief that differences between readings that are not manifest errors "are as likely to be authorial as scribal in origin" is "held in defiance of five centuries of textual criticism" and that in producing their edition they "take no account of even the most elementary indications of textual criticism."[70] Much as Lachmann and Greg have had their continuators, subsequent scholars have assimilated Kane to this tradition by predicating editions on allegiance to Kane's methods.[71] Ultimately, the work of Kane has further consolidated humanist textual criticism: The extension of his theories beyond *Piers Plowman* recuperates a tradition—the Middle English tradition—that might constitute a challenge to humanist assumptions and principles as entirely responsive to and consistent with them.

If there is a status quo in Middle English editing today, then, it is one based less on method and more on the central theoretical positions that I have traced back to the humanists. To put matters another way, since methodological considerations dominate textual-critical discussions of Middle English, the implication of these discussions, as of much textual criticism in general, is that the theoretical principles are given and constitute a critical horizon beyond which one cannot go. One could in fact speak of an implicit editorial model for most Middle English literature that rests on two assumptions, each of which betrays an attempt to accommodate humanist paradigms: that in the Middle Ages literature existed textually, aesthetically, and culturally much as it does in the modern (or Antique) period and that the goal of the editor of medieval works is consequently much the same as the goal of someone concerned with other literature.[72]

This implicit model is apparent in any edition that attempts to equate authoritative texts with the efforts of particular individuals, such as Chaucer, Henryson, Langland, Malory, Lydgate, or Gower. It is also apparent, however, in editions of anonymous works. The editor of *The Cloud of Unknowing,* for example, observes: "The present aim in recording all the variant readings of six manuscripts . . . is to attempt to determine the author's original text by comparing the readings of the best representative manuscripts of each group."[73] Similarly, the editors of

Seinte Katerine suggest, "The archetype of the three extant manuscripts was itself inaccurate and cannot have been the author's holograph."[74] Even in cases where application of this theory seems particularly difficult, as in the fifteenth-century *Tale of Jack and his Stepdame,* it has informed editorial procedure. This work survives in five manuscripts and five early printed editions, and a correct authorial text was somehow retrieved by recension from the ten copies presumed to be corruptions of this work, even though "there are only two lines in the entire poem on which all of the versions agree."[75]

In the last decade or so there have been several studies that by implication attempt to get outside the humanist paradigm to evaluate Middle English manuscript materials in ways that are more responsive to the distinctive cultural and literary determinants and qualities of these works.[76] Recent editorial and literary theorists of more modern literature like Jerome McGann, whose arguments I will consider in the following chapter, have perhaps inspired textual-critical work that closely attends to the circumstances of production, the demands of genre, and the particularities of individual works. A rejection of the totalizing of humanist textual criticism is apparent in studies that advocate methods conditioned by the specific generic characteristics of Latin tropes, commentaries, and *reportationes,*[77] as well as of Middle English translations, religious works, dramas, lyrics, and romances.[78] Several studies of individual works representing a variety of genres and modes of production have also appeared.[79] In the editing of Middle English romances in particular, Pearsall has been especially forceful and eloquent in arguing for the relevance of manuscript context in assessing and editing medieval materials and against the utility of modern editorial methods and the modern critical edition.[80] All of these studies are valuable both for their individual contributions and for the way they collectively suggest alternatives to the humanist model of textual criticism. But in many cases the analyses are limited only to advocating a specific editorial method in response to particular manuscript materials and do not extend to an account of why the materials might be in the condition they are. Moreover, the advocated method has increasingly become essentially diplomatic transcription, which, like Bédier's best-text approach, is nonetheless informed by unassessed humanist notions of the authoritative, lexical work.

Attempts to offer more radical critiques of received notions of textual criticism have been rather less successful. Stephen Knight argues for the editing of medieval works "with a consciously historical and socio-literary interpretation as the ultimate guide" and prefers readings that create "maximum possible historical tension," even if they are not by the acknowledged author of the work being edited.[81] Arguments like this are not cogent unless they can justify a historical lexical work over any other one and then defend the historically "tense" text as the historically valid one within a broadly cultural and literary context. Other arguments have been compromised by the ambivalence over historicity that has characterized textual criticism in general. Various and conflicting assumptions about editing, historicity, and cognition undermine the contention that modern editorial methods are inadequate for editing manuscript works because they are not sensitive to historical context and production, that any attempt to reconstruct a historical text is destined to failure, that a best-text edition (in Bédier's sense) has self-evident validity as a representation of "what at least one medieval reader actually read," and that, in accordance with modern Derridean thinking, editors should themselves participate in the "free play" of manuscripts, since it recreates a communal, socialized reception of works in the Middle Ages.[82]

Other critics have fully embraced humanist textual criticism and therefore humanist assumptions about literature. Patterson, for example, implies that not to edit the Kane-Donaldson way is not to edit at all and thereby essentially affirms the humanists' self-validating positions on textual criticism. After pointing out a number of intriguing parallels between Lachmann's editions and the Kane-Donaldson *B* text as cultural statements, Patterson concludes that textual criticism and editing are inherently New Critical in nature, as his definition of editing suggests: "The task of the editor confronted with the mass of lectional evidence is to 'read' the evidence as a New Critic would read a poem, and to produce as a result of his labors an interpretation that is, in fact, the poem itself." But such an argument does not take full account of the evidence of manuscript transmission, simplifies the development and complexity of editorial procedure and textual studies, and finally testifies only for the New Critical understanding of the character and limitations of textual criticism. Recent advancements in manuscript codicology and reception do indeed suggest the inadequacies of New Critical textual criticism but scarcely warrant the observation that the alternative to the

Kane-Donaldson approach "is not some other mode of interpretation, or some other kind of edition, but the refusal of interpretation entirely and an edition that, for all its claims to soundness and reliability, in fact represents an arbitrarily foreclosed act of historical understanding." Such a theoretical dichotomy preempts the deconstruction of a straw man (or men) and most clearly reveals the unacknowledged and debilitating premises of the New Critical position.[83]

Traditional, humanist principles are also apparent in a number of attempts to edit texts on the basis of presumed metrical regularity[84] or, in the case of Hoccleve's *Regement of Princes,* to transform the orthography of a work that does not survive in holograph into Hoccleve's own orthography on the basis of several other works that do.[85] Both these approaches tacitly equate the authoritative text with the authorial one, presume a lexical, idealist conception of the work, and attribute literary qualities characteristic of recent and Antique poets to those of Middle English. In this silence lurk a number of questions. If the "variety of alliterative patterning that we find in the surviving manuscripts is scribal in origin," it is nonetheless the only patterning in which most alliterative poems survive. What historical validity is there, then, in the "single, remarkably homogenous set of rhythmic and syntactic constraints" in which the poems are alleged to have been originally written?[86] If a tree falls in a forest with no one around—if a poet writes a meter no one reads—does it make a sound? In its flippancy, my question is not meant to challenge the integrity or achievement of recent developments in metrics, all of which seem valuable to me, but provocatively to foreground how the horizon of traditional textual criticism can resolve significant and complex theoretical issues into commonplace assumptions. Arguments about editing based on metrical regularity, in other words, assume certain humanist positions on the character of an authoritative text and certain attitudes toward the purpose of modern editions, but these assumptions, acknowledged or not, do not themselves preclude other ones or validate themselves.

Equally worth examination is the assumption that it is historically valid to speak of authorial accidentals for a vernacular text of the early fifteenth century, over three hundred years before the spread of regularized spelling for English; as late as the end of the seventeenth century, for instance, Milton was rather unconcerned about punctuation. Again, a number of questions lurk. To what extent can one conceptualize vernacular orthography in an age when there were no books or institutions to identify and regulate it? To be written, words obviously had to have (variant) spellings, but what cultural or linguistic reasons are there for regarding orthography as integral to vernacular works at this time? Assuming that the *Regement* could be printed in a text with orthography that approximates what Hoccleve would have written, would he, as a vernacular writer, have recognized the orthography as his and as a distinctive characteristic of the poem? It may in fact prove possible "to combine orthodox 'classical' base-text theory (stemmatics) with orthodox 'modern' copy-text theory to produce for the first time an edition of a Middle English work (surviving only in scribal copies) with *all* its auctorial features—accidentals and substantives alike—still intact in the edited, eclectic version."[87] But how valid are the assumptions that it is desirable to utilize the humanist-derived "base-text theory" and "copy-text theory" in the editing of a nonhumanist work, that modern "auctorial features" have meaning for a fifteenth-century vernacular work, and that a textual-critical notion of authors and the features that characterize them should be applied to individuals who were not *auctores* among their contemporaries?

In short, the issues involved in assessing the implications of contemporary editing of Middle English works are much larger than is often recognized, as are those involved in evaluating potential textual-critical procedures. Moreover, to point out that Middle English literature has been accommodated to the antagonistic demands of traditional textual criticism of course does not ipso facto obviate the value of or need for such accommodation. Having considered the consequences and implications of traditional Middle English textual criticism as the products of a variety of historical and ideological forces, I want in the following chapter to address directly these larger issues as they apply to Middle English materials. What is the character of an edited text as a critical production and as a site of interpretation? What responsibility does it owe in these regards to a historical work? How can the character of a historical work be determined? Should it be presented to the modern reader, and if so how? To what extent, for each of these questions, are there alternative answers?

❦

CHAPTER THREE

Editing, History,
Discourse

I T IS A commonplace that modern critical editions of medieval works, with their orthographic conventions, elimination of copying errors, reader aids, and uniformity, differ radically from medieval works, which materially exist in physically and lexically variable manuscripts.[1] Whether such editions falsify or even misrepresent the original works, however, depends on how one chooses to define the work and the objectives of a modern edition. Within the idealist, lexical conception of the work that has been predominant throughout textual-critical history, a modern critical edition is in fact completely comprehensible as a representation of an original work. From this view, the physical realization of a work in a particular document is not an intrinsic characteristic of that work. To Tanselle, for example, "messages may be inextricable from their media, but the medium of literature and other pieces of verbal communication is language, not paper and ink. . . . from the point of view of verbal communication, manuscripts and printed books are simply objects of utility." Therefore, "if one is reconstructing texts intended by their authors, one generally need not preserve these features [e.g., paper quality, leaf dimension, style of letters, margins] of documents, for they are not, except in unusual cases, part of the intended texts."[2] In a related vein, Steven Mailloux has argued that an author's most complete intentions are "best defined in terms of *the intended structure of the reader's response*" and that "the interpretive framework of reader-response criticism" should thus be utilized in editing.[3] For both Tanselle and Mailloux, the words the author intended reflect and in fact constitute the ideal work in the author's mind—or at least a fixed part of the work that the reader supplements—and that editors, accordingly, should attempt to recover in their texts.[4] By the same token, if the material existence of the historical work is an insignificant aspect of that work beyond the concerns of the editor, then the presentation and apparatus of the modern critical edition are presumed not to affect the character of the work itself or of the reader's responses to it. From this perspective, the material differences between the historical and modern realizations of a work are irrelevant to both editorial procedure and critical interpretation.

These differences are profoundly significant, however, in a view that sees material realizations as inextricable aspects of the work. The work may in fact be conceptually and philosophically distinct from a particular realization, the argument goes, but since readers' access to a work is only through a particular realization, for practical purposes it is impossible to differentiate readers' responses to a work from their responses to particular material realizations of that work. Moreover, documentary realizations themselves—in their size, color, layout, typeface, illustration, and construction—are thought to signify as complexly as literary texts. By extension, if different realizations elicit markedly different responses, the work itself might be regarded as different in each realization. Jerome McGann, for example, has shown how Byron's *Don Juan* was initially issued anonymously in an expensive limited edition so that only readers of taste and judgment would have access to the poem and that controversy might be averted. The poem was quickly pirated, however, in small, inexpensive editions complete with engravings. In one edition the poem was thus the product of an aesthete and appealed to sophisticated readers; in the other it was a bawdy romance that pandered to depraved imaginations.[5] While the idealist conception of the work presents the edited text as in effect the work itself, the materialist view would maintain that the physical characteristics of the original work, as much as its text, need to be recognized and recuperated.

This materialist conception of the work has recently had a number of advocates,[6] perhaps in part because it is consonant with larger movements in literary criticism, such as feminism and New Historicism, that have focused on the historical constructions, meanings, and receptions of literary works. In textual criticism this focus has been manifested as arguments about the socialized nature of the text, and these arguments represent the first serious challenge to the status of traditional notions of textual criticism that were initiated by the humanists and have been developed into Anglo-American clear-text eclecticism. Critics such as James Thorpe, Donald Pizer, D. F. McKenzie, and Jerome McGann, for instance, have argued that the authority of a text needs to be seen as more comprehensively contextual than has typically been the case. In McGann's formulation, "For an editor and textual critic the concept of authority has to be conceived in a more broadly social and cultural context. Authoritative texts are arrived at by an exhaustive reconstruction not of an author and his intentions so much as of an author and his context of work."[7] Hershel Parker, thus, has stressed the historical context of the creative act itself, which in his view has a beginning, a middle, and an end.[8] An author, according to Parker, cannot return to a work years after its original composition without tampering with the initial intention, and editors, therefore, need to respect the nature of intention as a function of a temporally limited creative act.

Other critics have explored the publishing and personal factors that contribute to the character of a printed text and have maintained that editors need to view texts as functions of historical contexts and thus ought to expand "authorial intention" to include the intentions (of a spouse or publisher, say) to which an author acquiesces. "The chief difficulties emerge," McGann maintains, "when textual criticism has the effect of desocializing our historical view of the literary work. When we make decisions about the condition and significance of various texts on the simple criterion of author's (final) intentions we foster serious misconceptions about the nature of literary production. Too many relevant aspects of the literary work are de-emphasized, or even abstracted from the critical view altogether, when we operate on such a principle."[9] Peter Shillingsburg says of such positions:

There is a fundamental shift in the concept of authority involved in this argument. . . . this argument simply vests authority for the text in a socio-economic environment which "contains" the author's initiating creative activity *and* the publisher's ongoing process of moving composition into production. The textual changes introduced by the production process are accepted by the editor, not because they are better, not because they are historical, not because they are sacred, but because they are social—representing a necessary bio-socio-economic relationship between author, publisher, and audience (including the editor).[10]

Not surprisingly, this "fundamental shift," inasmuch as it constitutes a partial rejection of the received tradition of textual criticism, has been challenged in several ways. Tanselle, for example, accepts in theory McGann's socialization of the text: "If one wishes to reconstruct how earlier readers reacted or to analyze their written reactions, there is no doubt that the physical features of the books they read are relevant and can in that sense be considered part of the 'texts.' "[11] Elsewhere he observes that "one obviously need not give preference to an author's intention, for what is done to a text by the author's friends, scribes, printers, and publishers is also a matter of history, and one can decide to reconstruct the version of a work resulting from the ministrations of any of them. Such a goal is as valid as that of recovering the author's intended text: each is valuable and serves a different historical purpose."[12] But in such a critique, concepts like work, text, author, intention, and scribe are presumed to be transhistorical constants, manifested at specific moments in history, rather than themselves historically constructed phenomena. In other words, the very notion that an "author" might "intend" a "text" is assumed not to be historically determined, and such an assumption is entirely consistent with humanist principles. Similarly, Parker's argument—that to "do as Pizer, Thorpe, and McGann do is to insist on integrity in something after integrity has been lost and to confuse two separate phases, the creative phase and the publishing, marketing phase[13]"—depends on seeing these "phases" as not themselves contextually defined. Thus, in these responses socialization is accommodated by being perceived not as a reorientation of textual-critical constants (author, work, text) but as a perspective that focuses on constants other than those with which textual criticism has traditionally—and by nature—been concerned. These constants are nonetheless still within the traditional purview of textual criticism so that socialization thus conceived poses no challenge to the transhistorical, humanist conception of the lexical, idealist work as the product of an individual author. Hence, while the Anglo-American tradition has perceived Bédier's work, which is actually consolidating, as a discontinuity, it has processed socialization not as a rupture but as a continuity, and in both cases it has sustained itself.

Though Tanselle and Parker offer cogent arguments, they critique the specifics of socialized views without entirely abandoning the theoretical framework of humanist textual criticism. But in some (if not all) hermeneutic endeavors, including textual criticism, there is a hierarchy of theories. When a number of theories obtain in what is regarded as a discipline, some of them are necessarily of different conceptual orders in such a way that each theory is framed in accordance with the limitations imposed on it by higher-order theories and in turn delimits the hermeneutic options of lower-order theories. The higher up in such a hierarchy one moves, in Roger Lass's words, the greater the consequences of any interpretive decision: "A factual error made by a historian in interpreting a document (e.g. a misreading) is usually quite easy to remedy. . . . But an error in the local theory itself (e.g. admission of a document that is not properly part of the record) can be much more damaging. And by the same token a general statement of the form 'X can be recovered from history by assuming Y' can be disastrous if the arguments for the recoverability of X or the assumption of Y are (either empirically or logically) unsound."[14] In textual criticism and literary interpretation, understanding of a historical reality and of the objectives of a modern edition must logically be higher up the theoretical hierarchy than methodological discussions, for in any edition method is always an extension—a concretization—of theory, however unacknowledged the latter may be. If one disagrees with the reading of a given line in an edition of a Middle English work (e.g., preferring *lene* to *leue* from a hand where *n* and *u* are interchangeable) but accepts the editor's understanding of historical reality, the disagreement is narrowly methodological; because of the extent of the theoretical agreement, such a disagreement seems to be potentially solvable (only *lene,* for instance, might fit within context) or generally recognizable as unsolvable (either reading might be possible). Even more is this true when two critics agree on method, in which case disagreement over a reading should in fact be absolutely resolvable.

By extension, for meaningful disagreements of opinion to take place, they must take place at the same theoretical level. Tanselle's and Parker's critiques of socialization do not entirely meet that requirement, and the fruitlessness of pursuing discussions that originate at different points on a theoretical hierarchy can be illustrated in a variety of ways. In his review of N. F. Blake's *The Textual Tradition,* for example, Charles Owen faults Blake for allegedly "ignoring aesthetic considerations" in his discussion of the Hengwrt manuscript.[15] But Blake's argument is situated farther up the theoretical hierarchy than the methodological level at which most of Owen's is situated: Blake's argument is an attempt to account in informed historical terms for the surviving manuscripts of the *Canterbury Tales* as predicates of the existence and transmission of Chaucer's text, and the methodology Blake uses is shaped accordingly. Blake's perception of the historical reality may be challenged, as may be the methods he utilizes. But to address only the methodological level without recognizing the more encompassing theoretical differences is to initiate a discussion very much at cross-purposes. On the other hand, the existence of any theoretical hierarchy does not preclude informed criticism of any level of that hierarchy, provided that the criticism emerges from a similar theoretical level. Thus, Patterson claims of the Kane-Donaldson *B* text of *Piers Plowman* that "criticism at the level of counterexample, which is virtually the only criticism that this edition has received, is in itself futile. In the last analysis, Kane and Donaldson's systematic interpretation of the data can be effectively challenged only by another, better system."[16] But this is to claim for the *B* text a paradoxical existence—that the edited text exists only at a theoretical level, not in a methodologically realized form. In fact, "criticism at the level of counterexample" is entirely valid, so long as the critic agrees, at least for the sake of the argument, with all the theoretical positions farther up the hierarchy.[17] The issue of a materialist conception of a work versus an idealist one is thus neither as simple as this very formulation suggests nor, more importantly and despite the rhetoric of many critics, absolutely resolvable.

At every point on the theoretical hierarchy of textual criticism, the choices editors make are not essentialist: Unless they transgress legal issues of plagiarism or libel, editors could in principle approach and present their material through any number of editorial techniques.[18] In practice, however, editors' choices are rather more limited, most generally by the institutions that sanction and sustain editorial activity. In the earliest, humanist days of textual criticism these institutions were the Church, the system of patronage, and the universities. The former two have of course become increasingly less influential. But the academic community (encompassing both scholarship and pedagogy) and, since the nineteenth century, the commercial publishing houses do assert diverse and sometimes conflicting demands on editors' decisions about editorial technique and the works they choose to edit.

The ways in which these relationships can reify theoretical propositions are sometimes startling. When Fredson Bowers wrote the initial directives of the Center for Editions of American Authors, for example, he not surprisingly incorporated the Greg-Bowers position on copytext as requisite for a good edition. The National Endowment for the Humanities agreed to fund the undertaking, but in so doing the N.E.H. in effect transformed the notion of copy-text from a theory to a fact. That is, it funded the C.E.A.A. from 1966 to 1976, and, since copytext had been present in the original documentation, the N.E.H. continued to look for evidence of the theory's employment in subsequent proposals. To obtain funding—and thus the means to continue and advance projects and, perhaps, their careers—editors needed to incorporate copy-text theory in their proposals and methods, regardless of the character of the materials with which they were working.[19] As a result, in D. C. Greetham's words, "virtually all of the three hundred or so volumes" to acquire the seal of approval of the C.E.A.A. or its successor the Committee on Scholarly Editions "have been constructed on Greg-Bowers principles of eclecticism and copy-text."[20] Particularly with the 1991 revisions of C.S.E. principles, copy-text theory and eclectic intentionalism have gradually become much less predominant in the editing of American literature, though their influence remains in the existence of the C.E.A.A. and C.S.E. editions that have already been produced and that are unlikely to be reedited in the near future.

But, again, in principle the theoretical hierarchy offers a broad range of options. Perhaps the highest level involves conception of the objectives of a modern edition: the decision whether the edition is primarily meant to be itself a contemporary work or to recuperate a work as historically constituted at some point. Examples of the former are the various seventeenth- and eighteenth-century modernizations of Chaucer's poetry, which attempt to present the poems in a modern format so that they can be read as modern poems. The historical orientation, however, has dominated textual criticism since the fifteenth century: Whatever the vicissitudes of method, almost every editor—particularly modern scholarly ones—has conceived the editorial task to be the recuperation of some earlier work. This task motivates both McGann and those interested in socialized texts as well as Tanselle and those interested exclusively in an individual author's actual words. The implication of this dominant motivation may well be that editing, like translation, is an inherently historical endeavor: Once editors and translators become more interested in creating new works than in recovering old ones, we can no longer conceptually differentiate their achievements from those of creative writers. Ezra Pound's *Seafarer* is a case in point. Pound does not really attempt a translation but structures a poetics suggestive of the Old English tradition and entirely reworks his source in order to offer a picture of cultural desolation in the early twentieth century.

As fundamentally an act of historical recuperation, textual criticism as it has been practiced thus begins at the same theoretical level as archaeology. This is a level that is defined in part both by the intention of the investigator and by the manner in which the recuperated object is presented. For archaeologists to perform archaeology when coming upon what they believe to be pot shards in a midden, they must attempt to reconstruct the pot that the shards once formed. The archaeologists may get the pot all wrong; or they may construct a pot out of what are in fact the fragments of a statue. But in either case they are attempting to reconstruct an object that they believe to be historical; the exhibition of this object as historical constitutes, in turn, a hermeneutic pretext for subsequent viewers of the object. Archaeology is not being performed, however, when the archaeologists disregard or defy what they believe to have been the historical source-form of the shards and use them to construct, say, a lamp—they are then primarily creating rather than recovering. Even if it should turn out that the shards in fact historically formed a lamp to which the construction is extraordinarily similar, the facts that the activity was not historically motivated and that the object is presented as a new work rather than a reconstructed one vitiate it as archaeological reconstruction.

Like a pyramid, the theoretical hierarchy of textual criticism becomes increasingly broader, offering increasingly more options, the farther one moves from its origin in historical motivation. At the very next level, for example, one faces at least two general options: to represent or to recreate the historical work. An edition that attempted to recreate the historical work would be one that attempted to present the contemporary *equivalent* of the historical work so that the responses of the modern reader would not be like that of a visitor to a museum, where the objects are patently not parts of the viewer's day-to-day world, but would parallel if not duplicate that of the historical reader. If it could be shown, for instance, that physical realization is an immanent aspect of a historical conception of the work but *not* of the modern conception, a modern editor who attempted to include this quality in some way would transform the effect of a historical work into something it was not historically. To borrow the terminology of linguistics, an editor would in so doing turn an unmarked work—one that fulfilled the expectations of its historical audience—into a marked one—one that, in its dependence on physical realization, constitutes an unusual reading experience for modern readers. Therefore, in such a situation the historically sensitive procedure, it might be argued, would be to recreate the unmarked quality of the historical text by *disregarding* physical realization.

If a work is represented, it is in effect displayed as an object of historical interest, like a museum display of some archaeological object. But as the comparison to museum displays suggests, there are still editorial options. One could devote relatively little attention to the historical contexts of the original work or of the modern edition and concentrate instead on the work as distinct from either manifestation, in the same way that a vase or statue might simply be placed on a pedestal without consideration of its historical functions or significances and without regard to the interpretive effects of its present display. Or one could take a more perspicuous view of the *edition* as work and attempt a broader duplication of the physical layout and design of the historical work—rather like the editorial equivalent of a diorama.

To effect a historical recovery—one step further down one portion of the theoretical hierarchy—an editor has at least three broad theoretical options: to recover a historical work on the basis of presumed historical principles, to recover it on the basis of recognizably nonhistorical aesthetic principles, or to recover it on the basis of allegedly transhistorical principles. Each of these options, in turn, creates still more alternatives that depend on a variety of theoretical and practical considerations. Editors would need, for instance, to take positions on the recoverability of the past, on the processing of the past by the present, and on the defining characteristics of a literary work in a given historical period, and they also would need to consider cost and audience for the edition.

Humanist textual criticism has followed the route of transhistori-

73

cal principles, while the advocates of the socialized text have for the most part been guided by presumed historical principles. But even they have sometimes adopted principles about authorship and text that seem essentially humanist in orientation. The argument that the authorial intention of a given work includes the opinions of a friend or publisher, for example, depends on and thereby valorizes the humanist notion of an author in order to *extend* consideration to the influence of others; this argument does not conceive the authorial principle as itself historically constructed. Moreover, if the traditional humanist view stresses the "spatial" character of a work—its existence at a given moment—while the various social approaches stress the "temporal"—its changing character through time—in practical, editorial terms both approaches share an essentially lexical-idealist conception.[21] By comparison, archaeology no longer concerns itself simply with the reconstruction of pots in isolation but with understanding such pots as they emerge from broadly social and cultural concerns. It also, in the words of two proponents of the "new archaeology," examines and emphasizes "theory as a practice which cannot be separated from the object of archaeology, itself indelibly social, and the present socio-political context of this practice, this mediation of past and present."[22]

A more rigorous attempt to recover a historical work on the basis of presumed historical principles would utilize historical factors to reach an understanding of how the abstract notions of author, work, and text were constructed in a given period and would then edit a particular text in view of these notions. Rather than rely on modern editorial conceptions of authorial intention, for example, an editor would attempt to determine what combination of what aspects of literary creation, production, and reception defined authorship in a historical period.

A brief glimpse here at a familiar example will usefully reveal specific social and cultural factors that potentially help to construct authors, works, and texts at any given historical moment.[23] Throughout the eighteenth and nineteenth centuries the social and literary characteristics of authors and texts were demonstrably shaped by nonliterary and noncreative actions like the Copyright Act of 1709, an increase in literacy, the development of the rotating printing press and of paper made from wood pulp (both of which made printed matter less expensive), the rise of parts publication, the moral and economic influence of Mudie's circulating library, the 1852 decision on the Bookselling Question (which enabled free trade), the restrictions placed on triple-decker novels by the circulating libraries in 1894, and the Net Book Agreement of 1899. During the course of this two-hundred-year period, through these social phenomena as much as through developments in literary theory, genre, or style, the "author" as a cultural entity transferred economic dependence from patron, to bookseller, to publisher, to (perhaps) literary agent, and in the process acquired for the first time in English history a distinct social and *professional* identity as a writer. In the words of *Fraser's Magazine* from March of 1847, by that time "literature has become a profession. It is a means of subsistence, almost as certain as the bar or the church. The number of aspirants increases daily, and daily the circle of readers grows wider. That there are some evils inherent in such a state of things it would be folly to deny; but still greater folly would it be to see nothing beyond these evils. Bad or good, there is no evading the 'great fact,' now what is so firmly established. We may deplore, but we cannot alter it."[24]

Such social constraints similarly contributed to the construction of works and texts in this period. The two dominant forms of publication for fiction in the nineteenth century, for instance, were parts publication and publication in a triple-decker, primarily for the circulating libraries. Both forms were responses to social determinants and, in turn, became social determinants themselves. The appearance of Charles Dickens's *Pickwick Papers* in parts publication, for example, was partially predicated both on an expanding market for fiction and on Dickens's need for a steady income. In turn, parts publication subsequent to the phenomenal success of *Pickwick*, Robert Patten observes, "became for thirty years a chief means of democritizing and enormously expanding the Victorian book-reading and book-buying public";[25] and it was the success of *Pickwick* that established Dickens as the writer whose financial success (however exaggerated) would become a model for a growing professional class.[26] The growth of Mudie's circulating library was similarly in part a response to the reduction in printing costs and to the increase of literacy among the poor in England and of a desire for moral guidance in fiction that was imputed to this group. At the same time, Mudie's library, which grew to be so powerful in part by compelling artificially inflated book prices for private buyers, manipulated the canon of works and authors printed and, with respect to the demands of the three-volume format, the nature of the novels' themes, plots, and characterizations. In the process, the "select" list of Mudie's library mirrored the values that it allegedly helped to foster: "The middle- or upper-middle-class reader who exchanged his volume regularly under Mudie's dome received, besides entertainment, confirmation or definition of many of his beliefs."[27] Such publishing constraints, in conjunction with the evolving legal status of texts through copyright laws, ultimately redefined "text" so that, in N. N. Feltes's view, "it might become a commodity like any other."[28]

The novels of Thomas Hardy in particular nicely illustrate how contextually conditioned the character of a historical work and author can be.[29] Like many Victorian novels, Hardy's works were initially serialized, and he frequently found himself still writing a story even after serialization had begun. He used the opportunity of the book's appearance in a bound volume to effect a number of substantive changes, and did so again in its preparation for his collected works. In each case, the text was suited to the demands of the format and of Hardy's evolving conceptions of his works and of himself as an author. The famous semi-mythic county of Wessex in fact represents a thematic layer that Hardy was able to work into the books consistently only when he sat down to revise them for the collected edition published in 1895–97—after the reception of *Jude the Obscure* had caused him to abandon novel-writing forever. And this thematic layer, thus predicated on the complex publishing history of his novels, became a determinant not only of the revised novels Hardy produced but also of Hardy himself as a writer: "What Hardy looked forward to most keenly was the opportunity to revise all of his fiction from a common standpoint, the standpoint of Thomas Hardy, delineator of Wessex. The collected edition offered him the chance to see his work as a whole thing, to place each text in the pattern of existence that Wessex had become for him."[30]

As even this limited survey suggests, the historical construction of authors, works, and texts intersects and potentially emerges from a wide variety of cultural attitudes and institutions. What is true for the eighteenth and nineteenth centuries is likely to be true for any chronologically and geographically determined period: From a *historically sensitive perspective,* the particular effects of literary, economic, social, and cultural factors belie the transcendence inherent in humanist textual-critical principles. But to identify the existence of these factors is of course not necessarily to demonstrate their relevance either to the historical notion of a work or to the work's recuperation in a modern edition.[31] That a work necessarily exists in a physical form, for instance, does not necessarily make it true that that form was historically perceived as essential to the work or that a modern editor generally interested in historical recovery—as every editor in the humanist tradition has been—misrepresents the work by not in some way recuperating its material realization. And the converse assumption of humanist textual criticism—that physical form is not relevant—also needs to be tested for individual historical contexts. Moreover, an editor interested in recovery through presumed historical principles needs to decide how to reconcile the sometimes competing demands of individual writers and larger historical frameworks. Should the accidentals of the works of Ben Jonson or William Cowper, for example, be granted special status because *they,* unlike most of their contemporaries, were particularly interested in preserving their own orthography and punctuation, or should the larger cultural indifference to such matters in the seventeenth and eighteenth centuries overbalance Jonson's and Cowper's concerns and lead the modern editor to display similar indifference? [32] Similarly, should the concern Shelley displays in a letter to the publisher Thomas Hookham about the placement of the title page, the paper quality, and the volume size of *Queen Mab*—selected "so as to catch the aristocrats: They will not read it, but their sons & daughters may"—predominate over any other indications about cultural determinants in these matters? [33]

If an editor elects a position on the textual-critical hierarchy that requires historically constructed conceptions of author, work, and text, it might be argued that such issues could be resolved through direct consultation of original historical documents or, barring that, of facsimile editions. There would still remain, however, the problem of defining the original work. A modern novel or poem may appear in any number of physically distinctive editions, while the manuscript manifestations of a medieval work typically vary still more widely, even assuming that a reader would have access to them: Which of these manifestations would be presumed to represent the historical work and why? An attempt to read a historical document of a work historically, furthermore, is compromised by the problems confronted in a hypothetical recreation of that work: The physical features and the responses they elicit that may have been unmarked in the Middle Ages may now be marked and vice versa. In essence, an original document is not an autonomous semiotic object, because its significances and meanings for its original readers were conditioned by the placement and definition of both those readers and the documents within larger social and institutional networks of the sort I outlined above. The simple act of a modern reader reading a medieval manuscript or a facsimile thereof, thus, does not provide unmediated access to the medieval work but rather constitutes a reading experience that is neither entirely medieval nor entirely modern.[34] In such a situation we would see a medieval document, but since we would not read it *as* medieval readers, the work to which we would respond would not be absolutely medieval. The limitations of an original document removed from the contexts out of which it emerged are especially clear in the poetry of Emily Dickinson. While all the poems are available in Thomas H. Johnson's edition, they are, in a strict sense, nonetheless impossible to edit. In transforming poems written on disparate bundles of envelopes and letters stitched together with thread and left in "Lady's Drawer" into the uniform format of a scholarly edition, Johnson renders a unique and private performance as a standardized, public one. But even when one reads the actual historical documents—Dickinson's envelopes—they arguably are not the same works they were originally, inasmuch as implicit in the modern reading is the recognition that the reading of the text is itself marked: We "normally" read poetry in printed books and magazines, and we "normally" do not at all read material not meant to be read.

A perspective that is equally unhelpful to historically minded critics and that betrays similar problems of historical sensibility has arisen in the wake of Marshall McLuhan's and Walter Ong's work on orality: That is, it has become common to speak of the electronic age as one of new orality and, consequently, to draw parallels between medieval and modern production and reception of literary works.[35] Computer technology, in the textual fluidity it enables, is thus seen as returning literary production to medieval practice, for it subverts the authority of any one version and can serve as the means to elevate readers to virtually collaborative status in the construction of literary works. Such a return is predicated, however, on the complete separation of texts and works not only from the cultural institutions and attitudes that enabled them but also from the technologies that realized them. Medieval readers had neither the technology for instantaneous and multiple textual access nor a cultural context that could in any meaningful way recognize collaboration between, say, St. Jerome and a late-fifteenth century vernacular writer. Since, again, texts, documents, and works are not autonomous semiotic objects, any resemblance between computerized publication and medieval literary production is thus as general and unhelpful as that between, say, deconstruction and nominalism, or Batman and Beowulf.

Another solution to the problems of presenting historically sensitive editions would be to produce a variety of editions, each, perhaps, reflecting a different version of a work.[36] But even with this approach, one would still need to be able to define the historical work and to distinguish one version of it from another, and one would also still be dependent on the institutional support that currently sustains editing and that is likely to limit editorial options. Only certain versions, in other words, would probably get printed, and the primary considerations in differentiating among versions would likely be not theoretical but economic and pedagogical.

Since its inception in the humanist period, textual criticism has been an inherently retrospective activity: It has looked back from the present to the past and attempted to reconstruct what it saw. As the moral vocabulary of textual criticism suggests, it has also been an inherently rehabilitative procedure—one that, in its retrospection and from the perspective of humanist ideology, saw ruin or corruption in need of correction. In Grafton's analysis: "The scholastics had read their texts as structures, systems of interlocking propositions that they tested for coherence as an engineer tests the load-bearing parts of a building. The humanists read theirs as clouded windows which proper treatment could restore to transparency, revealing the individuals who had written them."[37] Strictly speaking, retrospection is of course the only possible perspective on historical phenomena; and editing, as I discussed above, seems to be an inescapably historical activity, constrained in the same ways that historical scholarship in general is constrained. Historical criticism, therefore, provides yet another way to approach textual-critical problems.

From this perspective, an edition may itself be considered a historical narrative: As the historian selects and arranges a variety of historical phenomena into an account of past events, so the editor utilizes historicized textual and documentary evidence to construct an edition that in one sense describes the historical work. But since we cannot absolutely

79

recreate historical phenomena either as participants or as readers and since edited texts rather than original manuscripts are the most common formats for reading older literature, our access to history or original works is only through such historical or editorial narratives. Like a historical account, which both narrates and is history, an edition is thus simultaneously two ontologically distinct entities: a contemporary work—an edition—that is itself a site of interpretation and, in effect, the historical work it presumes to recuperate. The project of historians and literary critics alike is in fact understood as a response to historical phenomena (history or original works) and not simply to modern representations of them (historical acounts or editions); a literary critic, for instance, writes a book on the *Canterbury Tales* and not the *Riverside Chaucer,* even though the latter is inescapably the primary work.

In the modern era it has become increasingly clear that the historical phenomena that constitute history do not come as ready-made facts to the historian; it is the historian who supplies the interpretive categories that render the phenomena as facts and concomitantly enable interpretation of them. In the now classic statement by R. G. Collingwood: "History is not a spectacle. The events of history do not 'pass in review' before the historian. They have finished happening before he begins thinking about them. He has to re-create them inside his own mind, re-enacting for himself so much of the experience of the men who took part in them as he wishes to understand."[38] Consequently, whenever a historian "finds certain historical matters unintelligible, he has discovered a limitation of his own mind; he has discovered that there are certain ways in which he is not, or no longer, or not yet, able to think."[39] In this vein, textual criticism, as a type of historical criticism, affords the reenactment of a textual past as the critic is able to conceive and construct it.

In Collingwood's view, if the past is unintelligible, it is so primarily because of limitations in the critic's ways of thinking, and so such unintelligibility reflects not at all on the potential intelligibility of the past— on the past phenomena that might be identified and on the ways in which they might be thought about. This is the case because, Hayden White has further argued, historical scholarship and reconstruction predetermine what the object of study will be: "Before the historian can bring to bear upon the data of the historical field the conceptual apparatus he will use to represent and explain it, he must first *pre*figure the

field—that is to say, constitute it as an object of mental perception."[40]
There appears, however, "to be an irreducible ideological component in
every historical account of reality":

> To put it another way, the very claim to have distinguished a past from
> a present world of social thought and praxis, and to have determined the
> formal coherence of that past world, *implies* a conception of the form that
> knowledge of the present world also must take, insofar as it is *continu-
> ous* with that past world. Commitment to a particular *form* of knowledge
> predetermines the *kinds* of generalizations one can make about the present
> world, the kinds of knowledge one can have of it, and hence the kinds
> of projects one can legitimately conceive for changing that present or for
> maintaining it in its present form indefinitely.[41]

Consequently, the prefigurative act of the historian shapes not simply
the field to be studied but also, thereby, the terms that will define
and limit analysis: "It is also constitutive of the *concepts* he will use
to identify the objects that inhabit that domain and *to characterize the
kinds of relationships* they can sustain with one another."[42] The facts and
theories of history and historical scholarship are thus in essence always
self-validating and constitute a sort of charmed hermeneutic circle that
can be evaluated only by stepping outside of, and perhaps breaking,
the circle. For Collingwood, "in scientific history anything is evidence
which is used as evidence, and no one can know what is going to be
useful as evidence until he has had occasion to use it."[43]

I have argued that Renaissance humanism has been the essential
determinant of the way in which textual criticism, as the theoretical
framework for acts of historical narration, has prefigured its field and
methods of inquiry. The form of historical explanation that textual
criticism has typically provided, therefore, is fundamentally what White
calls the Mechanistic paradigm. Within this paradigm, the acts of historical agents are seen as manifestations of extrahistorical agencies, and
the historian "considers individual entities to be less important as evidence than the classes of phenomena to which they can be shown to
belong; but these classes in turn are less important to him than the laws
their regularities are presumed to manifest. Ultimately, for the Mecha-
nist, an explanation is considered complete only when he has discovered
the laws that are presumed to govern history in the same way that the
laws of physics are presumed to govern nature."[44]

In textual-critical terms, it was the totalizing orientation of humanism that determined that the dominant paradigm would be Mechanistic. The specifics of this paradigm were determined by the humanists' equation of the authoritative text with the authorial one and by their valorization of a lexical, idealist conception of the work. In the retrospective humanist tradition of textual criticism, these characteristics have been presumed to be transcendent laws of literary production that inevitably manifest themselves in specific historical epochs and that therefore motivate and define the objects, field, and methods of textual-critical inquiry. It is this very presumption that enables traditional textual criticism to tolerate the interpretive limitations that McGann and McKenzie have exposed. When their identification of textual-critical objects and their characterization of the relationships among them are seen as still within the field of traditional textual criticism, these objects and relationships cease to be challenges to other objects in the field, to the methods of inquiry, and to the field itself. There is nothing sinister or even necessarily debilitating about this situation. It is simply a reflex of what the humanists invented textual criticism to do, and their arguments have been consistently accepted at face value. Contemporary textual criticism's own ideological component—its maintenance of certain literary and cultural attitudes by and for academic and commercial institutions—both safeguards the principles of textual criticism and obscures their humanist motivation.

Earlier I suggested that retrospection was in fact the only possible perspective on historical phenomena. There are, however, two kinds of retrospection. In one kind—that practiced by the humanists and many contemporary textual critics—the retrospection is an actively backward and rehabilitative gaze: The critics' activity, in other words, is to look back and restore the work from the damage it has sustained in the passage of time. In the other, the retrospection is a historically situated gaze: The critics attempt to position themselves in the past in order to look about. This kind of historical explanation is what White calls the Contextualist paradigm. The Contextualist contends that events can "be explained by being set within the 'context' of their occurrence. Why they occurred as they did is to be explained by the revelation of the specific relationships they bore to other events occurring in their circumambient historical space. . . . the Contextualist insists that 'what happened' in the field can be accounted for by the specification of the functional interrelationships existing among the agents and agencies occupying the field at a given time."[45] This Contextualist paradigm, especially in the distinctive treatment of Michel Foucault, provides historical criticism with a solution to the problems I discussed earlier—one that from a historically sensitive perspective confronts equally the character of late Middle English writing and the consequences of its representation for a modern audience.

Foucault urges the rejection of traditional categories and methods of historical inquiry that are designed to suppress the discontinuities and ruptures of history and, concomitantly, to emphasize traditions and unities. In their place he substitutes an approach he calls archaeology, which "describes discourses as practices specified in the element of the archive," or "the general system of the formation and transformation of statements."[46] Archaeology, accordingly, examines not only the statements and the discourses they form but also the discursive formations that organize the statements into a discourse and distinguish it from other discourses in the archive. Foucault's archaeology thereby explores the ways by which historically situated disciplines and fields were constructed and sustained. To do this, to analyze a discursive field, "we must grasp the statement in the exact specificity of its occurrence; determine its conditions of existence, fix at least its limits, establish its correlations with other statements that may be connected with it, and show what other forms of statement it excludes."[47] In the process the conceptual and articulatory discursive practices that enable statements and discourses at a given period are, at least in theory, laid bare. Similarly exposed is their multifarious dependence on nondiscursive practices and institutions that determine who has access to the discourse, where this access is situated, what relation such individuals have to the discourse and others who participate in it, and what relation various discourses have to one another.

Foucault's objective is to realize a perception of discourses, their characteristics, and their consequences that is resistant to interpretation imposed by subsequent ideologies or other discourses and that enables historicized phenomena to be displayed and comprehended from within. His goal is

to substitute for the enigmatic treasure of "things" anterior to discourse, the regular formation of objects that emerge only in discourse. To define these

objects without reference to the *ground,* the *foundation of things,* but by re-
lating them to the body of rules that enable them to form as objects of a
discourse and thus constitute the conditions of their historical appearance.
To write a history of discursive objects that does not plunge them into the
common depth of a primal soil, but deploys the nexus of regularities that
govern their dispersion.[48]

For Foucault as for any historian, the reflexive problem remains: the
difficulty (if not impossibility) of accounting for the status and validity
of his theories. His solution is to reiterate archaeology's lack of interest
in teleology and to say to an imagined interrogator: "If you recognize
the right of a piece of empirical research, some fragment of history,
to challenge the transcendental dimension, then you have ceded the
main point."[49] If Foucault's solution here is not entirely satisfactory, the
problem is one that compromises every historical—and, for that matter,
contemporary—inquiry.

To critics interested in presenting a historical work according to presumed historical principles, Foucault's arguments about history offer
many possibilities. They confirm humanist textual criticism itself to
be a discourse, for instance, and not the value-free praxis it is often
presumed to be. Moreover, if one contends that definitions of abstract
concepts like work, or author, or text have meaning only in specific historical and social contexts, Foucault's positions suggest a way of gaining
a broadened historical understanding of such concepts and their specific
realizations at a given point in history, such as the late Middle English
period. This understanding emerges from an examination of the discourse of late Middle English manuscripts: the totality of extant documents and the discursive formations, institutions, and enunciations that
enabled and defined them. This discourse is not unified and monolithic
but varied and disperse, and in fact it is this same distinctive (but not exclusive) quality of dispersion that in part differentiates the discourse of
late Middle English manuscripts from other discourses. Foucault notes
of discourse in general that it is "from beginning to end, historical—a
fragment of history, a unity and discontinuity in history itself, posing the
problem of its own limits, its divisions, its transformations, the specific
modes of its temporality rather than its sudden irruption in the midst of
the complicities of time."[50] To identify and characterize this discourse
from within requires the exploration of a variety of concepts and in-

stitutions: medieval literary theory; manuscript enunciations of literary works; the intersections between the discourse of late Middle English manuscripts and other contemporaneous discourses such as those of learned Latin works, linguistics, theology, or political theory. The next two chapters of this book consider these very concepts and institutions, primarily as they are mediated by Middle English works, in order to reveal the construction of author, work, and text within the discourse of late Middle English manuscripts. Recognition of these constructions, in turn, offers theoretical and practical opportunities for the articulation of a specifically Middle English textual criticism.

By way of a conclusion to this chapter I want to offer another illustration. My example is again a familiar one—Chaucer—and my point of departure is simply some of the physical realizations in which Chaucer's compositions (particularly the *Canterbury Tales*) have appeared from about 1400 to the close of the eighteenth century. Rather than look retrospectively, however, I want to look prospectively: to begin in 1400 and to explore how these physical realizations reflect and condition the discourse in which Chaucer's works were recuperated, how they help to make him into the proverbial "father of English poetry." My intention is not to argue that the Chaucer(s) perceived from such a perspective are or are not the authentic Chaucer(s); it is to show that they are in any case historically constructed and identifiable and that these qualities emerge perhaps most clearly from a Foucauldian attempt to see from within.

The earliest extant manuscript of the *Canterbury Tales* is the Hengwrt manuscript, which probably dates to very early in the fifteenth century, or shortly after Chaucer died. It is a carefully written, though not particularly polished manuscript: There is little illustration, and, as I noted in the first chapter, portions of the text seem to have been copied rather haphazardly. The order of the fragments, in fact, follows no unambiguous artistic pattern and may well suggest the limited availability of *Canterbury Tales* materials to the scribe.[51] Whether this inferior ordering—coupled, it should be noted, with some clearly superior readings—represents the unfinished condition in which Chaucer left the *Tales* or is simply an accident or error in transmission is currently one of the most contested issues in Chaucer studies, and I have no intention here of even trying to address it. I do want to point out, however, that the less than refined presentation of Hengwrt and of the text it contains does parallel the situations for a number of Chaucer's other works at his death. Quotations by Thomas Usk and others in the 1380s and 1390s indicate that some of Chaucer's works clearly were known by contemporaries before he died. But very few works—including the three longest: the *Canterbury Tales, Troilus and Criseyde,* and the *Boece*—are extant in manuscripts written before 1400. In this regard, Chaucer fared less well than some of his contemporaries, since there are extant manuscripts of both Gower's *Confessio Amantis* and Langland's *Piers Plowman* that date to their author's lifetimes. The rough ordering of the Hengwrt text further resembles the situation for other Chaucerian compositions, for at his death the majority of Chaucer's works were unfinished to a greater or lesser degree: the *Canterbury Tales, Boece,* the *Legend of Good Women,* the *Romaunt of the Rose,* the *Astrolabe,* the *House of Fame,* and (if it is in fact by Chaucer) the *Equitorie of the Planetis.* Even if the Hengwrt scribe is responsible for confusing an ordering for the *Tales* that Chaucer himself designed, the work in its entirety is profoundly unfinished: It lacks the number of *Tales* that the *General Prologue* promises; there are insufficient links to make the order of the *Tales* unequivocal; and the pilgrims never get to Canterbury, much less back to the Tabard. As the earliest extant documentary realization of the *Canterbury Tales,* then, Hengwrt does not present Chaucer's composition in any way that elevates it over the work of other vernacular poets and thus offers an inauspicious beginning for the father of English poetry.

In the first decade of the fifteenth century, however, a burst of manuscript activity, producing numerous copies of many of Chaucer's works, implies a growing interest in Chaucer as well as a conviction that he was somehow superior to most vernacular English poets. To be sure, as I will discuss in the next chapter, Chaucer's interest in attaining auctorial status certainly invited this response, which also seems to reflect an early fifteenth-century movement to mediate English nationalism and linguistic and artistic self-consciousness through him.[52] But if Chaucer's own attitudes mark a special place for him within the discourse of late Middle English manuscripts, so does the increasing attention devoted to the collection, presentation, and transmission of his works. For texts of the *Canterbury Tales* and of the *Boece,* this attention concentrated on removing the indications of incompleteness by supplying missing tales, links, and rubrics and by designing an *ordinatio* commensurate with the status Chaucer's works were acquiring.

The presumption of Chaucer's artistic superiority also probably motivated attempts to reify and emblematize this superiority in documents and their design. Approximately ten years after Hengwrt was composed, for example, the same scribe wrote San Marino, Huntington Library MS Ellesmere 26.C.9 (Ellesmere), the elaborate presentation of which includes illuminations, marginal glosses, widely spaced lines, and the famous portraits that accompany each pilgrim's tale.[53] Physically, the manuscript thus helps to construct a *Canterbury Tales* vastly different from that in Hengwrt. If the latter is the sort of serviceable production characteristic of manuscripts of vernacular poetry in the early fifteenth century, the former, through its cost and effort, enunciates Chaucer's vernacular composition as uniquely worthy of the attention (and status) of the great *auctores*. The Ellesmere manuscript is thus the first clear documentary movement toward the placement of Chaucer in a preeminent position in the tradition of English poetry.

That this position very quickly gained currency is clear from a manuscript compiled about fifteen years after Ellesmere: Cambridge, Cambridge University Library MS Gg.4.27. Two features of this manuscript are striking with regard to the establishment of Chaucer as England's premier poet. First, the manuscript contains the remnants of an illustration pattern of portraits similar to that surviving in Ellesmere. What is striking, and what further attests to Chaucer's growing status, is that these portraits were not modeled on the Ellesmere ones: In reflecting a distinct tradition, they imply a growing audience for Chaucer's works, which in turn suggests and invites an even broader contemporary sense of respect for the poet. The second striking feature of Gg.4.27 is that the manuscript is a Chaucer compendium that includes the *Canterbury Tales,* the *Troilus,* the *Legend,* and the *Parliament of Fowls.* This type of anthologizing was rare if not unprecedented in Middle English manuscripts, which typically were organized by theme, genre, or, simply, availability of texts. It adumbrates, however, a distinctly humanist organization that equates an author with his works and that implies the self-evident artistic and moral superiority of the author and his works.

By the time Caxton set up his press in Westminster in 1476, then, Chaucer's works were already being physically realized in documents that accorded him special status. In the fifteenth century, manuscripts of Lydgate's and Gower's poems often equaled if not exceeded those of Chaucer's in terms of lavishness of presentation. But, significantly, as I noted in the previous chapter, only Chaucer's compositions, in part for ideological and political reasons, have remained continually in print since the early sixteenth century. In other words, if initially Chaucer had competition for the fatherhood of English poetry—if in the early sixteenth century Stephen Hawes could still regard Lydgate as "the moste dulcet sprynge / Of famous rhetoryke"[54]—the Reformation conceptually eliminated many of his competitors, while the printing press served to emblematize and solidify his now unique status.

The first of the post-Reformation editions was William Thynne's *Workes*, which was initially printed in 1532 and reprinted several times thereafter. The layout of the book is unremarkable. But its inclusion of all the compositions then believed to be by Chaucer extends the humanist tradition (foreshadowed in Gg.4.27) of collecting all the works of a noble auctor and strengthens the connections between this tradition and vernacular literature by establishing (uniquely for Middle English writing) the entire oeuvre as the standard format for approaching a specific writer. After this time, it was not until well into the eighteenth century that any of Chaucer's compositions was issued independently rather than in the collected works. A similar extension emerges from Brian Tuke's dedication of the volume to Henry VIII, which likens Chaucer's linguistic and literary accomplishments to those of the great auctores: "For though it had ben in Demosthenes or Homerus tymes / whan all lernyng and excellency of sciences florisshed amonges the Grekes / or in the season that Cicero prince of eloquence amonges latyns lyued / yet had it ben a thyng right rare & straunge and worthy perpetuall laude / that any clerke by lernyng or wytte could than haue framed a tonge before so rude and imperfite / to such a swete ornature and composycion / lykely if he had lyued in these dayes."[55]

The early modern reading of Chaucer, as manifested in Renaissance editions, is thus distinctly ideological, recuperating Chaucer both as a courtier and as a prophet of the Reformation. Among the spurious works included in Thynne's 1532 volume, for example, are several courtly ballads, *The Flower of Courtesy, The Assembly of Ladies, The Complaint of the Black Knight,* and *The Remedy of Love;* and when in 1561 John Stow nearly doubled the size of the canon, courtly compositions predominated among the many spurious works he added. Already by Thynne's second issue of 1542, the courtly impulse had been joined by a Protestant one that attributed the antipapist *Plowman's Tale* to Chaucer, and this same impulse would lead to the inclusion of *Jack*

Upland in 1602. Most generally, such an ideological recuperation, and thus Chaucer himself, served nationalistic purposes, as in the connections Tuke draws between the quality of Chaucer's works and that of England itself:

> Under the shylde of your [Henry's] most royall protectyon and defence it [the volume] may go forthe in publyke / & preuayle ouer those that wolde blemysshe / deface / and in many thynges clerely abolyssh the laude / renoume / and glorie hertofore compared / and meritoriously adquired by dyuers princes / and other of this said most noble yle / wherunto nat onely straungers under pretexte of highe lernyng & knowlege of their malycious and peruers myndes / but also some of your owne subiectes / blynded in foly & ignorance / do with great study contende.[56]

This tradition of elevating Chaucer's status among English poets is even stronger in Thomas Speght's various editions of Chaucer's works, which were produced at a time when the humanist movement had long since been firmly established in England. While Thynne's title page had referred merely to "Geffrey Chaucer," the title pages of Speght's 1598 and 1602 editions boldly announce that Chaucer is an "Ancient and Learned English Poet," a characterization that in 1687 is supplemented with the adjective "Excellent"; this last printing also asserts that the best manuscripts were used, and that some works never before printed are included. In his preface Speght affirms Chaucer as the progenitor of and model for subsequent English poets by indicating his desire to "set out *Chaucer* with a Coment in our tongue, as the *Italians* haue *Petrarke* and others in their language;"[57] the comparison with Petrarch and Italian is compelling here, inasmuch as Italy, since the time of Dante, had offered the most progressive vernacular literature. The humanist impulse is further apparent in Speght's belief that Chaucer's works would be responsive to and ought to be approached with the same methodological rigor accorded to ancient *auctores*:

> It were a labor worth commendation, if some scholler, that hath skil and leisure, would confer *Chaucer* with those learned Authors, both in *Greek* and *Latin,* from whom he hath drawn many excellent things; and at large report such Hystories, as in his workes are very frequent, and many of them hard to be found: which would so grace this auncient *Poet,* that whereas diuers haue thought him vnlearned, and his writings meere trifles, it should appeare, that besides the knowledge of sundrie tongues, he was a man of great reading & deep judgement.[58]

The edition includes a Life of the poet, an argument prefaced to each work that outlines the contents and background of what follows, explanations of "Old and Obscure Words," translations of incorporated Latin and French, and a list of authors whom Chaucer cites by name. Together, this material recapitulates a very humanist Chaucer, one who is presentable in (and by implication worthy of) the same format as an Antique poet. If already as early as Ellesmere, then, the presentation of Chaucer's works began to reflect and condition a preferential and unique response, his claim to be the father of English poetry is further elevated and emblematized more complexly in Speght's edition.

Kynaston's 1635 translation of the *Troilus, Amorum Troili et Creseidae Libri duo priores Anglico-Latini,* is the culmination of the humanist response to Chaucer, though the desire to bring Chaucer outside of the narrow confines of England and introduce the world to him bespeaks nationalistic impulses as well. As the contrived structure of *Amorum Troili et Creseidae* suggests, Chaucer's status as the father of English poetry was precarious, since it could be maintained only by linguistically bifurcating Chaucer's poem. This precariousness would pass when the anxieties attendant upon English humanism ceased, when the present no longer needed to define itself actively in terms of the past. By the early eighteenth century, in fact, Chaucer's compositions had become the concerns of antiquaries without endangering his preeminence in the newly defined tradition of English poetry. This conception is apparent in John Urry's 1721 edition of Chaucer's complete works.

A large, folio volume, Urry's edition would impute status to Chaucer in its cost alone, though its contents are even more significant in the creation and continuation of Chaucer's reputation. The title page conditions the reader's response to what follows by stressing the thoroughness with which the edition was allegedly prepared and by depicting Chaucer's tomb, thereby inscribing Chaucer's monumental status within a monument to his preeminence among English poets. An author portrait, which portrays a very Augustan-looking Chaucer, is followed by a long and heavily documented Life wherein Chaucer, in the manner of a folk tale, is presented not simply as an English gentleman (as Speght had done) but as the unpromising youth who rises to greatness: "In his early years his Temper and Inclination were somewhat too gay and loose. . . . Towards the latter part of his Life, the gay Gentleman gave way to the grave Philosopher and pious Divine."[59] Just as the author portrait depicts an eighteenth-century Chaucer, so the Life attributes to him the requisite qualities of a contemporary gentleman: "In one word, he was a great Scholar, a pleasant Wit, a candid Critick, a sociable Companion, a stedfast Friend, a grave Philosopher, a temperate Economist and a pious Christian."[60] The Life is followed by the "Testimonies of Learned Men concerning Chaucer and his Works" (ironically including Gower and Lydgate); in effect, these testimonies define a literary history at the forefront of which stands the author of the *Canterbury Tales*. Chaucer's position is soldified by the inclusion of the greatest number of works ever attributed to him and by the elaborate critical apparatus: a preface outlining the edition's methodology and the publication history of Chaucer's works; attention to layout in the form of arguments and engravings; a seventy-three-page glossary, which includes line numbers to illustrate usage; translations of Latin and French words and quotations; a record of the authors Chaucer cites; and an errata page and a page of additions to the glossary. For all its textual faults, the Urry edition displays a thorough recuperation of Chaucer as a figure who is not simply a Middle English vernacular poet (as in Hengwrt), or a mediation of cultural self-consciousness (as in some early fifteenth-century manuscripts), or an index of nationalistic impulses (as in Thynne), or an emblem of humanist paradoxes (as in Kynaston) but a figure who embodies all the requirements of the consummate eighteenth-century poet.

Thus, by the time Thomas Tyrwhitt published his edition of the *Canterbury Tales* in 1775, typically regarded as the first truly scholarly edition of the poem, Chaucer's character, reputation, and destiny had already been decided. From the moment he died, through changing, sometimes incompatible ideologies and a variety of cultural forces reflected in the presentation of his works, he was steadily transformed from a Middle English writer presented much like any other Middle English writer into the father of English poetry, from whom the history of English literature extends. If Chaucer's poems respond to the analysis of humanist textual criticism, therefore, it is because this analysis, consistently recuperated throughout English literary history, has come to prefigure them as responsive. Chaucer's position in English literature has in this way become so broadly based that an argument against this position—an argument for another father or for no father at all—must take as its point of departure Chaucer's preeminence; the onus, in other words, is on those who would prove Chaucer does *not* deserve the status he has. To sit down in the 1990s and look back at Chaucer's works through the *Riverside Chaucer* is merely to confirm the position his works have acquired. To look from within, in Foucault's sense, even as briefly and selectively as I have here, is to recognize the origins, consequences, and intersections of Chaucer's position with other discourses; to see his position as an optional choice at a variety of historical moments; to see the present valorization of Chaucer's authorial texts, despite the weight of the traditions perceived to support it, as itself still an option. It is from this perspective, then, that the following chapters will look at the discourse of late Middle English manuscripts.

❦

CHAPTER FOUR

Authority

Fredson Bowers expressed the traditional position on textual criticism when he defined it as the "attempt to determine what the author wrote." In articulating the humanist equation of the authoritative text with the authorial one, such a definition imputes unambiguous and transcendent significance to the concept authority, but even within only a literary context "authority" embraces several meanings. It can be used in reference to the individual or individuals who created (or "authored") a literary work; to the legal or cultural entitlement certain individuals or institutions may have to a particular work or text (their "authoritativeness"); to the claim imputed to certain texts to represent accurately the original texts from which they are judged to derive (their "authenticity"); to the validity of what a work or text states about a certain topic and of its right to make such statements in the first place (its "authorization"). While each of these references is distinct from the others, they clearly can and do overlap and occur simultaneously. In the modern period in particular, the individuals who are most responsible for the creation of a particular work are likely to be the ones who have legal entitlement to it; and according to Greg-Bowers copy-text theory, their own documents—holographs, typescripts, and corrected proofs— are judged the best representatives of what they actually intended to

write, particularly with respect to accidentals. The authorized characteristics of a work's positions and observations are rather less relevant
in modern creative writing, because this kind of authority is typically
understood to be empirically and culturally verifiable. We may thus
speak of the authority of a scientist or scientific work, and also of a
theologian and a political scientist. But while a specific literary critic
may be judged an authority *on* the works of Elizabeth Gaskell, for example, the domestic situations fictionalized in Gaskell's *Sylvia's Lovers*
can make no claim to authorization. Gaskell may echo views that were
institutionally authorized, and she may be considered by some to be
the best writer on such topics, but the very fact that she wrote fiction
precludes the verifiability of her novels.

The fact that there are overlaps between these various senses of authority thus does not mean that they are always synonymous. T. S.
Eliot, for instance, may legally and culturally be considered the author
of *The Waste Land,* but he always maintained that Ezra Pound's extensive contributions to the poem—leading to elimination of over half
of the original thousand or so lines of the original draft—were the
reason for its critical success. And though a holograph manuscript of
Theodore Dreiser's *Sister Carrie* is extant, the revisions that were initiated by others but accepted by Dreiser problematize, if not undermine,
the authority of this document.[1] The relationships among these significances of authority are in fact various and complex, and at any given
historical period what finally determines where the significances overlap
and which significance takes precedence over another are the cultural
institutions and discourses that generate ideology: politics, the market
place, and religion, for example. More specifically, the author function,
to use Foucault's terminology, is constructed from a variety of legal and
cultural discourses, social practices, and institutional frameworks, all of
which can be manifested in and sustained by rhetorical strategies.[2] Such
discourses, practices, frameworks, and strategies, in turn, are themselves
historically constructed and in part mutually constitutive.

Eliot remains the sole nominal author of *The Waste Land* because,
like the manager of a factory, he can be said to have overseen in a
sense what Pound produced; because the romantic myth of the solitary genius conceives literary production as distinctively individualistic;
because this myth in turn is consonant with the valorization of the individual, which Foucault sees as the preeminent social characteristic of
the past two centuries; and because academic interpretive discussion,

defined and informed as it is by all these discourses, still typically assumes the integrity of the author in the creation of literary *texts* (but
not *works,* in various critical senses) and on the basis of this assumption has already constructed itself too much through efforts like the
analysis of the works of Eliot in particular to countenance challenges
to his authority. It is understandable—though as I shall suggest later,
not justified—if critics who have devoted their careers to identifying
and analyzing Eliot's artistry would feel their own integrity challenged
should this artistry be Pound's as well as Eliot's.

Since the relationship between the various kinds of authority is culturally generated and historically determined, the balance effected at
one moment by one culture need not be the same as that effected at
another moment by another culture. Furthermore, the construct of authority perceived by some members of a culture need not be the same as
that perceived by others; I would venture, for example, that in the 1990s
conceptions of authority not only vary widely within literary studies
but also differ significantly between the literary community and the
general public. While Bowers's equation of the authoritative text with
the authorial one makes perfect sense as a principle of humanist textual criticism, therefore, it need not be relevant to the discourse of late
Middle English manuscripts. To determine what constitutes authority
within this discourse is the purpose of this chapter, and to do so it is
necessary to determine the relations between the various significances of
authority that the discourse specifies. What, for instance, are the character of and relations between Middle English writers' authorship, their
authoritativeness over the texts they produced, and the authorization
of these texts?[3] How does the discourse construct the author? What
would an authorial vernacular text be, and could it be equated with the
authoritative one? Within a Foucauldian analysis of a discursive field,
such determinations emerge from recognition of a work's conditions of
existence, of its correlations with other works connected to it and with
other discursive fields, and of the types of works that are excluded from
the field. In order to make such determinations, I offer in the following
pages a number of disparate examples of discourses, genres, works, and
techniques. These are meant to be representative rather than exhaustive, since my intention is to open up the disparities in the discourse of
late Middle English manuscripts, not to silence and consolidate them.

Latin literary criticism is one discursive field that co-existed and cor-
related with the discourse of late Middle English manuscripts, and its

positions on authority are both well articulated and official. In calling them official I mean that they were produced within and sustained two of the most socially and politically powerful institutions in the Middle Ages: the church and, by extension, the universities. Accordingly, they were profoundly conservative positions that precisely defined which writers had access to authority in such a way as to preempt challenges to received opinion. In this regard, one can speak of positions on literary authority as reflections of a medieval ideology of authority: a hierarchical construct whereby the powerful remained in power and the powerless not only were denied the means by which they might alter their positions but also were confronted by a theoretical system that mandated their situation. The conventional sociology of the three estates, for example, represented social stratification as divinely inspired; the indigent were assured that their lack of access to property and opportunity was literally and figuratively Heaven-sent, since as workers they were serving the common good and laboring in the humble fashion that Christ himself had set as a model for humanity. Until camels could pass easily through the eyes of needles, the poor had the promise of the greater chance for salvation as compensation (and rationalization) for the worldly power of the wealthy. Similarly, the systems of patronage and ecclesiastical preferment provided the opportunities for the ambitious to rise in society, but in doing so these systems sustained their own hierarchies: To rise in the hierarchies meant to submit to the ideology of hierarchy and to the fact that any individual within the hierarchy was necessarily positioned above some but below others.[4]

For literary authority, the empowered were the *auctores*: those Latin writers whose compositions were made venerable by their antiquity and enduring by their language.[5] They were ancient poets and rhetoricians like Vergil, Ovid, and Quintilian, and learned commentators like St. Augustine and St. Jerome. These writers were in part officially *auctores* because they had been able to create original literary matter, for an *auctor*, etymologically, is one who increases.[6] Indeed, one of the most common medieval ways of distinguishing among various writers' contributions to a text is quantitative. In St. Bonaventure's well-known formulation:

The manner of making a book is fourfold. One person writes the words of another, neither adding nor changing a thing; and this person is called simply a scribe. Someone else writes the words of another and supplements them, but not with his own words; and this person is called a compilor. Someone else writes the words of another and supplements them with his own words, but the other's words are primary and his own are used for clarification; and this person is called a commentator, not an author. And someone else writes the words of another as well as his own, but his own are primary, while the other's are used for clarification; and this person ought to be called an author.[7]

In light of other aspects of medieval literary theory, however, discrimination among the quantitative contributions of these various bookmakers could be difficult. The rhetorical processes by which translation and commentary, for example, responded to and recuperated an auctorial work could in effect displace the original.[8]

What enabled indisputable identification of auctores were the literary qualities and the culturally and institutionally sanctioned ethical truths (*auctoritates*) of their works. These elicited the distinctive exegetical responses of glosses, commentaries, and discussion in university lectures, and the existence of such institutional responses served to confirm the auctorial status of writers. There is thus something circular in this theoretical framework: Auctores were those known and named writers whose works had *auctoritas*, and *auctoritas* was identified as the characteristic quality of the work of an auctor. Such circularity reflects the conservative, preemptive, and self-validating character of medieval views on authority, which made it difficult if not impossible for a contemporary writer to acquire auctorial status. As A. J. Minnis points out, "No 'modern' writer could decently be called an *auctor* in a period in which men saw themselves as dwarfs standing on the shoulders of giants."[9]

Significantly, vernacular writers are nowhere represented in this well-known conceit, as if to image the official suppression of and disinterest in conceptions of authority in nonauctorial, noninstitutionalized writing. Furthermore, while official positions on this topic institutionally and theoretically excluded vernacular writing, Middle English writers themselves offer very few direct comments. No Middle English literary manifesto or apologia was probably ever written, and certainly, with the exception of prologues justifying the procedures in specific translations, of which the Prologue to the revised Wycliffite Bible is the best known, none exists. It is still possible to describe the conditions of existence of late Middle English works from within the discourse, though the indirection of this aspect of the discourse of late Middle English manuscripts compels a similar indirection upon me: a focus on rhetorical strategies Middle English writers use to mediate larger cultural concerns in representing themselves as narrators and authors and in addressing their authority for the texts they produce. Such a focus reveals that these strategies are in part predicated on medieval sociology, institutions, and literary theory and that, consequently, Middle English writers did to an extent recognize and accept the inferior and non-authoritative status accorded to vernacular writing. But the common assertion that late-medieval writers had no understanding of authority or an authoritative text belies and simplifies a complex and dynamic situation.[10] There is a great deal of variety in the strategies writers use—and therefore in their conceptions of literary authority—and several of these strategies suggest that the absence of official authority was itself, in fact, a significant condition of existence for late Middle English works, shaping both stylistics and thematics. To put matters another way: Since Middle English writers were officially denied auctorial status, a diminished sense of self for both narrators and authors informs and, more importantly, *enables* Middle English writing.

The impact of official positions on the character of vernacular writing is clear in a common trope in which Middle English writers use the Antique writers and auctores in order to define themselves; the recognized auctores, that is, are often presented as constituting a fixed reference standard that inevitably reveals the inadequacies of vernacular writers but to which they aspire. Thus, in the *House of Fame* the figures Chaucer sees upon the pillars of Fame's castle wrote in Greek, Latin, and Hebrew, while in the conclusion to *Troilus and Criseyde* the writers to whom he declares his little book to be subservient are Vergil, Ovid, Homer, Lucan, and Statius; and the writers Gower itemizes in books 4 and 7 of *Confessio Amantis* are also all ancient auctores.[11] A similar common trope of self-identification involves vernacular writers declaring that they are inadequate to accomplish the task at hand and that only a genuine auctor would in fact be able to do so. It is this trope Dunbar plays on in the *Golden Targe* when, upon seeing one hundred ladies enter a field, he indicates the indescribability of the scene by observing that accurate depiction would be beyond the powers of even Homer and Cicero:

> Discrive I wald, but quho coud wele endyte
> How all the feldis wyth thai lilies quhite
>   Depaynt war brycht, quhilk to the hevyn did glete?
> Noucht thou, Omer, als fair as thou coud wryte,
> For all thine ornate stilis so perfyte;
>   Nor yit thou, Tullius, quhois lippis suete
>   Off rethorike did in to termes flete:
> Your aureate tongis both bene all to lyte
>   For to compile that paradise complete.
>
> (64–72)

Middle English awareness of the nonauthorial vernacular writer would also account for the overwhelming anonymity of Middle English works.[12] For every Chaucer, Gower, and Dunbar whose name accompanies his works, there are many more writers who evidently thought it was unnecessary, perhaps inconceivable, to attach their names to their lyrics, romances, and treatises. This situation is especially significant in light of the fact that one of the requisites of auctores, it should be recalled, is that their names be known. In this regard, auctores and vernacular writers in part defined each other through their opposition: If auctores were characteristically named writers who sustained the dominant institutions in various ways, then nonauctores must characteristically not have been. A diminished sense of authorial identity also underlies the prevailing narrative mode of Middle English poetry: first person, but typically by a nondistinctive narrator who either does not figure in the action of the poem or who serves merely as a vehicle for the reader's emotional responses. The "I" of romances, for example, generally records action in which it is not involved, as in the cases of *King Horn, Havelok, Floris and Blauncheflour, Sir Orfeo, Sir Gawain and the Green Knight,* or the alliterative *Morte.* The latter begins with the poet perfunctorily asking that "grett glorious Godde"

> wysse me to werpe owte   som worde at this tym
> That nothyre voyde be ne vayne,   bot wyrchip till Hym
>   selvyn,
> Plesande and profitabill   to the pople þat them
>   heres.
>
> (1.9–11)

The narrator is completely removed, however, from the events of the story.

Rhetorical strategies that mediate the exclusion of the vernacular from institutional authority could, of course, be used very effectively. In fourteenth- and fifteenth-century Middle English secular or religious lyrics, for instance, the anonymous "I" is often developed as a vehicle for the reader's emotional responses to the poem. In the secular lyrics, the narrators may provide few circumstantial details because the addressee could be presumed to know already who the writer was,[13] but the details they do provide are in any case so general as to enable the poem to function not only for the writer's own reputed love situation but also for that of anyone who might read the lyric. Such is the case with the conventional details of love-longing in spring-time for the most beautiful but unresponsive of women in poems like *De Clerico et Puella, Whan þe Nyhtegale Singes, Alysoun,* and *The Meeting in the Wood,* all from the early fourteenth century and recorded in London, British Library MS Harley 2253: They specify without specification, as does a late lyric like Dunbar's *Bewty and the Presoneir.* Even lyrics as potentially personalized as the fifteenth-century *My Gentle Cock* and *Jolly Jankin,* which elliptically recount amorous encounters and impregnation, resist particularization: The described "gentle cock" could belong to any man, while the encounter between Jankin and Alison, though admittedly done cleverly, is nevertheless one between conventionally named characters in the public and common setting of a Christmas service.[14] The effectiveness of these strategies is clear from the fact that the broad applicability that characterizes such secular lyrics ultimately gives them much of their purpose.

In religious lyrics the nondistinctive "I" furthered the meditative quality of the poetry and was an especially valuable conceit in enabling the reader to experience specific emotions and feelings.[15] The "I" of religious Middle English lyrics is in fact a major feature of the genre's affective stylistics, but it is so only because its lack of specificity—in comparison to the lyric voices in Donne's *The Flea,* for example, or Keats's *Ode to a Nightingale,* or Eliot's *The Love Song of J. Alfred Prufrock*—neither provides the reader with a hermeneutic perspective nor allows the "I" itself to serve as a site of interpretation. In numerous poems on the crucifixion, for example, the "I" gives immediacy to the poem and provides for a sympathetic response from the reader without specifying itself or its own authority in any way:

> Quanne hic se on rode
> ihesu mi lemman,
> An be-siden him stonden
> marie and Iohan,
> And his rig i-suongen,
> and his side i-stungen,
> for þe luue of man;
> Wel ou hic to wepen
> and sinnes for-leten,
> yif hic of luue kan,
> yif hic of luue kan,
> yif hic of luue kan.[16]

Even the self-reflexive conclusion of Dunbar's *The Passioun of Crist* does nothing to alter the transparency of the narrator and the meditative quality that it induces:

> Than wrayt I all without delay,
> Richt heir as I have schawin to 30w,
> Quhat me befell on Gud Fryday
> Befoir the crose of sweit Jesu.
> (141–44)

The "I" of *Pearl* shares these qualities. The personalization of the experience through the dreamer's paternal relationship to the Maiden certainly enriches the poem, but it is his posture as the uncomprehending yet insistent mortal that gives the poem its emotive power and, at least in the Middle Ages, its universality. In this regard, the dreamer's petulance is indeed more thoroughly and convincingly delineated than are the characteristics of the narrators in many lyrics, yet the differences are significantly of degree, not kind. Like Dunbar and the author of *Quanne hic se on rode,* the dreamer, when he asks and learns about the merits of heavenly rewards, can still serve as a vehicle for the reader's affective response to the ideas and emotions of the poem.

Some Middle English writers, to be sure, do explicitly involve their narrators, though their treatment is still largely perfunctory and therefore still a mediation of institutionalized views of authority. The narrators may offer details about themselves or even name themselves, in either case historicizing the work and thereby strengthening its credibility for medieval readers. Such a strategy realizes the highest aspirations for vernacular literature, since it presents the work as *historia* rather than *fabula,* and it is not surprising, accordingly, that so far as we can tell the name of the narrator typically seems to be that of the writer as well. But the recognition that fictitiously named narrators are rare in late Middle English provides few interpretive insights, for in almost every case—Chaucer being the most notable exception—there is no extratextual evidence in the form of documents or letters to corroborate anything the poems may claim about the narrator-poet. If some Middle English writers have the auctorial characteristic of having known names, then, their lives remain anonymous enough to prevent the construction of an *accessus ad auctorem,* which would both confirm and reflect auctorial status. More importantly, in many instances the fact that the writers are named or even that they provide details about themselves is irrelevant to the objectives and stylistics of a work and therefore bespeaks no claim for authority on the writers' part.

The mid-fourteenth-century poet Laurence Minot, for instance, names himself in two of his poems:

> MINOT with mowth had menid to make
> Suth sawes and sad for sum mens sake;
> The wordes of sir Edward makes me to wake,
> Wald he salve us sone mi sorow suld slake;
> War mi sorow slaked sune wald I sing:
> When god will sir Edward sal us bute bring.
>
> . . . . .
>
> Thus have i mater for to make,
> For a nobill prince sake:
> Help me god, my wit es thin!
> Now LAURENCE MINOT will bigin.[17]

All of Minot's poetry offers an extremely partisan—not to say jingoistic—account of Edward III's battles with the French and the Scots. These isolated instances of naming do nothing to establish the credibility or authority of Minot, who apparently did not personally witness any of the events he describes, nor do they alter the propagandistic orientation of the poems or even contribute a self-contained theme to them.

Robert Mannyng, in his translation *Handlyng Synne,* displays a similarly perfunctory sense of self. In a passage Mannying himself creates at the beginning of the poem, he exhorts all Christians to flee from sin and in the process names himself, his residence, and his intended audience:

And to gode men of brunne,
And specyaly alle be name:
Þe felaushepe of symprynghame.
Roberd of brunne gretyþ 30w
Yn alle godenes þat may to prow.
(58–62)

Yet even though he couples this specificity with a brief account of his life and also notes that 1303 was the year in which *Handlyng Synne* was composed, Mannyng the author does not insert Mannyng the narrator thematically or rhetorically into the translation, which conventionally uses exempla to illustrate Christian topics such as the Ten Commandments and the Seven Deadly Sins. This very conventionality, indeed, seems to work against a more prominent rhetorical role for the narrator, as do the romance conventions in *Sir Launfal,* at the end of which Thomas Chestre perfunctorily identifies himself as the author. Equally perfunctory is the naming of the writer in poems like the Middle Scots *Ratis Raving* and *The Buke of the Howlat,* both from the fifteenth century. The former purports to be the advice of a father to a son; but rather than the personal and anecdotal focus that such a situation would seem to invite, the father's advice is consistently conventional (e.g., suggesting that the son speak courteously), and the identification at the end of the poem seems peripheral: "For now is endyt this matere / The quhilk is ratis raving cald" (1800–1801).[18] *The Buke of the Howlat* similarly identifies the writer only in the final stanza, while throughout the rest of the poem the narrator serves as a non-participating observer of an owl's complaint about its unattractive appearance and harsh treatment.[19]

Conventionality also moderates (even eliminates) the narrator's prominence in the early fifteenth-century poems of John Audelay. Throughout these fifty-five poems and the Latin rubrics that connect them, Audelay, a chaplain at Haghmond Abby, is named numerous times, the first occasion being near the end of the second poem:

I nel not wraþ my God at my wetyng,
As God haue merce on me, syr Ion Audlay,
At my most ned.[20]

The poems themselves, however, are relentlessly nondistinctive and conventional religious lyrics of devotion in which the "I" is the same unpersonalized "I" of meditative poems on the crucifixion. Paradoxically, Audelay's self-references, most often by way of a conclusion to a poem, extend this depersonalization by characteristically noting his deafness and blindness. Rather than specify the historical John Audelay, the self-references turn his condition into a metaphor as they come to suggest formulaically that the author of the poems is the prototypical sinner, blind and deaf to his own sins and to the salvation of Christ. For example:

> Y made þis wit good entent,
> In hope þe raþer 3e wolde repent.
> Prayes for me þat beþ present;
> My name hyt ys þe blynde Awdelay.
>
> . . . . .
>
> Al þat redis reuerenly þis remyssioune,
> Prays to blisful Bregit, þat merceful may,
> Fore hom þat mad þis mater with dewocion,
> Pat is boþ blynd and def, þe synful Audelay.[21]

This formulaic quality furthers the lack of specificity, which in turn enables readers sharing the meditative experience to recognize the same recalcitrant traits of a sinner in themselves.

Similar rhetorical strategies also inform both Langland's *Piers Plowman* and Gower's *Confessio Amantis*. Langland the author, of course, names himself on only one occasion and then only cryptically: " 'I haue lyued in londe,' quod I, 'my name is longe wille' " (*B*.15.152). The various conventional details that the narrator of the *B* version provides about himself—such as his appearance as a hermit (e.g., Prologue, 1–4 and 8.1–2) and his aging (11.46–48 and 20.180–85)—help to establish the dreamer as an affective vehicle for the reader's vicarious participation in his experiences. Even the domestic account of his wife Kit and of his existence as an itinerant cleric that occurs in passus 5 of the *C* version does less to individualize the narrator and assert his claim for a special kind of authority than to demonstrate pointedly the very ordinariness of Long Will's life: He is a critic, not a revolutionary, and the criticism he articulates emerges from the lowest social class. As the narrator of *Confessio Amantis,* Amans is not so much ordinary as typical—a learned, Christian courtier. While in the Prologue he provides some information about himself in an account of the motivation behind the poem and while Gower eventually identifies Amans as himself (8.2321), Amans indicates that his own experiences in love are meant to serve as an example for others (Prologue, 61–92). Since it is Genius who defines the course of the *Confessio* by telling the various stories and by instructing the narrator, Amans's experience is here not presented as unique and personal but as instructive and universally applicable. The reader, that is, is meant to learn about virtue and vice along with Amans.[22]

In their narrative postures, then, Middle English writers mediate the strong influence of medieval social practices, literary theory in particular. Their very sense of self—their anonymity as writers and nondistinctiveness as narrators—is in part determined by their nonauctorial status. Even when they name themselves, it is typically in a perfunctory way with no implication that in so doing they have anything in common with recognized *auctores*. And this is to say that their rhetorical strategies recognize and accept that vernacular works were precluded from authorization and vernacular writers from authorship and authoritativeness. Indeed, the fact that Middle English writers like Audelay effectively exploited rhetorical strategies of self-presentation represents an accommodation, not rejection, of institutionalized literary theory. The discourse of late Middle English manuscripts is thus defined as much by what it excludes—a strong sense of authority—as by what it admits. But the situation can be described more pointedly than this. A conception of diminished authority enabled Middle English works because it provided vernacular writers with a position from which they could speak in the larger discourse of medieval literature and therefore with an identity from which they could define and project their rhetorical strategies. By sustaining the identity of *auctores*, Middle English writers sustained their own nonidentity, but also, in turn, made the distinctive narrative voice of much Middle English poetry possible; it was largely this voice, then, that articulated late Middle English literature.

Accommodation of the nonauthorial, nonprestigious status accorded vernacular writing also appears in the rhetorical strategies late Middle English writers use to stress that their compositions did not originate with them but with an accomplished authority or *auctor* on whom is predicated any claim the work may have to be authorized. At the same time, in shaping their works according to the dictates of social practice and literary criticism, vernacular writers achieved the greatest possible credibility for their efforts. In translations, for example, one common trope stresses the original writer's responsibility for controversial or contentious opinions. After a twenty-line diatribe against women in the *Troy Book,* Lydgate underscores that the expressed opinions are not his but those of Guido del Colonne, whom he is translating:

> Þus Guydo ay, of cursid fals delit,
> To speke hem harme haþ kau3t an appetit,
> Þoru3-oute his boke of wommen to seyn ille,
> Þat to translate it is ageyn my wille.
>
> (2.3555–58)[23]

In the *Fall of Princes* Lydgate similarly disavows the antifeminism of his auctor Bochas (i.e., Boccaccio),[24] and it is of course this same trope of credibility through denial that Chaucer's Nun's Priest uses to comic effect when speculating that it may have been the coldness of women's counsel that led to Chauntecleer's downfall: "Thise been the cokkes wordes, and nat myne; / I kan noon harm of no womman divyne" (*Canterbury Tales* 7.3265–66).

Another narrative strategy that accommodates the demands of both social practice and medieval literary criticism even as it appropriates the latter's conception of an authoritative work is that which presents the vernacular work as having been written at the directive of a genuinely unimpeachable authority. Lydgate, for instance, indicates that the *Troy Book* was written at the command of Henry V, *Saint Albon and Saint Amphibalus* at that of John Bostock, abbot of St. Albans, and *The Legend of Seynt Margarete* at that of Lady March.[25] In these instances, the directive may have been real enough as a manifestation of the patronage system, but the fact that such socially motivated commands could be converted into effective literary tropes is clear from the way Audelay and Chaucer use them. In the concluding poem to the first part of his book, Audelay maintains that his writing is the working of "þe Hole Gost" and was inspired by a "mon" who appeared to him in a dream and assured him that God would take vengeance on the pride of mankind; Audelay writes to warn the unrepentant.[26] And Chaucer uses the trope in the *Legend of Good Women,* where Alceste commands him to devote his efforts to composing stories of good maidens and wives; her authority is supplemented with that of Anne of Bohemia, to whom Chaucer is directed to deliver the poem.[27]

A related trope, found particularly in dream visions, generates and validates the narrative of a poem through an authoritative character who instructs or guides the first-person narrator. This is the situation in the late fifteenth-century *Court of Sapience,* wherein the narrator, upon losing an imaginary game of chess to Fortune and the World, dreams that Sapience, Intelligence, and Science appear to him, instruct him in theological matters, and then conduct him to the Castle of Sapience. This is also the case in Hoccleve's *Regement of Princes,* where a very learned beggar appears to Hoccleve in a dream. After instructing Hoccleve on a number of matters including faith and the value of poverty, the beggar, like Alceste in Chaucer's *Legend,* specifies what the poet is to write for Henry V:

> "Write him no thyng þat sowneth in-to vice;
> Kythe thi loue in matere of sadnesse;
> looke if þou fynde canst any tretice
> Groundid on his estates holsumnesse;
> Swych thing translate, and vnto his hyhnesse,
> As humblely as þat þou canst, present;
> Do thus my sone." "fadir, I assent."
>
> (1947–53)

The narrative of *Confessio Amantis* is similarly generated by a double-faceted authority: It is Richard II (in the early version) who inspires the poem to be made, and it is Genius whom Amans asks to direct the discussion and who ultimately tells all of the stories.[28] In *Pearl* this narrative trope is manipulated for theological and rhetorical effect, since in that poem the validating authority of the Maiden highlights how much the dreamer's young daughter, over whom he once had paternal authority, has been transformed.

But though there are thus a good many rhetorical strategies in late Middle English literature that accept and accommodate official positions on authority, there are other strategies that implicitly reject these positions—that attempt to appropriate what the discourse of late Middle English manuscripts typically excludes—by presuming authority for vernacular writers and works. Some poems, for example, are clearly constructed around the writers' strong sense of their historical selves. Hoccleve's *Complaint* is one such personal poem—extraordinarily so— that recounts his mental breakdown and the suspicions he encountered from his friends over whether he had recovered;[29] his *Regement* details his twenty-four years in the Privy Seal and the difficulties he had in getting his annuity payments; and his *La Male Regle* offers an account of his dissolution, which, though general in many ways, is also highly personalized: "Be waar, Hoccleue, I rede thee therfore, / And to a mene reule thow thee dresse" (351–52). In a different vein, *The Flyting of Dunbar and Kennedie* displays Dunbar's strong identification of himself with his poetry (and the same is true for Kennedie), as does his *To the King,* wherein he complains that the "sonne of rakyng Muris" has corrupted his poems:

> That fulle dismemberit hes my meter
> And poysonid it with strang salpeter,
> With rycht defamows speiche off lordis
> Quhilk with my collouris all discordis,
> > Quhois crewall sclander servis ded.
> > > (8–12)

The fourteenth-century mystic Richard Rolle has a similarly strong sense of himself and of his writings, so strong, in fact, that the defining direction of Rolle's writing career can be viewed as a struggle for spiritual as well as literary authority. By insisting on his fidelity to the Church Fathers in the Prologue to his English Psalter, Rolle preempts criticism of his intentions and abilities and imputes integrity to his work: "In expounynge I folew haly doctours, for it may cum into sum envyouse mans hand þat knawys noght what he suld say, þat wille say þat I wist noght what I sayde, and so do harme till hym and tille other if he despise þe werk þat es prophetabil till hym and other."[30]

This nontraditional imputation of integrity, even authority, to vernacular works that informs some of Rolle's writings also emerges from other Middle English compositions. For example, in San Marino, Huntington Library MSS HM 111 and HM 744, both of which are Hoccleve manuscripts written by Hoccleve himself, Hoccleve acted as a *compilator* of his own works, thereby privileging his status as a writer.[31] And in the *Kingis Quair,* James I implies that his poem is an autonomous work by imagining its reception by posterity:

> Allace, and gif thou cummyst in the presence
> Quhare as of blame faynest thou wald be quite,
> To here thy rude and crukit eloquens,
> Quho sal be thare to pray for thy remyt?

No wicht, bot geve hir merci will admytt
Thee for gud will, that is thy gyd and stere,
To quham for me thou pitousely requere.

(1359–65)

Reginald Pecock, a mid-fifteenth-century opponent of the Lollards, also articulates a strong conception of his own works. On several occasions he refers to them by name, and in the *Donet* he expresses concern that his books had gotten public currency in an unpolished, unauthorized form:

> "Þe donet of cristen religioun" and "þe book of cristen religioun" and oþire suche of doctrine and of officiyng whiche, bifore þe deuyce and setting of þis present book, ben runne abrood and copied aȝens my wil and myn entent, as y haue openli prechid at poulis, and þat bi vncurtesie and vndiscrecioun of freendis, into whos singuler siȝt y lousid þo writingis to go, and forto not haue go ferþir into tyme þei were better examyned of me and approuid of my lordis and fadris of þe churche, y wole to be as noon of myn; but in as moche as in me is, y wole þei be rendrid vp aȝen, and bettir formes of þe same be to hem deliuered, whanne dewe deliueraunce þerof schal be made.[32]

Integrity might also be imputed to vernacular works simply through citing them by name. In his *Testament of Love,* for example, Thomas Usk refers to "the boke of Troilus,"[33] and Henry Scogan, in his *Moral Balade,* introduces paraphrases from the *Wife of Baths Tale* with "Chaucer . . . sayde" and "Chaucer sayth."[34] Lydgate similarly refers by name to Chaucerian works on a number of occasions.[35] An especially striking testament to vernacular integrity is Lydgate's attribution of specific *words*—the refrain of his *A Thoroughfare of Woe*—to Chaucer:

> O, ye maysters, that cast shal yowre looke
> Vpon this dyte made in wordis playne,
> Remembre sothly that I the refreyd tooke
> Of hym that was in makyng souerayne,
> My mayster Chaucier, chief poete of Bretayne,
> Whiche in his tragedyes made ful yore agoo,
> Declared triewly and list nat for to feyne,
> How this world is a thurghfare ful of woo.

(184–91)

Of course, such an attitude toward Chaucer (and sometimes Gower and Lydgate) and his works was shared by several fifteenth-century writers, who assign auctorial status to Chaucer in a number of ways. Not only is he identified with specific works but the works themselves are perceived as having an integrity that exists into the future. Thus, in the *Regement* Hoccleve observes:

> But nathelees, yit hast þou [death] no power
> His name sle; his hy vertu astertith
> Vnslayn fro þe, which ay vs lyfly hertyth,
> With bookes of his ornat endytyng,
>
> (1970–74)

Elsewhere Chaucer is recuperated as a mentor and model for specific English poets[36] and, more broadly, for English poetry in general:

> Daunt in Itaille, Virgile in Rome toun,
> Petrak in Florence hadde al his plesaunce,
> And prudent Chaucer in Brutis Albioun
> Lik his desire fond vertuous suffisance.[37]

Such recuperations make sense only if one is able to grant to English poetry a literary tradition with an originator and continuators, as in fact is the case in the *Troy Book* (5.3531–39), the *Kingis Quair* (1373–79), Dunbar's *Timor Mortis conturbat me,* and the *Court of Sapience:*

> O Gower, Chaucers, erthely goddes two,
> Ofthyrst of eloquent delycacye,
> With al youre successoures fewe or moo,
> Fragraunt in speche, experte in poetrye,
> You, ne yet theym, in no poynt I envye;
> Exyled as fer I am from youre glorye
> As nyght from day, or deth from vyctorye.
>
> (50–56)

But to grant such a tradition to English and such status to Chaucer makes sense, in turn, only if one is willing to concede literary integrity to the vernacular.

Thus there is obviously a great deal of variation in the rhetorical strategies late Middle English writers used within the constraints of in-stitutionalized official discourse. One constant in this variation is the

conditioning of rhetoric by the received view of authority. At one extreme, as in many of the lyrics, writers seem to have complied entirely
by effacing themselves as narrators and authors; and at the other, as
particularly in the works of Chaucer and those who explicitly patterned
their writings after his, writers challenged the theoretical status quo by
presuming to act in some of the postures of the genuine *auctores*. Some
insights on the significance of these extremes and the variety of possibilities between them emerge from the correlations between the discourse
of late Middle English manuscripts and contemporaneous vernacular
discourses.

While throughout medieval Europe the vernacular was less prestigious than Latin, English writing in general seems to have been particularly constrained by the dictates of literary theory and social practice.
For instance, the anxiety over literary authority that is betrayed by a
number of Middle English rhetorical strategies is absent in other vernacular discourses. Chaucer's Welsh contemporary Dafydd ap Gwilym,
writing within a much stronger vernacular tradition, displays none of
Chaucer's authorial anxiety. In the French tradition, in which already
in the twelfth century Chrétien de Troyes had spoken confidently as a
vernacular authority, writers like Machaut and Froissart were so com-
fortable with their status and recognition as writers as regularly to
use anagrammic signatures, while earlier, in the beginning of the fourteenth century, the Italian vernacular tradition had been validated by
Dante's creative and critical efforts. If fifteenth-century manuscripts
of Chaucer's and Hoccleve's works were the first compilations of the
works of individual English vernacular writers, such French compilations were already apparent in the fourteenth century.[38] And in Old
Norse literature, a prose tradition had been well-established in the
twelfth century by Ari Þorgilsson, while central to the long history
of skaldic verse was the identification of specific writers with specific
poems, written in response to specific events and often for specific individuals.

Also suggestive is the fact that auctorial strategies in other vernacular literatures are sometimes structurally distributed along generic lines.
Though most Old Norse skaldic (or court) poems can be assigned to
a known writer, there is not a single name that can be legitimately attached to any of the Eddic poems about the gods or the heroes of the
Hunnish and Burgundian legends. A similar division obtains in the

sagas: All but one of the family sagas (such as *Njal's Saga*) are anonymous, but many of the kings' sagas (such as Snorri Sturluson's *King Harald's Saga*) have authors' names connected to them. In Old French literature, the genres of fabliaux and chansons de geste are typically anonymous, while the romance genre is not.[39] But in Middle English literature no such structural principles obtain. A romance like the alliterative *Morte* is authorially unselfconscious, while one like the *Troilus* clearly is not; and as narrators, a partisan of the court like Minot is an insignificant narrative feature of his poems, while one like Hoccleve figures distinctively and prominently in his. One might argue that religious writers, such as Rolle and Pecock, tend to have the more developed sense of their own authority. But even leaving aside the counterexamples of Audelay and *Pearl,* this argument would only paradoxically affirm the absence of authority in Middle English works, since these writers were the ones closest to the Latin tradition and its notions of authorization. Rolle's most important and authorially ambitious writings, indeed, are in Latin.

The variation between and within vernacular literatures like Welsh, Italian, French, Norse, and English confirms Foucault's contention that the author function "does not affect all discourses in the same way at all times and in all types of civilization."[40] The most general conclusion one might draw is that traditional textual criticism's transcendent principles of authority are belied, from a historically sensitive viewpoint, by the Middle Ages. But how, then, does the discourse of late Middle English manuscripts in particular construct authority? How can Audelay's position be reconciled with Hoccleve's? Is the discourse characterized by so many divergent views on authority that no significant and editorially useful generalizations can be drawn? The more stable sense of the authorial function in Norse and French seems to support such an argument.

This same discursive divergence, however, may be the answer to the question it raises. If the structural distribution in French and Norse implies for these literatures a stability in the enactment and significance of the author function that is lacking in Middle English, a significant feature of the character of authority in late Middle English literature was its *instability.* Not only was the character of authority unstable, however: It was contested. English writers in general present literary authority neither as an issue beyond critical examination nor as one to be taken for granted. For a number of Middle English writers authority in fact serves as a thematic and narrative focus. Relying again on rhetorical strategies as mediations of cultural concerns, I want to examine the contest these writers wage over authority at some length, both because the detail helps to show how Middle English writings variously represented authority and because the very fact that the issue is so contested ought to be factored into any definition of Middle English authority.

The contest over authority is perhaps most visually prominent in Gower's *Confessio Amantis,* where the English text is supplemented with an extensive body of Latin poems, rubrics, and glosses. These, too, were written by Gower and constitute a commentary on the poem that simultaneously imputes auctorial status to Gower. In a marginal gloss early in book 1, for example, Gower observes: "Henceforth, just as in the persona of others whom love constrains, the author, pretending to be Amans, intends to write the various passions of those same people, one after the other in various sections of this book."[41] In a diglossic situation that recapitulates the larger literary condition of late-medieval England, the Latin of the commentary frames and validates the English of the poem and the achievement of Gower as writer. Also indicative of Gower's ambitions is the fact that in revising the passage from the first recension wherein Richard II causes the poem to be made, Gower did not substitute the directive of another authority; though he calls himself "burel" in the second recension, it is nonetheless Gower himself who decides to compose the *Confessio* "for Engelondes sake."[42] Thus, if Amans is a rather nondescript narrator, Gower is nonetheless a sophisticated and presumptive author. Yet the important point is that the indirection of the commentary-and-poem format reveals the tenuousness of this presumption: It is less an attitude informing the structure of the poem than an anxiety motivating it.[43]

Chaucer's presumptions to auctorial status are diverse and well-known: the catalogs of his works in the Prologue to the *Man of Law's Tale,* the "Retractions," and the Prologue to the *Legend of Good Women;* the sense of the integrity of his own works in *Chaucers Wordes unto Adam* and the concluding stanzas of *Troilus and Criseyde;* and the strong self-consciousness about himself as a writer that emerges both from the distinctive persona he develops through several works and from the metacritical machinations of *Sir Thopas,* the *House of Fame,* the *Legend,* and the *Troilus.* The attempt by writers like Lydgate and Hoccleve to recuperate Chaucer as an auctor, thus, is probably in no small part due to Chaucer's own invitation of this response. To Chaucer as well as Gower, however, auctorial status is a contested issue. But while in Gower's *Confessio* the fact and character of this issue are negotiated in the layout and design of the poem, in Chaucer's works the negotiation takes place in his conception of his own literary production, both in translations and original works.

Chaucer's position on translation, not surprisingly, is nominally Hieronymic, recognizing a distinction between word-for-word and sense-for-sense translation and preferring the latter. In the verse introduction to the *Tale of Melibee,* for instance, Chaucer echoes this position with a medieval commonplace when he observes that despite different narrative techniques the four Evangelists "alle acorden as in hire sentence" (*Canterbury Tales* 7.947). He uses this example to forestall the criticism of those who recognize the differences between his version of the *Melibee* and other versions:

> in my sentence,
> Shul ye nowher fynden difference
> Fro the sentence of this tretys lyte
> After the which this murye tale I write.
> (961–64)

Similarly, by way of an introduction to the *Canticus Troili* Chaucer indicates that the "sentence" was his primary concern but that in the event he was able to transfer the words as well:

> And of his song naught only the sentence,
> As writ myn auctour called Lollius,
> But pleinly, save oure tonges difference,
> I dar wel seyn, in al, that Troilus
> Seyde in his song, loo, every word right thus
> As I shal seyn.
> (*Troilus and Criseyde* 1.393–98)

Even when speaking through the rhetorical posture of one of his characters, Chaucer voices the conventional theory. In the Prologue to her tale, for instance, the Second Nun explicitly acknowledges her composition to be a "translacioun" (*Canterbury Tales* 8.25) and later observes:

> Yet preye I yow that reden that I write,
> Foryeve me that I do no diligence
> This ilke storie subtilly to endite,

For bothe have I the wordes and sentence
Of hym that at the seintes reverence
The story wroot, and folwen hire legende,
And pray yow that ye wole my werk amende.

(8.78–84)

While Chaucer's expressed position on translation may thus appear both conventional and uncomplicated, it is problematic nonetheless, for none of the works in which he claims to have adopted the Hieronymic posture can be considered unequivocally a sense-for-sense translation. In the *Melibee,* R. W. V. Elliott points out, there is "a heavy infusion of tags, clichés, and repetitive phrases—the prose equivalents of the clichés in *Sir Thopas,*" so that Chaucer creates a "kind of mock-didactic style which . . . makes fun of the *tellyng* without ridiculing the *moralite.*"[44] By modern standards the *Troilus* is not a translation at all. And though at the level of the individual line the *Second Nun's Tale* is Hieronymic, at the larger level of the composition itself it is not, for Chaucer has gathered the "senses" from two different texts and thereby created by implication his own source and thus his own sense.[45] A work like the *Boece* diverges in still other ways from the Hieronymic ideal, for if it is a close translation, it is a close translation not of the Latin *Consolatio* but of a source that Chaucer compiled from the larger *Consolation* tradition, so that as with the *Second Nun's Tale* the source of what Chaucer wrote exists only as it is implied by his composition. Chaucer himself, that is, is in a fundamental way the author of the very sense that he translates.[46]

The divergence between Chaucer's expressed position on translation and his actual procedure is particularly striking in light of the fact that the positions he articulates in works modern scholars regard as original compositions to a large extent replicate his Hieronymic view of translation. For instance, in the *Parliament of Fowls,* an original composition, Chaucer describes the writer's role in creating texts with the metaphor of a field being plowed:

For out of olde feldes, as men seyth,
Cometh al this newe corn from yer to yere,
And out of olde bokes, in good feyth,
Cometh al this newe science that men lere.

(22–25)

By comparison, in the Preface to the *Astrolabe,* which of course is a translation, Chaucer similarly conceives his role: "But considre wel that I ne usurpe not to have founden this werk of my labour or of myn engyn. I n'am but a lewd compilator of the labour of olde astrologiens, and have it translatid in myn Englissh oonly for thy doctrine" (59–64). My point here is not simply the obvious one—that both translations and original compositions, medieval or modern, can have sources. It is, rather, that in discussing his own responsibility in the production of each type of work, Chaucer maintains, through a variety of rhetorical postures, that what he writes is largely determined by the character of the work he is rewriting. But to call this attitude simply a reflection of the humility topos is to obfuscate the key points: that Chaucer explicitly characterizes his own role in the production of both original and translated works as secondary to that of whoever wrote his "source" and that as a vernacular writer Chaucer evidently chose deliberately not to emphasize the originality or invention of his compositions. Rather than the anxiety of influence, it was the anxiety of *originality* that Chaucer, like Rolle and other vernacular writers, articulates.

Another set of examples will clarify these points. In the *General Prologue* Chaucer defends his right to speak "pleynly . . . in this mateere, / To telle yow hir wordes and hir cheere" (727–28) by noting:

> Whoso shal telle a tale after a man,
> He moot reherce as ny as evere he kan
> Everich a word, if it be in his charge,
> Al speke he never so rudeliche and large,
> Or ellis he moot telle his tale untrewe,
> Or feyne thyng, or fynde wordes newe.
>
> (731–36)

The restrictions involved in producing a work and the faithfulness of a writer to his source (in this case imagined reality) are again stressed—here explicitly—and these same stresses emerge from Chaucer's justification for his procedure in the *Melibee,* which I cited earlier. A similar articulation of his responsibility in the production of his own compositions occurs in the *Troilus:*

> Forwhi to every lovere I me excuse,
> That of no sentement I this endite,
> But out of Latyn in my tonge it write.

> Wherfore I nyl have neither thank ne blame
> Of al this werk, but prey yow mekely,
> Disblameth me if any word be lame,
> For as myn auctour seyde, so sey I.
>
> (2.12–18)

While Chaucer's procedure is certainly not the same in the *Miller's Tale,*
for instance, the *Melibee,* and the *Troilus,* he characterizes his procedures for and contributions to both imaginative works and translations
in the same way.

Such a characterization in part reflects broader medieval conceptions
of a work, which I will consider in detail in the next chapter. Here,
I want to stress that Chaucer's articulations of this issue serve as jus-
tifications for his literary project but also that there are fundamental
deceptions in this justification, because he is not the Hieronymic translator he claims to be and because he in turn uses this misleading posture
of a translator to legitimate his original writings. This deception is perhaps most prominent in the *Troilus,* which, strictly speaking, is neither
a translation nor an original composition: Chaucer pretends it is the
former, though the extent of the changes he works on Boccaccio's *Il
Filostrato* renders it the latter. Chaucer's view of himself as a legitimate
author is made explicit at the famous conclusion of the poem, where
he reveals an authorial concern for the preservation of his actual lexical
construct by praying God "that non myswrite the, / Ne the mysmetre"
(5.1795–96). Such an authorial posture is also evident in the stanza preceding the one in which Chaucer expresses this textual concern; for if he
enjoins his "litel bok" to "subgit be to alle poesye; / and kis the steppes
where as thow seest pace" genuine auctores, he also implies that his
"litel . . . tragedye" is only one step below the works of "Virgile, Ovide,
Omer, Lucan, and Stace" (1790–92). But since this "conscious regard
for posterity, and for the accurate transmission and true understanding
of the text," as Pearsall has noted, is "quite exceptional in the English
poetry of the Middle Ages,"[47] it is not surprising that Chaucer should
expressly deny himself auctorial status in the same poem in which he
implicitly claims it. In the Proem to book 2, which I quoted earlier,
he refuses any responsibility for his achievement by insisting he is only
a translator. In this denial Chaucer rhetorically mediates the cultural
constructions of vernacular writers as incapable of true poetic invention
and of vernacular texts, in comparison with those of the auctores, as

insubstantial and ephemeral. Such a mediation again occurs in book 3, when Chaucer observes,

> if that ich, at Loves reverence,
> Have any word in eched for the beste,
> Doth therwithal right as youreselven leste.

> For myne wordes heere and every part,
> I speke hem alle under correccioun
> Of yow that felyng han in loves art,
> And putte it al in youre discrecioun.
> To encresse or maken dymynucioun
> Of my langage, and that I yow biseche.
> (1328–36)

Chaucer's expression of the conceptual and productive similarities between the works he produced as translator and those he produced as original writer articulates a view of the two procedures not as separate but rather as two ends of a continuum on which new works were created from old ones. To be simply a vernacular writer precluded Chaucer from exercising his unique literary genius; but to be an auctor was culturally impossible. In conceiving literary production in general as translation to a greater or lesser extent, Chaucer utilized a variety of rhetorical strategies that enabled him to negotiate the ideology of authority and act as that paradoxical creature, the vernacular author. As a translator, whether actual or not, Chaucer obtained not simply texts, stylistics, and ideas. He obtained status and authority as well, for if the sources he translated—or claimed to translate—had prestige, this prestige necessarily became a part of his own works; the *Troilus* acquired poetic achievement from Chaucer's genius, but it acquired respectability from Lollius' alleged authorship.[48] As accomplished an author as Chaucer might be, his narrative personae and his conceptions of literary production depend on a tension between the actual cultural status of vernacular writers and Chaucer's presumptive status. His is a rhetorical posture that is meaningful only if he lacks the many auctorial attributes he sometimes thereby appropriates. In this way, the complexity and insistency of Chaucer's negotiation of vernacular authority—the mere fact that it takes place at all—ultimately testifies to the issue's contested character in late Middle English literature.

The contest over literary authority also takes place in fifteenth-century responses to Chaucer. References to him as the Vergil of English and echoes of his positions on the potential of vernacular literary authority occur throughout the century, but they do not suggest that his achievement by itself had changed the cultural status of late Middle English writers or even that the issues with which he was engaged were fully understood. For instance, George Ashby's *Active Polity of a Prince* opens with strong statements about Chaucer, Lydgate, and Gower as the progenitors of English poetry and about the need to further the vernacular tradition they established:

> Maisters Gower, Chauucer & Lydgate,
> > Primier poetes of this nacion,
> Embelysshing oure englisshe tendure algate,
> > Firste finders to oure consolacion
> > Off fresshe, douce englisshe and formacion
> > Of newe balades, not vsed before,
> > By whome we all may haue lernyng and lore.
>
> Alas! saufe goddes wille, & his pleasaunce,
> > That euer ye shulde dye & chaunge this lyffe,
> Vntyl tyme / that by your wise pourueunce
> > Ye had lafte to vs / sum remembratife
> > Of a personne, lerned & Inuentif,
> > Disposed aftur youre condicion,
> > Of fresshe makyng to oure Instruccion.   (1–14)

The subsequent ten stanzas of the Proem talk personally of Ashby's inability as a writer and his age, and he even names himself at one point (22). This auctorial self-consciousness is matched in the Latin prose paragraph introducing the poem, wherein in the manner of an *accessus ad auctorem* it is specified that George Ashby wrote the poem for Edward, Prince of Wales, that Ashby was formerly a Signet clerk, and that the poem is divided into three parts—past time, present time, and future time.

Yet when the poem proper begins in stanza thirteen, none of this authorial self-consciousness is included. Ashby assumes the posture of the nondistinctive lyric narrator, and the poem presents only medieval commonplaces, advising Edward, for instance, to think on the virtue of his ancestors, to be honest and avoid procrastination, and to keep good servants and watch out for traitors. A poem that opens with innovative recognition of vernacular authors and literary traditions thus becomes a conventional one shaped by the restrictions of medieval literary theory. Ashby follows a similar procedure in *A Prisoner's Reflections:* Seventeen very personal stanzas specifying his imprisonment in Fleet prison, his debts, and his enemies are followed by thirty-three stanzas of general advice about being wary of fortune and recognizing life as a pilgrimage. The reverse of this situation in the *Kingis Quair* results in the same effect. James I validates the experience of the poem by initiating it with the reading of the Latin *De consolatione philsophiae,* the work of an auctor. But he concludes by recommending his book to Gower and Chaucer as the founders of the English vernacular tradition:

> Vnto th'inpnis of my maisteris dere,
> Gowere and Chaucere, that on the steppis satt
> Of rethorike quhill thai were lyvand here,
> Superlatiue as poetis laureate
> In moralitee and eloquence ornate,
> I recommend my buk in lynis sevin—
> And eke thair saulis vnto the blisse of hevin.

(1373–79)

For both Ashby and James I, authority and vernacular tradition make incompatible claims in the formation of English poetry, so that in a vernacular poem the two may coexist but not overlap. As in the *Troilus,* they dialectically contend with each other, and it is this contention that finally enables the poems.

Other ways in which the issue of literary authority was contested in the fifteenth century inform the poems of Hoccleve and Lydgate. As two figures squarely in the Chaucerian tradition, both of whom claimed to have known Chaucer personally, these poets might seem to be in the best position to process and incorporate Chaucer's own contested ideas on vernacular authorship and authority. However, while they clearly were aware of the fact that Chaucer was interested in these topics, they seem neither to have regarded the issues as resolved nor even to have recognized and exploited the thematic, rhetorical, and theoretical uses to which Chaucer put them.

Hoccleve's poetry displays ambivalence toward the issue of literary authority—recognition simultaneous with only mild interest. A poem like the *Complaint* and the sequence of poems to which it belongs (known as the *Series*) suggest a high degree of authorial self-consciousness, but the narrative role of the beggar in the *Regement of Princes* seems conditioned by medieval literary theory, while Hoccleve's various begging and commemorative poems avoid the issue entirely. In the *Regement,* this ambivalence toward authority is in fact emblematized—both literally and figuratively—in the famous Chaucer portrait introduced in stanza 714.[49] In the portrait in London, British Library MS Harley 4866, Chaucer emerges from a windowlike picture frame in the page to point to the lines that refer to him. The very existence of this unusual marginal portrait of a historical writer pointing self-reflexively at the verses that describe him is itself a testament to the extraordinary status Chaucer as an individual poet had already acquired among certain fifteenth-century writers.[50] Even more suggestive, however, is the placement of the figure: The head and torso are within the frame, while the right arm extends naturally outside and across it to enable the index finger to direct the reader's gaze to the text of Hoccleve's poem. Imagistically, Chaucer stands behind the text on the page but also emerges to constitute a connection between Chaucer and his works—which inspired Hoccleve—and Hoccleve's poem. This image is thus a richly symbolic representation of both the intertextual fields from which any work emerges and of the nascent establishment of an idea of English poetry that is mediated not simply by works or themes but also by individual writers. Yet as much as this juxtaposition of text and picture in the *Regement* might suggest a sophisticated position on vernacular literary authority, the credibility of such a position is undermined by the fact that Hoccleve does so little with the juxtaposition. He incorporates the picture primarily to point to something extratextual—the reality of the historical Chaucer—just as "The ymages þat in þe chirche been, / Maken folk þenke on god & on his seyntes" (4999–5000).[51] One has the sense here of a missed—or unnoticed—opportunity that becomes even stronger if one speculates on what Chaucer might have done with a portrait of Lollius at the end of the *Troilus.* It is an opportunity that perhaps could have arisen only because Hoccleve had a sense of Chaucer's struggle for vernacular authority but was unrealized precisely because the struggle remained unresolved.

In the *Siege of Thebes,* his contribution to the *Canterbury Tales,*

Lydgate's position on authority is far less ambivalent than Hoccleve's. Indeed, his presentation of the vernacular writer as mere translator of an auctorial story is insistently traditional. Lydgate does not, for instance, indicate the way in which Edippus kills Laius, because "the story / writ not the maner howh" (582), nor does he describe what happens after Polyneices and Tideus go to bed with Adrastus' daughters, "For it is nat declared / in my boke" (1505). The limitations imposed by the authorial book are also clear in the account of the battle between the Thebans and the Greeks in part 3, where Lydgate declares:

> Of her fightyng / nor her slaughter in soth,
> Mor to declare / than myn Autour doth.
> (4252–54)

It is not Lydgate's stated position on literary authority (one Chaucer also adopts on occasion) that compromises the credibility of this posture, nor is it the fact that the *Siege* is scarcely a slavish translation. Rather, it is that this insistence continually foregrounds the topic of literary authority without any local or general rhetorical purpose. It is as if Lydgate derived from Chaucer the strategies of talking about authority but not the thematic and narrative purposes to which these strategies were put.[52]

Much of the time the references to Lydgate's author and authorial book are essentially metrical fillers that rather statically occupy a half-line before or after the caesura but that are not extensions of the surrounding themes or narrative matter. For example, in a brief *occupatio* after Eteocles expresses his disappointment that Polyneices should want to claim the throne and banish him from Thebes, the reference to Lydgate's story exists solely for the rhyme it enables:

> Al that he spak /, who that couth aduerte,
> Of verrey scorn, Rooted in his herte;
> As it sempte /, the story can ȝou teche,
> By the surplus / sothly of his speche.
> (1993–96)

Similarly, there is no metatextual significance when Lydgate refers to himself as reader in his account of Tideus' encounter with Ipsiphyle and King Lycurgus' son:

> And in hir Armes / a litil child hadd she . . .
> Sone of the kyng / born forto succede,
> Called ligurgus / in story as I rede.
>
> (3030, 3033–34)

Other rhyme-motivated references to Lydgate's author or book or to other books include "the story kan reherce," "the story telleth vs," "be recorde of wryting," and "as bookes specifye." In all, there are some twenty-six such postcaesura half-lines in the *Siege* that exist apparently only for the sake of rhyme.[53]

In eight instances, it is the half-line before the caesura that contains the metrically motivated metatextual allusion.[54] In describing the guests summoned by Adrastus to his daughters' weddings, for example, Lydgate notes:

> And thyder cam ful many lusty knyght,
> Ful wel beseyn / and many lady bri3t,
> From euery Coost / and many frecssh sqwyer,
> Þe Story seith / and many comunere.
>
> (1657–60)

Or when Tideus first appears in the tale, Lydgate observes:

> Of aventure / ther cam / a knyght ryding,
> The worthiest in this world lyvyng,
> Curteys, lowly / and right vertuous,
> As seith myn autour / Called Tidyus.
>
> (1263–66)

On eighteen occasions these references occupy an entire line, as in the record of Edippus' reign: "And as myn autour writ / in wordys pleyn, / by Iocasta he had sones tweyn" (877–78).[55] And at the conclusion to the second part of the poem, Lydgate's metatextual digression fills three lines:

> As the story / shal clerly determyne,
> And my tale / her-after shal 3ou lere,
> 3if that 3ow list / the remenaunt for to here.
>
> (2550–52)[56]

Even in these longer passages, the references are self-contained and could be removed without the poem being materially affected. The filler quality of Lydgate's allusions to authors and books perhaps becomes clearest, however, when one compares them to Chaucer's treatment of the same topic. For instance, the famous stanza about Lollius that introduces the *Canticus Troili* of book 1 of the *Troilus* is thematically significant in the way it juxtaposes incongruent theory and practice: Chaucer insists there is only a "tonges difference" between himself and his Latin "auctor," when in fact he here blends one of Petrarch's sonnet's into Boccaccio's *Il Filostrato*. [57] And this juxtaposition, in turn, figures in a larger thematic exploration of the narrator's role in the poem. To be sure, not all of Chaucer's metatextual references are contextually motivated; the fact that the Franklin, in dating the concealment of the rocks off the coast of Brittany to December, chooses the date "as thise bookes [him] remembre" (*Canterbury Tales* 5.1243) seems in no way significant. What is significant, though, is the desultory appearance of such perfunctory remarks; when Chaucer repeatedly refers to his sources—as is the case in the *Troilus* but not the *Franklin's Tale*—there is always a discernible rhetorical effect.

Another type of passage in the *Siege* that puts the issue of authority to perfunctory use is that which juxtaposes the auctor's book with other accounts of the same story. After attributing the building of Thebes to King Amphioun, for instance, Lydgate asserts:

> But sothly ȝit / Some expositours,
> Groundyng hem / vpon olde auctours
> Seyn that Cadmvs / the famous olde man,
> Ful longe afor / this Cite first began.
>
> (293–96)

Or when discussing Ipsiphyle's lineage Lydgate states:

> Hir fadres name / of which also I wante,
> Thouh some seyn / he named was Thoante,
> And some bokes · vermes ek hym calle.
>
> (3194–96)

Such allusions curiously impute unanimity among patently divergent authorial books. Even when the accounts diverge radically, Lydgate's rhetoric reconciles or downplays the differences, thereby implying that literary authority and authorial opinions are by nature consistent with each other because they reflect the transcendent truths of life.[58] For instance, when Tideus, one of the poem's heroes, enters Argos,[59] Lydgate is careful to qualify any moral disapproval that might attend his banishment from Caledonia:

> And he, allas / out of that Regioun
> Exiled was / for he his brother sclowe,
> As Stace of Thebes / writ the manere howe,
> Al be that he / to hym no malys mente.
>
> (1270–73)

The books cannot be reconciled in the account of Tideus' refusal to enter Thebes in part 3, which some books are said to attribute not to prudence but to folly. There, Lydgate relies on the immediate textual authority of his book and simply states the difference of opinion without exploiting the thematic potential of such differences:

> Though some bookes / the contrarye seyn:
> But myn Autour / is platly ther-ageyn,
> And affermeth / in his opynyoun,
> That Tydeus / of hegh discrecioun,
> Of wilfulnesse / nor of no folye,
> Ne wold as tho put in Iupartie
> Nowther hym-silf / nor non of his ferys.
>
> (3971–77)

A useful way to approach such metatextual passages, again, is through comparison to similar passages by Chaucer. Book 5 of the *Troilus,* for example, is in part characterized by the various ways in which the narrator distances himself from his story by stressing its conditional nature: His tale, he insists, is only one version of one historical incident, created from complex and sometimes discordant intertextual fields. The narrator alerts the reader to some stories, which he cannot confirm, that indicate Criseyde gave Diomede "hire herte" (1050); in Cassandra's lengthy equation of Diomede with the boar in Troilus' dream (1457–1519), the poem foregrounds the complex narrative background and potential of the smallest part of any story; the conditional nature of this *Troilus and Criseyde* is again apparent when the narrator refers readers interested in Troilus' "worthi dedes" to other versions of the story (1770–71) and also gives notice of his own future compositions (1772–78); and Chaucer underscores this conditionality when he affirms

125

a place for his poem in a literary tradition in which the *Troilus* co-exists with the other works to which he has alluded. Such metatextual motivations, however, are entirely lacking in corresponding passages in Lydgate's *Siege*. The conflicting views about the founder of Thebes or the name of Ipsiphyle's father seem more idle curiosity than inquiry into the problematic nature of origins; Statius' account of Tideus' exile, latent with potentially negative criticism, is quickly bypassed, so that his version becomes consonant with Lydgate's and the discordancy of the poem's intertextual background is mitigated; and the blatantly differing versions of Tideus' motivation in part 3 are simply stated and thus accommodated without consideration of the limitations of a narrator's viewpoint or the conditionality of any narrative.[60]

My intention here is not to find fault with Hoccleve or Lydgate for what they did or did not do with the rhetorical strategies and metatextual issues that interested Chaucer. Rather, I want to lay open the inconsistent fashion in which the *"idea* of English poetry" (to use A. C. Spearing's phrase)[61] developed in the fifteenth century: Two of the writers whom we typically and justifiably see as most responsible for the transmission of Chaucerian poetics and an English literary tradition were not ubiquitously responsive to that aspect of Chaucer's writing that perhaps best justified this same poetics and literary tradition. It is their responses, more than Chaucer's formulations, that are the ways by which the idea of English poetry—the acceptance of vernacular authorities and authors—came into being. These responses of inconsistent recognition and implementation characterize an idea that is important but not yet fully understood and accepted in the fifteenth century, an idea, in fact, that is in part important *because* it was not yet fully understood and accepted.

The late Middle English contest over vernacular authority is perhaps clearest in the *Moral Fables* of Robert Henryson, for there, in the fable of *The Lion and the Mouse,* it is dramatized. This is the seventh fable of the thirteen in the collection,[62] and by this point Henryson has effected two important emphases in the collection. First, having announced his interest in literary authority in the Prologue, he has gradually and self-consciously begun to assert his own rhetorical importance in the tales he tells. For example, in the *Moralitas* to *The Sheep and the Dog,* which precedes *The Lion and the Mouse,* he claims to have been a viewer of, a participant in, the events he narrates (1282–85). And second, he has gradually shifted the focus of his concern from the foolishness of one cock (in the first fable) to the issue of God's presence in this world (in the sixth). Given its subject and this emphasis on Henryson's rhetorical significance in his own moralizing poem, then, the seventh fable can profitably be examined for the way its rhetoric mediates the late medieval conflict over authority.

The Lion and the Mouse opens with cluster of literary conceits and devices: In a "ioly sweit seasoun" (1321) of late spring, early summer the narrator "rais and put all sleuth and sleip asyde" to go to "ane wod . . . allone but gyde" (1326–27), where he confronts a *locus amoenus* in which he has a dream. While such a cluster emphasizes Henryson's self-consciousness as a narrator, it is also in this overtly, even overdetermined metatextual context that Aesop appears. In the ancient poet the Scots writer confronts both the specific writer of whom he claims to be only a translator and also, more generally, one of the genuine *auctores* of medieval culture.[63] Even though Aesop was an *auctor* considered especially valuable for adolescents, the meeting itself thus has the potential to be emblematic of a broader meeting between *auctores* and *makers*. In this regard, it is noteworthy that such a meeting between *maker* and *auctor* is unprecedented in the Aesopic tradition in general and in the *Moral Fables* in particular. Furthermore, even in comparison to generally similar encounters, such as that between Dante and Vergil or Gavin Douglas and Mapheus Vegius, Henryson's experience is distinguished by the rhetorical and thematic complexity with which the encounter is treated.

That this meeting between *maker* and *auctor* is in fact representing larger cultural issues becomes more apparent when, after Aesop appears, he is described as the very emblem of the conventional poet:

> Ane roll off paper in his hand he bair,
> And swannis pen stikand vnder his eir,
> Ane inkhorne, with ane prettie gilt pennair,
> Ane bag off silk, all at his belt he weir.
>
> (1356–59)

This is not the misshapen Aesop of legend but a distinguished, imperious figure "with ane feirful face" (1361).[64] There is thus an immediate contrast between the ancient writer, who confidently advances towards Henryson ("he come ane sturdie pace" [1362]), and Henryson

himself, who is still reclining "amang thir bewis bene" (1346). Significantly, Aesop speaks first (1363) and sits down *beside* Henryson (1366),
thereby both imaging his superiority once again but also implying a certain familiarity with the Scots writer. The language here is especially
striking in this regard. Aesop's first words are "God speid, my *sone*"
(1363, emphasis added), and that "word" (1364) is not only pleasing to
Henryson but also well known ("couth") to him. Whether the intended
meaning of *word* is "utterance" or "single lexical item," the implication
is that Henryson has customarily viewed Aesop as his figurative father,
the name with which he initially addresses him ("Welcome, father"
[1366]) and which he later reprises with a reference to Aesop's "father-
heid" (1399); in turn, throughout the Prologue Aesop refers to Henryson as his "sone" (1370, 1382, 1388). To be sure, such language might
be used between any social or ecclesiastical superior and subordinate,
but the wider cultural context here implies a more specific application:
Henryson affirms Aesop as his figurative father in the sense that the
genuine auctores are the fathers of the vernacular makers and nascent
authors. Indeed, if the Scots poet presents the ancient as his father, he
also regards him as his "maister" (1367, 1377, 1384), and throughout
the dialogue Henryson's language is deferential and includes both rhetorical concessions (e.g., "Displeis 3ow not" [1367]) and the invariable
use of the honorific plural pronouns "3e" and "3ow." Furthermore, the
syntax he uses to phrase his final request to Aesop is as elaborately cir-
cumspect as that used either by Beowulf or by Sir Gawain for their own
respective famous requests:

> "3it, gentill schir," said I, "for my requeist,
> Not to displeis 3our fatherheid, I pray,
> Vnder the figure off ane brutall beist,
> Ane morall fabill 3e wald den3e to say."
> (1398–1401)[65]

Given the profound respect that Henryson evinces for Aesop, it is
perhaps not surprising that he conducts himself as an innocent by asking Aesop to declare his "birth . . . facultye, and name" (1368). It is
surprising, however, that Aesop reveals his "winning is in heuin for ay"
(1374), inasmuch as the historical Aesop was unambiguously pagan. But
in converting Aesop to a Christian now residing in Heaven, Henryson
eliminates the one potentially complicating aspect of his author's back-

ground and in effect provides, through Aesop's eventual acquiescence to Henryson's demands, divine confirmation of the theoretical positions he here dramatizes. It is also perhaps surprising that Henryson should now, after he himself has clearly recognized the "fairest man that euer befoir" (1348) he saw and after this "man" has clearly identified himself (1370–76), additionally demand that Aesop clarify his literary accomplishments in order to confirm his identity. Yet Henryson thereby forces himself (and the reader) to pause and consider the qualities and accomplishments of this representative auctor, and Henryson's questions thus further the discussion of literary authority in the passage:

> "Ar 3e not he that all thir fabillis wrate,
> Quhilk in effect, suppois thay fen3eit be,
> Ar full off prudence and moralitie?"
>
> (1379–81)[66]

When Henryson asks Aesop for a composition that meets one set of criteria put forth in the Prologue to the *Moral Fables*—that the work be both rhetorically pleasing ("ane prettie fabill" [1386]) and ethically beneficial ("Concludand with ane gude moralitie" [1387])—Aesop refuses. But he does so not because the composition Henryson requests is theoretically impossible—not because poetry cannot be simultaneously rhetorical and ethical—nor because it is impertinent for a maker to make such a demand of an auctor but because, in Aesop's words, " 'quhat is it worth to tell ane fen3eit taill, / Quhen haly preiching may na thing auaill?' " (1389–90). As Aesop elaborates this view (1391–97), it becomes clear that from his now-divine perspective the corruption and decadence of the world have rendered useless his ethical "taillis" if not ethical instruction itself. Despite what would seem to be the unchangeable and irrefutable nature of his position, however, the narrator does in fact persuade him to tell a tale, not by the cogency of any further arguments but simply by the power of his own rhetoric. As a result, during the course of the dialogue Henryson moves from passivity, when he remains reclining to meet Aesop, to activity, when he is not silenced by Aesop's objections but is in fact able to silence them through rhetoric.

In this regard, it seems especially significant that the fable Aesop tells is *The Lion and the Mouse,* for this fable and its *Moralitas* offer the most explicit political and social commentary in all of the *Moral Fables.*[67] Henryson may well be "cautious" in having Aesop tell this traditional story of a mouse that, having been freed by a lion, in turn releases the lion from a net in which it has been trapped.[68] But in view of the way that the Prologue to the fable foregrounds the issue of literary authority, another motivation for this particular tale at this particular point in the *Moral Fables* is possible. In telling a fable that is moralized as an account of the ideal social balance between king and commons, Henryson, through Aesop, confidently assumes what would become the Renaissance role of the adviser to and supporter of a prince.[69] It is this role that Aesop, in his final paternal and authorial gesture, explicitly transfers to the vernacular poet:

> My fair child,
> Perswaid the kirkmen ythandly to pray
> That tressoun of this cuntrie be exyld,
> And iustice regne, and lordis keip thair fay
> Vnto thair souerane lord baith nycht and day.
>
> (1615–19)

As rhetorical representations of larger cultural concerns, Henryson's unique dialogue with Aesop and the subsequent telling of *The Lion and the Mouse* thus enact a usurpation of authorial voice and authority by a vernacular writer. Up to this point in the *Moral Fables* Henryson has feigned to be merely a translator, passing on the text of an auctor. By drawing Aesop into a narrative that purports to be the translated text of Aesop, Henryson renders Aesop and his work part of the fiction and, consequently, undermines the authority that is imputed to him as an auctor and the efficient cause of the fables. Moreover, in silencing Aesop's objections and evidently compelling him to tell a story and in relying on rhetoric alone to achieve this end, Henryson appropriates for himself the dominant, authoritative role in the dialogue. Having usurped the rhetorical voice of his auctor—that is, authorship—Henryson thus by extension usurps his responsibility for the *Fables*—his authoritativeness. Moreover, since Aesop tells a fable of social criticism and since Aesop's composition is exposed as the production of Henyrson himself, the Scots poet also assumes Aesop's ability to make ethical utterances that have authorization. What Henryson dramatizes, in effect, is the birth of the vernacular author whose father is literary authority and whose mother is vernacular language ("mother toung" [31]). The *Moral Fables* is thereby in part a poem motivated by cultural and linguistic anxieties over the status of vernacular writers. In order to replace Aesop, his father figure, Henryson first needs to legitimate a familial connection between the Antique or patristic fathers and the vernacular sons. But of necessity, for Henryson's rhetorical resolution of the conflict over authority to make sense, it requires a cultural context in which the issue is not yet resolved. Indeed, this attempt at legitimation, which would not receive broad institutional support in England for at least another hundred years, only serves to confirm the fact that the authority of the vernacular writer was still, in the late fifteenth century, a contested issue.[70]

While the conception of literary authority that informs the discourse of late Middle English manuscripts varies in kind and the uses to which it is put, it is nonetheless possible to offer some general conclusions about its character. In the official discourse of late-medieval literary criticism, *auctoritas* was viewed as the characteristic utterance of a select group of authorized individuals and was one of the ways by which the dominant Latin culture of the Middle Ages validated itself. One implication of official positions on literary authority is that complete overlap was understood to exist between authority as it referred both to the individual who created a work and to that individual's cultural entitlement to the work. If one supplements "cultural" with "legal" here, one has a description that also largely applies to modern writers, though this supplement is very significant indeed. In all medieval traditions, vernacular as well as Latin, legal discourse does not figure in the construction of the author function; authors as legal entities and the copyright laws that define and sustain them by establishing propriety over texts are distinctly post-Renaissance developments. Official medieval notions of literary authority and modern ones diverge even further by the fact that in the Middle Ages the creative and entitlement aspects of authority overlapped with that of the validity of the work. For a work to have authorship, it also needed to have authoritativeness and the institutional authorization of the church and the universities. A work that lacked any one characteristic necessarily lacked all three and was therefore beyond the pale of institutionalized literary criticism.

Still another important divergence between medieval and modern notions of literary authority is that writers were stratified according to the language in which they wrote. Vernacular writers, accordingly, were neither theoretically defined as auctores nor professionally constituted and institutionally sanctioned as such, and in medieval culture it was only the auctores who had legitimate entitlement to create and delimit literary works. Their names might be known and they might unarguably have composed works, but vernacular writers could not have official authorship; like Chaucer or John Capgrave, they might have a very protective attitude toward their works, but they could not have authoritativeness; and their writings might be unquestionably orthodox and ethical, but they could not have authorization. As the development of the very word *auctor* suggests, the discourse of authority was exclusively in and about Latin. The Middle English form, *author,* is of course a Latin derivative, and this linguistic borrowing, first preserved in English in the late fourteenth century, would seem to imply a semantic and cultural borrowing as well. The earliest native approximate, *scop,* had died out by the early thirteenth century, leaving English without a privileged term to refer exclusively to what we would call a vernacular author; *maker,* significantly, applies as well to a woodworker as to a vernacular writer.[71] If a concept can gain at best limited currency in a language without a word to designate it, the very idea of authorship was thus presumably imported from Latin.

Middle English rhetorical strategies like the nondistinctive "I," the perfunctory naming of the poet, or the invocation of an officially authoritative figure reflect the correlation between the discourse of late Middle English manuscripts and larger cultural practices, especially the discourse of Latin literary criticism. Similarly, the exclusion of authority from vernacular discourse is manifested in the trope of the authorizing figure who controls a narrative from within, just as the hierarchical structure of medieval society and the nonprofessional status of vernacular writers led to the dependence on patrons. More general accommodations of Middle English literature to the constraints of literary criticism occur as well. The paean to Christian virtue with which Chaucer concludes the *Troilus*—his most metacritically self-conscious work—presumes to recuperate the poem as the sort of ethical lesson typical of *auctoritas.* And if in the *Confessio* Amans opens "up the possibility . . . that love need not disqualify one from *auctor*ship,"[72] he is able to do so only because Gower works through the traditional Latin voice of a commentator.

These accommodations underscore a significant aspect of the vernacular writers' understanding of authority: Their general strategy was not to attempt to establish a different kind of authority for the vernacular but to appropriate for Middle English literary authority as it was conventionally defined. To be sure, Hoccleve's psychological self-examination in the *Complaint* and critical self-consciousness in the *Series* do suggest a severance of auctor from *auctoritas* and a view of authorship, authoritativeness, and authorization as not being synonymous: It is not Hoccleve's ethical character that entitles him to speak in the *Complaint* but his problematic recovery from madness. Yet as Hoccleve's *Regement of Princes* and Lydgate's *Siege of Thebes* suggest, the character of literary authority remained a contested issue in the fifteenth century. Moreover, when Henryson explored the issue in the *Moral Fables,* he did not dramatize the creation of a new type of authority but the usurpation of the traditional kind. In short, the role of great auctores is *expanded to include* Chaucer, Gower, and Lydgate, not replaced by a solely vernacular tradition.[73]

The contest over authority does not seem to have exercised English writers much longer after Henryson was writing in the 1470s. Skelton might be considered the earliest writer whose works betray neither anxiety on the issue nor the rhetorical influence of it. The easy narrative archness of poems like *Phyllyp Sparowe* and *Agaynst the Scottes,* which incorporate the responses of antagonists to the poems themselves, and the pride Skelton displays at being a "laureate" in poems like *Agenst Garnesche, Against Dundas,* and *Speke Parott* bespeak satisfaction in both himself as a writer and the poems he writes. Skelton's sense of authority, significantly, still owes much to medieval arguments. While the *Garlande or Chapelet of Laurell* proclaims Skelton's place in the tradition of great poets, for instance, the tradition is represented as one extending back through Chaucer, Gower, and Lydgate to the Antique writers. Thus, if his work is an endpoint of sorts in the vernacular writers' quest for literary authority, the desired position was, again, the one the received auctores already occupied.

At the outset of this chapter I suggested that the expansion of the authorship of *The Waste Land* to include Pound as well as Eliot could be perceived as a challenge by some critics: If Eliot's artistry is really the artistry of Eliot and Pound, the argument might go, then discussions of the former are obviated. This is not the case for Eliot, however, any more than it is for Gower, Chaucer, or any late Middle English writer. If authority and the author function are contextually defined, then for any historical work criticism can always use at least two sets of contextual definitions: Those that applied at the time the work was written and those that apply at the time the critic is writing, and in each of these sets there may well be alternatives and variations. For Eliot, who composed *The Waste Land* only seventy-odd years ago, the sets would seem to be largely the same; the complicating factor is that the poem was received in a tradition that incorporated the romantic myth of the solitary genius, though its production was not consistent with this myth. Even so, the critic still has a choice between perceiving Eliot's poetry as postromantic thought has argued poems ought to be perceived and reading it as it was in fact written. A critical decision to follow one approach or the other is determined by personal preference or institutional influence, not by hermeneutic validity.

For late Middle English writers, the choice is more clearly between two different sets of contextual definitions of authority. Modern textual criticism has relied on the priority of its own presumptively transhistorical definitions and has therefore depended unselfconsciously on the authority of vernacular poets. Not coincidentally, those writers whose aesthetics are the most responsive to modern critical methods or whose sense of authorial identity seems the strongest—Langland, Chaucer, and Gower in particular—are the writers on whose works the greatest textual-critical effort has been expended. Writers whose works are more resistant to such methods and more typical of medieval aesthetics and literary attitudes—writers like Minot and Lydgate—appear in very old, essentially diplomatic editions. All readers are of course entitled to their preferences, but the actualization of literary taste as editorial method does not necessarily and exclusively validate either the literary taste or the editorial method. Since writers do not autonomously define themselves and their works, Langland's aesthetics or Chaucer's authorial anxiety are largely irrelevant to the kind of authority that would have determined the works' transmission and that medieval readers would have expected and perceived. The anxiety that motivates much of Chaucer's metatextual exposition, indeed, is occasioned by the consequences of the denial of auctorial status.

The rhetorical strategies and the contest over authority in Middle English writing of the fourteenth and fifteenth centuries give no indication that in historical terms vernacular writers had any claim to be authors, either as they were then culturally constructed—combining authorship, authoritativeness, and authorization—or as textual criticism has defined and utilized them. This status would not be granted to vernacular writers until well into the Renaissance, when they of course no longer wrote in Middle English, and after, significantly, the humanists had championed their notions of literary authority. For late Middle English vernacular writers, to equate the authoritative text with the authorial one is to grant them the very quality that their own desires indicate they did not have and whose absence in part enabled their writings. Since the lack of authority was a condition of existence for the discourse of late Middle English manuscripts, the authority imputed by modern textual criticism undermines the motivation and significance of such rhetorical strategies as the nondistinctive "I" and themes such as the contest over authority. Ultimately, the accommodation of Middle English literature to humanist principles on authorship does not simply obscure the author function of vernacular writing: It obliterates it.

The parallel between the production of Middle English literature within the constraints of medieval cultural practice and its reception after the Middle Ages is striking. That is, humanism compelled Middle English literature into an untenable position wherein its champions (if any) could not claim for it the qualities and attendant prestige of humanist literature, but neither could they declare the independence of Middle English from humanist literary values without merely confirming the nonprestigious status the works had been accorded. In a similar vein, in the fourteenth and fifteenth centuries vernacular literature was precluded from the various yet simultaneous kinds of literary authority, but there was no opportunity or forum in public venues like the court, the church, or the universities to effect a challenge to the critical status quo or to demonstrate a claim to a distinctive vernacular kind of authority. For Middle English writers, the only alternative— the alternative that accounts for the ways in which vernacular works rhetorically negotiate the issue of literary authority—was to accept the official literary-critical view of vernacular writing, thereby creating a cultural space for themselves even as they confirmed the official view of vernacular literature and, more generally, the medieval ideology of authority.

CHAPTER FIVE

Work and Text

Sₒₘₑₜᵢₘₑ ₗₐₜₑ ᵢₙ the Middle English period the following anonymous "punctuation poem" was composed:

> Trvsty . seldom to their ffrendys vniust.
> Gladd for to helpp . no Crysten creator
> Wyllyng to greve . setting all þeir ioy & lust
> Only in þe plesor of god . havyng no cvre
> Who is most riche . with them þey wyl be sewer
> Wher nede is . gevyng neyther reward ne ffee
> Vnresonably . Thus lyve prestys . parde[1]

The sense of this little poem is curiously ambivalent. If the metrical lines are regarded as syntactic units, the poem depicts the avarice of priests, but if the syntactic unit is defined by the caesura, the poem recounts their selflessness and virtue. Since the manuscript pointing (reproduced above) emphasizes this ambivalence, both writer and scribe—presuming they were different people—were well aware of the poem's conceit. Moreover, since even minor alterations in lexicon, syntax, and perhaps punctuation would undermine this conceit, a fixed text was inherent in the poem's composition and essential in its transmission.

This late-medieval example of dependence on and exploitation of a fixed text contrasts sharply with one of the popular fifteenth-century carols on ivy. This poem is in part an explanation of the mystical significance symbolized in the word *ivy*, which appears in this spelling throughout the carol. Accordingly, *i* is said to represent "Jhesu" and *v* is likened to "wurthy wyffe." Inasmuch as in the Middle Ages *i* and *j* were largely conditioned orthographic variants—with *j* often appearing in word initial and final positions, *i* everywhere else—the disparity between *i* in "ivy" and *j* in "Jhesu" is perhaps only apparent. But for the graph *v* to be likened to "wurthy wyffe," the reader must make a rather contorted abstraction between orthographic representations and phonetic realizations. The derivation of *ivy* from Old English *ifig* indicates that pronunciation with [v] must have been the norm even in the medieval period, and in native English words in Middle English, in fact, *v* typically indicates the voiced labiodental fricative.[2] The graph *w* in "wurthy" and "wyffe," on the other hand, implies the semivowel [w]: Both words are derived from Old English, where [w] was represented by the character wynn, which was gradually replaced by *w* in the Middle English period. Though in late Middle English the graph *v* can be used as a representation of [w], this is typically the case only in words of French or Latin derivation. The "likening" between *v* and "wurthy wyffe" depends, then, on the reader recognizing that *v* in contexts *other* than that of "ivy" could stand for [w], and that this [w], in turn, was often represented by *w* and was, therefore, the initial sound of "wurthy" and "wyffe."

The fifth stanza of this carol states:

> The thyrd letter is an E;
> I lykyn to Emanuell,
> That is to sey, "Cryst with vs be
> And euermore for to dwell."[3]

Though the form "ivy" appears three times within twelve lines before this stanza, here the poet implies an *e* for the last letter of the word, an inconsonance between the word and its likening that was again neither insignificant nor unavoidable. Spellings of "Emanuell" with an initial *i* (hence *y*) are recorded, so that the poet's "ivy" might have been used in support of "Imanuell." Conversely, the recorded form *ive*, which in fact offers the most logical representation of the pronunciation [ive] from which Modern English [aɪvi] presumably arose, contains an *e* for "Emanuell." As in the disparity between *v* and the significance he wished to see in that graph, the poet's sense of orthographic correspondence was evidently strong enough to require an *E* for the beginning of "Emanuell" and to insist here that the "thyrd letter is an E," but was apparently not troubled by the correctable disparity between this *E* and the *y* that figures in all of his other spellings of "ivy."

These two fifteenth-century examples imply radically different conceptions of work and text. On the one hand, the punctuation poem requires a strong sense of the integrity of the text and its determinative influence on the character of the work; but on the other, the actual letters of the carol's text, so to speak, are less important than the spirit that informs them and gives them (and the work) life. While it is certainly possible to define and evaluate these conceptions in the abstract or in accordance with contemporary reading strategies, historically sensitive consideration depends on recognition of the poems' conditions of existence. To judge one or both poems as representative of late Middle English poetry, that is, or even to assign them any historical meanings, we need to know the linguistic, bibliographical, and social codes that constructed the discourse of late Middle English manuscripts and through which English literature was negotiated in the later Middle Ages. Within the discourse, it is this negotiation that circumscribes conceptions of work and text, the focus of the present chapter.

Traditionally, it will be recalled, textual criticism has seen the work as a "message or experience implied by the authoritative versions of a literary writing" and a text as "the actual order of words and punctuation as contained in any one physical form, such as manuscript, proof, or book."[4] Both works and texts are nonsubstantial and not equatable with or limited to any of the specific documents in which they may be manifested. Furthermore, as I argued in chapter 1, in practice a predominant idealist, lexical conception of the work has rendered the text preeminent in textual-critical understandings of the work: The recovery and presentation of the authoritative, authorial text have been the primary concerns of theoretical and practical developments since the Renaissance and have defined editors' tasks in their efforts to edit a work. From a traditional textual-critical perspective, the work is, in effect, the correct text. Since a contemporary reader's access to a historical work is typically only through a modern edited text, the text comes to stand as the most significant and accessible part of the historical work, which the modern reader may in turn remake into a contemporary one. The modern text is thus viewed and used as an inherent, even originary, feature of the historical work.

Traditional textual criticism's equation of the authoritative text with the authorial one was a logical consequence of its origin in humanism: The humanists' valorization of individual, human achievement dictated that the medieval situation of authority in a divine power that acts through human endeavors would yield to a focus on the contribution and determining influences of earthly writers.[5] In the same vein, the traditional concentration on the text of a literary work, excluding extratextual phenomena to such an extent that the text comes to stand for the work—that the work is understood to be etiologically lexical—is also an unproblematic extension of humanist thinking. Such concentration upon the text was a logical consequence, for example, of humanist ideology. The humanists' conception of language as the door to reality and their attendant interest in empirical linguistic studies dissociated them from medieval thinkers like the *modistae* and made them inevitably interested in the specific words of specific texts. Their view of language and language studies as part of a moral project further validated this interest and safeguarded it from theoretical challenges.

On a purely practical level, moreover, the advent of print offered a technology that was almost ideally suited to the humanist emphasis on the text. Print, for example, radically altered the documents that enunciated literary works both by precluding many of the distinctive strategies and characteristics of medieval manuscripts and by facilitating exploitation of specifically textual phenomena. Medieval use of documentary spatialization had extended to nontextual phenomena, but from very early on handwritten glosses, illuminations, and historiated initials disappeared from typeset books. Woodcuts and changes in typeface could at best approximate some of the functions and effects of these medieval techniques, and it was not until well into the sixteenth century that both books and broadsides (in picture poems, for example) no longer attempted to duplicate manuscripts but developed their own pragmatic strategies. The strategies for exploiting the spatialization of a document were clearly both sophisticated and distinctive in the early modern period, but the important point is that they were essentially textual, involving the physical appearance of letters (in roman, black letter, or italic fonts), punctuation, and margins, and layout features like pagination, paragraphing, chapter titles, and running heads.[6]

Within given volumes, furthermore, printed production regularized and stabilized these same textual features. Similarly, typographic production, compared to chirographic, resulted in far less graphic variation within the texts of individual documents and even, as roman type became predominant in all books in the sixteenth century, between documents. As bibliographers have amply demonstrated, to be sure, early printed books were not universally regular; once printing had begun, for instance, a line or page could be reset, so that two copies of the same issue of the same edition might have differing texts. Even with the proliferation of stereotyping in the nineteenth century, typeset texts were never unalterable, since the plates could be damaged, changed, or corrected.[7] While recognizing that, either intentionally or accidentally, printed texts could undergo alteration, sometimes radically so, I am simply noting that the *degree* of alteration was typically much less than that in manuscript technology. Another way to describe the situation is to say that if it takes a Hinman Collator to detect different textual states of the same issue or work, then the states must be physically and textually very similar indeed, far more similar, certainly, than for the Hengwrt and Ellesmere manuscripts, say, of the *Canterbury Tales*. If in absolute terms variation in print production is much less than that found in manuscript traditions, print transmission is even more relatively stable in the areas of formatting and physical appearance. And given the fact that Renaissance printers typically set copy from previous editions, works were transmitted overwhelmingly *as texts* in a *unilinear fashion*. Since in all these ways realization in a document constituted a text as something relatively lexically fixed and physically regular, the text became the most prominent feature and time-consuming concern of most early printed books for both producers and consumers. Printed books, in turn, contextually could elicit the expectation of regularity in a way manuscripts could not.

To examine concepts of work and text in the discourse of late Middle English manuscripts from within the discourse itself, I need to consider their correlations with these humanist positions, with the principles of Latin literary criticism, and with the institutions and nondiscursive practices and technologies that enabled the production of Middle English works. In the discourse of Latin literary criticism, a work was also theoretically understood to be nonsubstantial, but it was distinguished from a work in the textual criticism of the humanist or contemporary periods by a number of other qualities that are reflected in its relationships to both texts and documents. At the foundation of the medieval conception was a relationship between words and things that differs radically—if not diametrically—from that of much poststructuralist thought, which often figures reality as a projection of language. To the medieval point of view, behind the book of nature as well as the books of men lay the absolute truths of the divine author, the prelinguistic verities of the physical and metaphysical world that can be read in the signs that are traces of them. This ideology thus validated and safeguarded itself, much as medieval views on authority did. In the famous words of Allanus de Lisle: "Every created thing of the world is like a book, a picture and a mirror for us—a faithful sign of our life, our death, our condition, and our fate."[8] Language and, by extension, literary works are ways for humans to acquire a sense of the absolute truths of existence, but they are products of a fallen world that, since the Tower of Babel, has linguistically drifted farther and farther from the Adamic language.[9]

As a system of signs, language was thus regarded as necessary but also inadequate and unreliable, so that when medieval writers attempted to represent prelinguistic truths in human language they were destined for—and expected—failure to a greater or lesser extent. The failure might be due simply to the inadequacies of language or to the writers' own limitations in style and thought (a recognition also expressed in the humility topos), or it might be due to the imperfections of scribal transmission, or it might be due to the fallibility of a reader's understanding. What could not fail or change were the absolute truths that the work attempted to recuperate. According to medieval literary theory, *intentio auctoris* was "the intended meaning 'piously expounded' and rendered unimpeachable,"[10] and since an auctor by definition was one who had *auctoritas,* the meaning as well as the exposition was necessarily pious. This *auctoritas* coincided with the *res* of a literary work and was what the auctores themselves produced (or, perhaps, transmitted), while the *verba* and document in which it appeared—the *liber scriptus*—were the products of scribes. Throughout the Middle Ages the distinction between *dictare* (the composition of a work) and *scribere* (the writing of a text) is in fact carefully maintained, though, as in the case of Hoccleve, the same individual could perform both activities. This notion that a work has both *res* and *verba,* Mary Carruthers notes, "posits an 'idea' or 'meaning' that lies 'within' or 'behind' speech as some sort of construct partly independent of and greater than the words from which it is constructed."[11] It is just such a distinction, of course, that Chaucer articulates in the preface to the *Melibee,* where he stresses that though the evangelists may differ in their *verba,* they "alle acorden as in hire sentence" (*Canterbury Tales,* 943–48)—the *res* of Christ's life. If a medieval work was nonsubstantial, therefore, it was nonetheless in a sense fixed by the truths it was presumed to express. Since the mental conception of a *res* remains prior to the *verba* and is not affected in any important way by them, what was not fixed was the *text.* For a medieval reader, when there was disparity between the *res* and the *verba* of a literary work, the latter was inevitably judged in error and emended or supplemented, if not completed, by the reader's own understanding. When such a supplement was physically incorporated into the texts of subsequent documents, it thereby altered the *verba* (but not the *res*) for other readers.

In textual-critical terms, the key point is that in its production a work was thus theoretically instigated and determined less by a specific text or the human intentions (final or otherwise) of a specific individual and more by this core of prelinguistic truth that was presumed to be manifested in various literary works much as in various features of the natural world or in various events of human history. Emendation of inevitably flawed human texts against this unimpeachable divine work takes various forms. Generically, hagiography is in part defined by such an orientation, for the specifics of individual lives are far less important than the manifestations of generic and ethical constants like temptation by nonbelievers or the reliance on God's deliverance: Rather than the individual's actions defining her or his life, these manifestations define the life as that of a saint. In medieval views of history, what was known were the eternal truths and what needed to be known was not whether but how they appeared in specific historical incidents. For medieval historians, Ruth Morse points out, "the clear light of historical truth meant a rhetorical presentation of what was believed to have happened. Or, a plausible narration of what was likely to have happened—which could mean the attribution of speeches or deeds to 'villains' of the whole story or period who were perhaps not *actually* present at the scene or scenes described. This implies, too, that characterization may precede events."[12] The negotiation between the known and unknown inevitably resulted in the formulaic quality of much medieval historical writing, and it also accounts for the medieval habit of supplementing perceived gaps in the historical record by claiming the antiquity of newly produced documents and by altering historical documents.[13] To the modern scholar such activities constitute forgery, but within medieval conceptions of work and text, they are emendations of the *verba* so as more accurately to reflect the *res*.

Such theoretical conceptions of work and text are in fact manifested in original works, commentaries, and translations, all of which subjugate textual remaking to the prelinguistic ideas that surpass and inform both works and texts. While the works auctores produced were theoretically original with them, for example, the auctores were able to produce them only by searching their memories and also whatever books were available and then ruminating on this information.[14] As one considers each of the other possible ways of contributing to the production of a medieval book—those of a *commentator,* a *compilator,* and a *scriptor*—it becomes clear that remaking is not simply the dominant trope in medieval presentations of literary composition but the principle that enabled it:

> For out of olde feldes, as men seyth,
> Cometh al this newe corn from yer to yere,
> And out of old bokes, in good feyth,
> Cometh al this newe science that men lere.
>
> (*Parliament of Fowls,* 22–25)

If auctores overtly took possession of another's literary work by transforming it into their own, even while retaining many of the other's *verba,* commentators and translators covertly did so by much the same means. Commentators, through the rhetorical strategies of poets and ad hoc devices such as restructuring the syntax of their original for their lemmata, substituted their own *verba* and intentionality for those of another in the very maneuver of claiming to offer exposition. As commentary material for academic works proliferated in the later Middle Ages, physically as well as conceptually commentaries could displace and transform the original works they accompanied, all the while sanctioned by the view that since the commentaries were not altering but merely clarifying and affirming the *res* of the auctor, the work remained unchanged.[15] Translation similarly represented itself as subservient to auctorial works that it in no way changed. In fact, through both rhetorical and exegetical strategies late-medieval vernacular translators displaced their originals and, as I suggested earlier in my discussion of Chaucer's literary theory, cleared a space for themselves in the discourse of medieval literature.

The character of a work in the later Middle Ages was also in part constructed through the work's reception by its readers; if at an *interpretive* level much contemporary criticism shares this attitude, at a *productive* level—in the conception of how the textual-critical work comes into being—it does not. Within the ethical poetic of the later Middle Ages, reading, as well as writing, was a moral, active, and essentially meditative experience. Thus, if writers sought to supplement and correct the *verba* of a work according to the *res* they understood to lie behind them, readers did so, too, albeit mentally. In Carruthers's analysis, "Reading is to be digested, to be ruminated, like a cow chewing her cud, or like a bee making honey from the nectar of flowers. . . . It is both physiological and psychological, and it changes both the food and its consumer." The medieval use of rumination as a metaphor for both reading and writing underscores this quality of reading as a " 'hermeneutical dialogue' between two memories, that in the text being made very much present as it is familiarized to that of the reader." [16] The text itself, moreover, was not limited to the original words of an original writer but included the interpretations that literally and traditionally accrued to it, as is suggested in the *Confessio* (1.270–71), the *Book of the Duchess* (333), and *Piers Plowman* (B 5.276, 12.294, 15.82, and 17.10). In *A Procession of Corpus Cristi,* Lydgate even dramatizes such a conception when he merges historical biblical events with Scripture and the interpretations thereof by describing a procession that begins with the events of the Old Testament and moves through John the Baptist and the evangelists before concluding with the patristic fathers and Thomas Aquinas.[17] George Ashby reflects a similar merger in his *Active Policy,* which states that his ignorance of Scripture extends *especially* to the glosses:

> Right so though I haue not seien scripture
> Of many bookes right sentenciall,
> In especial of the gloses sure,
> I woll therfor kepe true menyng formal.
>
> (50–54)

Through dialogue with such a broadly conceived text, the reader preserves the *res* of a work at the expense of its *verba.* On a more pragmatic level, the layout and design of medieval manuscripts also in-

vite the reader's active participation in the construction of a work—
in processing illuminations, for instance, and their relationships to the
accompanying text—even as the advent of print and its elevation of the
black and white text foreclosed these kinds of interpretive participation
and rendered reading a more passive experience.[18] This inclusion of the
reader's contribution to the construction of a work is implicit in the
very concept *intentio auctoris,* which situates the intention of a work in
part within the understanding of individual readers, and also underlies
one of the most popular rhetorical strategies of the Middle Ages: allegory. More so than simple description or narration, allegory depends on
the reader to supplement the work with what is not said—to complete
the *verba* of a manuscript from the reader's own storehouse of images,
tropes, and social phenomena—and is thus a strategy that subordinates
a work and its writer to the interpretation of its readers.[19] Without the
reader's supplement, the work fails not only to succeed but to be.

One of the conditions of existence for late Middle English works,
then, is that they not be found in explicit disagreement with these theoretical principles, and to a large extent this condition could be easily met.
These official positions, unlike those on authority, did not expressly
exclude the vernacular work, which thus did not need to become a contested issue in and of itself. But since vernacular writers were excluded
from being auctores, their works could not be presumed to have *auctoritas*—an insubstantial yet unassailably ethical and determinative *res*
behind them. Middle English works could be formally framed by the
conceptions of Latin literary criticism, but only without the motivations
for such a frame: They might be determined by the idea that an absent
constitutive *res* is variously realized in any text but not by an authorized
res itself, however unambiguously moral they might nonetheless be.

The Middle English language, particularly in its correlation with
Latin and the institutional generation of ideology, also helped to construct the character of late Middle English writing in ways that need
to be factored into any Middle English definitions of work and text.
Broadly stated, for medieval England linguistic attitudes had always
been at least twofold: Latin was the language of tradition, authority, and
power; the vernacular was the language of the people, impermanence,
and change.[20] In pragmatic terms, these differences were enabled by and
emblematized in the long and developed traditions of grammar and
rhetoric that exclusively characterized Latin in the Middle Ages. Since
even by the Anglo-Saxon epoch there were no native speakers of Latin,

and since from antiquity Latin had had a highly codified prescriptive grammar, it was in a very real sense a dead language, despite the fact that it continued to be spoken in universities and monasteries. Indeed, in a world of continual flux, the necritude, so to speak, of Latin was evidently a cherished quality, and it was in part to assure the geographic and chronological transcendence this quality enabled that Latin grammars proliferated throughout the Middle Ages. Hence, Dante speaks of

> the art of grammar, which is nothing else but a kind of unchangeable identity of speech in different times and places. This, having been settled by the common consent of many peoples, seems exposed to the arbitrary will of none in particular, and consequently cannot be variable. They therefore invented grammar in order that we might not, on account of the variation of speech fluctuating at the will of individuals, either fail altogether in attaining, or at least attain but a partial knowledge of the opinions and exploits of the ancients, or of those whom difference of place causes to differ from us.[21]

As Dante and others were well aware, Latin of course did change, both in respect to its development into Vulgar Latin and thence the Romance languages, and in respect to Latin as the spoken medium of the church and the universities. But the language of the *texts* of the ancients and the Church Fathers was fixed because it had already been written, and the dissemination of the grammars of Donatus and Priscian (among others) and the evaluation of grammar as the first of the seven Liberal Arts testify to the universal perception of this fixity.[22] The long rhetorical tradition of Latin served much the same purpose: The codification of rules for preaching, letterwriting, and the composition of poetry assumes the legitimacy of Latin as a medium of communication and thereby furthers its linguistic fixity.

At the same time these traditions were embracing and constituting Latin as a prestigious language distinct in form and function from any of the vernaculars, other changes furthered a general divergence of the textual from the oral. Twelfth- and thirteenth-century developments in punctuation and word division, for instance, aided the stabilization of texts and the demarcation of *written* language as a distinctive linguistic variety with its own determinants, pragmatics, and discursive functions.[23] In indexing and cross-referencing systems, this nascent individuality of written language coalesced with the prestige of Latin: Developed specifically for Latin works like encyclopedias and preaching manuals, such devices stabilized Latin texts at the same time they facilitated access to them.

Together, the prescriptive grammar and stylistics of Latin, the identification of an auctor with his writings, and the cultural status of Latin compositions yielded texts that were imbued with the qualities of prestige, stasis, and, insofar as they had been produced in accordance with various linguistic and poetic rules, regularity. Ultimately, grammars and rhetorics also served an ideological function, symbolizing and characterizing the power of a language, whether ecclesiastical, civil, or literary. Within this cultural framework, grammatical and stylistic studies of Latin were far more than linguistic diversions: Right or wrong grammar and rhetoric meant right or wrong understanding—and hence preservation—of tradition, culture, and God. By the same token, a language that lacked the stabilizing and symbolic influences of grammatical and rhetorical traditions could not be the language of power.

Within the discourse of late Middle English manuscripts there are ample recognitions of the cultural prestige and ideological power of Latin in comparison to the vernacular. Throughout *Piers Plowman,* for instance, Latin is presented and recognized as the elite language of authority in the scriptural quotations that shape Langland's vernacular poem. Latin is the language of angels and the learned that excludes the unregenerate like Lady Mede and Sloth; it is the language whose linguistic authority, as well as the authority of all the institutions and practices Latin sustains, that Langland by the very act of writing his critique in English presumes to challenge.[24] Moreover, just as vernacular poets define themselves in terms of their inadequate relation with *auctores,* so expression of the linguistic inadequacies of English is a rhetorical strategy that paradoxically creates a cultural space for English. In Hawes's *The Pastime of Pleasure* Dame Grammar defines the parts of speech so as expressly to omit English:

> all the eyght partes in generall
> Are laten wordes / annexed properly
> To euery speche for to speke formally.
>
> (593–95)

And in the *Court of Sapience* the poet explains his rhetorical deficiencies by citing the inadequacies of English in general:

> For to al makers here I me excuse
> That I ne can delycately endyte;
> Rude is the speche of force whiche I must use:
> Suche infortune my natyf byrth may wyte.
>
> (1.36–39)

In contrast to Latin, Middle English was thus represented as, and presumably understood to be, a living, unstable language, for recognition of diachronic change and synchronic variation is a persistent theme throughout the period. Perhaps the most famous instance is in the Proem to book 2 of *Troilus and Criseyde:*

> Ye knowe ek that in forme of speche is chaunge
> Withinne a thousand yeer, and wordes tho
> That hadden pris, now wonder nyce and straunge
> Us thinketh hem, and yet thei spake hem so,
> And spedde as wel in love as men now do.
>
> (22–26)

But several other passages or works also acknowledge the diverse character of the Middle English language: Trevisa's excursus in his translation of the *Polychronicon* about the diversity of English dialects; the similar excursus in Osbern Bokenham's *Mappula Angliae;* the dialectal exercise of Chaucer's *Reeve's Tale;* and Caxton's remarks on English dialects in his preface to the *Eneydos.*[25] For the most part, however, such passages are borne more of idle curiosity than of rigorous inquiry. When genuinely systematic linguistics was practiced, such as by the *modistae,* it was concerned with the authorial language: Latin.

As the language of daily transactions and popular diversions—as a language culturally less prestigious and institutionally less powerful than Latin—English offered neither opportunity nor intrinsic reason to stay even temporarily this ephemerality by means of prescriptive or descriptive grammar. Thus, while systematic grammars of Latin proliferated throughout the Middle Ages, no similar interest was displayed in Middle English grammar outside of passing remarks by Latin grammarians (like John Leylond) who wrote in Middle English.[26] The very idea of linguistic fixity and correctness may have had to be imported from Latin, for in Middle English (as well as Old French and Middle Welsh) a common word for a grammar book is, significantly, *donet* (MW *dwned*), a derivative of the name of the Latin grammarian Donatus. In any event, English was not described in any systematic way until well into the sixteenth century, when grammarians like Roger Ascham and Thomas Wilson began to discuss English rhetoric and usage, while others, like Sir John Cheke and William Bullokar, offered prescriptive discussions of orthography. Even at this date English was scarcely accorded its own linguistic identity, since these early accounts of English grammar, like early accounts of most vernaculars, depended heavily on Latin terminology, paradigms, and analyses. Other grammatical confirmations of social stability and prestige took even longer to develop; the first dictionaries date to the seventeenth century, and truly regularized orthography to the eighteenth. As the sixteenth-century arguments over inkhorn terms suggest, this status was not easily acquired.

Since as a linguistic medium Middle English was constructed as ephemeral, it is not surprising that, again in contrast to Latin, English elicited little stylistic discussion. Theoretically, Middle English readers might describe the style of a Middle English work (though such descriptions are exceedingly rare), but without a sense of linguistic correctness and incorrectness, they had no native paradigms within which to evaluate it. In this regard, Middle English again generally resembles other vernacular traditions in the Middle Ages. For example, while early in the fourteenth century Dante expressed a high opinion of Italian when he composed his influential *De vulgari eloquentia,* a more representative medieval view is that of Petrarch, who in a letter to Boccaccio admits that on occasion he is inclined "to give all my time to writing in the vernacular" but stresses that the vernacular has only the *potential* for excellence: "Latin is of course the loftier language, but it has been so developed by ancient geniuses that neither we nor anyone else can add much of anything to it. The vulgar tongue however has only recently been formulated. It has been mishandled by many and tended by only a few; rough as it is, it could be much beautified and enriched, I am sure." [27] There were some early localized attempts to stabilize English grammar and style, such as the group of early thirteenth-century religious works known as the Katherine Group, or the late twelfth-century homilist Orm, who precisely articulates his own orthography. But the linguistic regularity and self-consciousness of these examples are exceptions to the general absence of concern for such matters as they relate to English. Moreover, the correlation between Middle English and other vernaculars indicates that English in particular was characterized by lateness in the development of formal grammar and rhetoric. The Icelandic *First Grammatical Treatise* of the mid-twelfth century discusses phonology and orthography, while Sir Raimon Vidal's *Razos de trobar* of about 1200 offers a grammatical analysis of Provençal. In addition to *De vulgari eloquentia* several stylistic works from other vernacular traditions survive: for Icelandic, *Skáldskaparmál* and *Háttatal* of Snorri Sturluson's *Prose Edda* of the mid-thirteenth century; for Provençal, Joifre de Foixà's *De la doctrina de compoindre dictatz* of the latter part of the century; for Welsh, the *Bardic Grammar* of the early fourteenth century; and for French, the various manifestations of the *seconde rhétorique* of the late fourteenth century.

A vernacular writer was of course free to use the techniques of Latin rhetoric, and in fact it was in part through the incorporation of such techniques that written English gradually acquired codes of stylistic correctness. Perhaps the most influential figure in this regard was Chaucer, whose eloquence was praised and style imitated by fifteenth-century writers as diverse as Lydgate, Henryson, and Caxton. But that Chaucer is again not representative of prevailing late-medieval literary theory and practice is underscored by the fact that the stylistics of poetic composition in English apparently did not receive extended treatment similar to Dante's of Italian or Snorri Sturluson's of Icelandic until George Gascoigne's brief *Certain Notes of Instruction Concerning the Making of Verse or Rhyme in English,* written in 1575.

During the Middle English period, changes in English culture transformed and were reflected in its language and institutions, as through the 1362 Statute of Pleading, which dictated that all court pleading should henceforth be conducted in English, or the 1422 decision of the Brewers' Guild to keep all subsequent records in English, or Henry V's concerted effort (apparently as part of a political program) to use English and avoid French during the Hundred Years' War.[28] Though in this way the vernacular did figure in new social practices, in the Middle Ages it never achieved the discursive and nondiscursive power of Latin. The cultivation of Chancery English in this period, for instance, did initiate the creation of a vernacular standard. But while Chancery embodied the reduction of variation that is requisite for standardization, it was not circumscribed by the concomitant requirement of the ideology of standardization. Chancery ultimately became a consciously selected variety with an elaboration of function and broad acceptance, yet it still displayed more internal grammatical and orthographic variation than Latin, it lacked visible social confirmations of prestige in the form of grammars and rhetorics, it was not taught, and it was not (or, more generally, English was not) the dominant language in two of the most powerful institutions of the period: the church and the universities.[29] In legal discourse the functions of English were restricted through the end of the Middle Ages: Despite the 1362 Statute, law French was not officially abandoned in English courts until 1731, up to 1490 petitions passed by both Houses of Parliament had to be translated into French in the process of being made public, and French was (therefore) a common language for legal yearbooks and works on land tenure. In education, Latin remained the dominant language through the seventeenth century, when Christopher Cooper could still publish a Latin grammar of English (*Grammatica Linguae Anglicanae*) and Milton could still hold the position of foreign language secretary (specifically Latin) to the Council of State. In the medieval period, the exclusion of English from such powerful social and institutional practices was reflected in the absence of grammars and rhetorics and helped to confirm the necessity of such practices for linguistic prestige. In this way the absence of grammatical and rhetorical standards in the late Middle English period both generated and was generated by ideology.

One indication of the precarious and ideological status of the English language in the late-medieval period is the politicization of the Lollards' translations. Their use of English made the Bible and theological discussions accessible to a thitherto unreachable audience and thus potentially destabilized both institutions and ideology. In its emphasis on language, the institutional response to this potential (and its realization) was categorical. Archbishop Arundel's 1407 Constitutions, indeed, expressly forbid translation of the Bible into English as well as possession of vernacular translations dating to Wycliff's lifetime. Moreover, Anne Hudson points out, "by the time of bishop Alnwick's investigations in 1429, knowledge even of the elements of religion, of the creed, the Pater noster or the Ave in English constituted accepted evidence of heresy." [30] And in the mid-fifteenth century Pecock, who was himself eventually accused of heresy, attributed much of the Lollards' success to their use of English and maintained that English was the best language for refutations of Lollardy, thereby politicizing English from a different direction.[31]

Another indication is the frequent claim that English has every bit the communicative potential of any other language. Both Usk and Lydgate express the belief that English readers need to have works in their own language,[32] but perhaps the strongest testament to linguistic relativism occurs in the preface to Chaucer's *Astrolabe,* where he tells Lowys:

> Latyn canst thou yit but small, my litel sone. But natheles suffise to the these trewe conclusions in Englissh as wel as sufficith to these noble clerkes Grekes these same conclusions in Grek; and to Arabiens in Arabik, and to Jewes in Ebrew, and to Latyn folk in Latyn; whiche Latyn folk had hem first out of othere dyverse langages, and writen hem in her owne tunge, that is to seyn, in Latyn. And God woot that in alle these langages and in many moo han these conclusions ben suffisantly lerned and taught, and yit by diverse reules; right as diverse pathes leden diverse folk the righte way to Rome. (27–40)

The very assertion of this relativism of course bespeaks a situation where the idea is not widely accepted, perhaps even actively resisted. Indeed, the contested character of the idea is clear from the fact that in the Prologue to the revised Wycliffite Bible the Lollards echoed the idea of linguistic relativism as a rationale for their much-politicized program of translation.[33]

Not only was the contest over English never resolved in the Middle Ages, but the political ramifications of vernacular language in fact extended well beyond the Middle English period. In the preface to his 1574 translation of Ramus's *Logike,* for example, Roland Makilmenaeum still felt the need to acknowledge that Moses wrote in Hebrew, Aristotle in Greek, and Cicero in Latin: "Shall we then thinke the Scottyshe or Englisshe tongue, it not fitt to wrote [*sic*] any arte into? no in dede." After pointing out the inadequacies of Latin for rendering Hebrew and Greek and the ways in which Cicero accordingly amplified his native tongue, Makilmenaeum suggests English should not scruple at similar borrowing and tells the story of Anacharsis among the Athenians, "who called his Scithian tongue barbarous, yea sayethe he, Anacharsis is barbarous amongst the Athenienses, and so are the Athenienses amongst the Scythyans, by the which aunswere he signified that euery mans tongue is eloquent ynoughe for hym self, and that others in respecte of it is had as barbarous."[34] By 1614, when Richard Carew published *The Excellencie of the English Tongue,* some arguments assumed the legitimacy of English in order to assert its *supremacy* over other languages, but such assertions necessarily implied the still-contested character of vernacular language. Ultimately, English's rise in prestige as a written medium required the full political implications of the Reformation and proclamations like the 1549 First Act of Uniformity, which mandated public use of the Book of Common Prayer and reserved Greek, Latin, and Hebrew for private religious observance.[35]

In short, written Middle English, perhaps more so than any other medieval vernacular, in effect was paradoxically denied that period's status of written language. In a state of continual flux, the vernacular lacked the grammatical and rhetorical regularity that was used to assess the quality and correctness of any piece of writing. In both stylistic ways and social functions, in fact, Middle English was still very much an oral language juxtaposed to the written language of Latin.[36] Furthermore, without the institutional and ideological functions of Latin, English lacked social opportunities for expanding its discursive practices and its ideological reach and for thereby acquiring the qualities and purposes that framed expectations of authorized writing. Even if a manuscript text of an auctor is by modern standards inaccurate, as an auctorial text in the auctorial language it would have elicited in the Middle Ages recognition and expectation of the possibility of textual correctness or incorrectness. There are no medieval linguistic contexts that would have fostered similar expectations for Middle English.

In order to expose other conditions of existence for late Middle English works, I turn now to two specific examples. These examples—London, British Library MS Harley 2253 and Chaucer's *Boece*—are disparate in composition, transmission, and audience; the one is a manuscript containing an anonymous collection of popular lyric poetry, both secular and religious, while the other is a prose translation by the best-known writer of the English Middle Ages and is squarely in the genre of late-medieval academic translation.[37] Together, however, these examples reveal much about the correlations between medieval cultural practices (particularly Latin literary criticism) and the discourse of late Middle English manuscripts in regard to conceptions of work and text and also about the linguistic codes through which late Middle English literature was negotiated. Specifically, the Harley lyrics offer insights into the relations between words and text, and the *Boece* into those between text and work.

MS Harley 2253

Probably produced around 1340 near Ludlow, this manuscript is among the most famous and most discussed in Middle English studies. Like most fourteenth-century vernacular manuscripts, its decoration is restrained, consisting mostly of paragraph marks and enlarged letters accented with red at the beginning of each piece. What distinguishes Harley 2253 among English manuscripts is the ambitiousness of the collection, which contains 116 distinct items of prose and poetry in Latin and French as well as English.[38] Furthermore, the English secular lyrics, the artistry of which has been all but universally praised, represent the earliest surviving collection of this type of poetry.[39]

Here my interest is in some of the English lyrics and with what the layout of the words in the manuscript reveals about their status as texts. Both single- and double-column formats are used for these poems, and two metrical forms predominate: a balladlike stanza with rhyming patterns involving three lines (e.g., *a a b a a b c c b c c b*),[40] and a stanza relying on rhyming patterns involving couplets and quatrains (e.g., *a b a b c c d d*).[41] For the most part, the texts of the former group of poems are laid out to reflect the metrical units, but those in the latter group are arranged in long lines each of which contains two rhyming periods and roughly twice as many syllables as those in the balladlike stanzas. There is, moreover, a correspondence between the patterns of layout and meter: typically, the balladlike stanzas appear in the double-column format, the other stanzas in the single-column one. Layout also influenced text selection, since five of the balladlike poems are grouped together in a sequence of double-column pages extending from f. 70v to f. 73r.[42]

The fact that textual layout, the physical appearance of individual poems, and the character of the text of Harley 2253 as a whole mutually determined one another is significant by itself and reflects the attention devoted to design that is apparent elsewhere in this manuscript.[43] Even more significant are what these mutual determinations imply about the integrity and character of individual Middle English texts. For example, the stanzaic patterning in which all the Harley lyrics appear in modern editions is not present in the manuscript. While the rhyming scheme may well be considered inherent within the texts of the poems, in medieval terms such stanzas are realized only, if at all, through a reader's actualization of the *work*. As Middle English poems, in other words, their stanzas exist conceptually and not physically, as I take to be requisite in modern editing and poetics. Moreover, on six occasions poems are written as prose in order to accommodate space limitations. By writing *The Lover's Complaint* as prose, for instance, the scribe was able to fit it into the last third of f. 63v and thereby begin a new poem at the top of f. 64r; and by writing *A Spring Song on the Passion*, a French lyric, and the macaronic *Dum Ludis Floribus* as prose, he was able to fit all three poems on f. 76r, enabling himself to begin f. 76v with another French poem.[44] Space limitations, however, were not always a necessary rationale for textual presentation. On f. 114v and f. 115r *The Man in the Moon* is laid out as prose, even though the scribe clearly had enough room to write the poem in long lines; the bottom portion of f. 115r was in fact left blank. Since in all these instances arrangement of the words and lines can be accommodated to the demands of space and even, perhaps, scribal whimsy, the implication is that the accommodations do not affect the *res* behind the *verba*. In Harley 2253, unlike in those manuscripts that bracket rhymed couplets, the status of the words as metrical patternings and their physical appearance in lines are not intrinsic to the text or (consequently) the work.

Modern editors, however, have given priority to meter—and hence the text—as a determinative of the Harley lyrics in ways other than the imposition of stanzaic layout. The common editorial treatment of the poems involving couplet rhyme schemes, for example, is to print what appears as one line in the manuscript as two.[45] The rationale for this division is that the words at what would be the caesura in the long manuscript lines are viewed as participating in the rhyming pattern.[46] When this is not the case in three poems, G. L. Brook and Carleton Brown—the editors of the most scholarly editions—leave the lines long.[47] Two of these poems, however, could be printed like the other long-line poems, for they bear traces of an original rhyme scheme at the caesura that is suggestive of the *a b a b a b a b* pattern found in other English poems in the manuscript:

> Suete ledy, þou wend þi wod,
> > sorewe þou wult me kyþe.
> Ich am also so sory mon
> > so ich was whylen blyþe.

In a wyndou þer we stod
we custe vs fyfty syþe;
few biheste makeþ mon
al is serewes mythe.

. . . . .

When þe nyhtegale singes
þe wodes waxen grene;
lef ant gras ant blosme springes
in Aueryle, y wene.
ant loue is to my herte gon
with one spere so kene
nyht ant day my blod it drynkes,
myn herte deþ me tene.[48]

The erasure of this putative scheme through transmission further in-validates traditional textual criticism's conception of the text. To the scribe, if not the writer, rhyme (hence lexicon), stanzaic patterning, and lexical arrangement—features central to modern editorial perspec-tives—were not in fact integral to the medieval character of the text. Thus, whether the internal rhyme scheme survives in some poems and not others through chance, whimsy, or editorial design, the presence of the same meter and layout for both rhymed and unrhymed poems undercuts any historical claim for the intergrity of a poetic line based on rhyme.

Similar evidence is provided by the layout of *Iesu, for þi Muchele Miht, I Syke When Y Singe,* and *An Autumn song,* which appear one after the other in the manuscript. The implications of their layout become clear only through consideration of several of the poems that precede them. The top of f. 77va begins with a French poem in short lines and is accordingly formatted in double columns. The double-column format continues through an English poem in short lines and another French poem all the way to the bottom quarter of f. 79rb. Characteristically, the scribe then began one of the balladlike English poems (*Dialogue between the Virgin and Christ on the Cross*), which extended to the top quarter of f. 79vb. At this point, rather than begin another poem of short lines (which would seem the most logical decision) or leave the remainder of the folio blank (which the scribe does do elsewhere, as after *The Man in the Moon*), he began one of the longer-lined poems,

specifically *Iesu, for þi Muchele Miht.* In order to accommodate it to
the available space, however, for each stanza the scribe wrote only the
first two lines (representing four lines in modern editions) as customary long lines—and then only with some difficulty; for the rest of the
stanza he used the shorter, rhyming lines into which contemporary editions divide all the long lines of the poems typically written in single
columns. Thereby, he utilized the poem to fill the available space on
f. 79vb, and by adopting the same procedure for *I Syke When Y Singe*
on f. 80ra and a similar procedure for *An Autumn song* on f. 80rb,[49] he
managed for each of the three poems to occupy a single column of the
double-column format. On f. 80v the scribe reverted to single columns
for one longer-lined poem and the beginning of another.

The scribe's reasons for reverting here and not on f. 80r to the
long-line layout, or for not continuing the contorted double-columned
format, may well be rooted in design: a desire not to juxtapose a double-
column format on f. 79v with a single-column one on f. 80r. Such
procedures, in any case, again have clear implications for Middle English
concepts of text. If the text is determined more by layout features and
available space in the document than by any intrinsic lexical qualities,
then the physical appearance of a text is neither inherent in it nor significant in its makeup. It is the readers, in fact, who have to perceive
and formulate the lines and stanzas of the Harley lyrics, supplementing the text with both metrical patterns and the unexpressed words
and ideas between it and the *res* behind them. The assumption that
modern editions enunciate is that medieval readers did perform such
gestures—that they perceived the formal qualities of poetry in ways
resembling contemporary perceptions—but the evidence of this manuscript, at least, does not support such an assumption. Paradoxically,
while the texts of these lyrics are necessarily made up of words, the constitution of these words into any specific text is not a condition of the
texts' existence.[50]

The *Boece*

One of the most popular and influential works of the Middle Ages,
Boethius's *De consolatio philosophiae* was translated into several vernaculars, sometimes more than once. One of these translations is the *Boece,*

which Chaucer wrote around 1380 and which in turn was transmitted with some enthusiasm in the fifteenth century: Ten manuscripts or fragments survive, as well as the editions of Caxton and Thynne, each of which derives in part from a no longer extant manuscript. At first glance, the transmission of the *Consolatio* and the *Boece* would seem to be both unambiguous and responsive to humanist textual criticism's conceptions of author, work, and text. Boethius, whose works were set texts in medieval universities, was a recognized auctor and the author of the *Consolatio,* an imaginative and original work about the character of fortune, fate, and free will. The text of this work survives in hundreds of documents and was converted into several vernacular translations, each of which also survives in numerous documents from which the individual works of translation could be reconstructed. Chaucer, while not an auctor, is the author of the *Boece,* a work in part defined by the words he used to render Boethius's Latin.

The transmission of the *Consolatio* and the *Boece* is far more complex than this glance would seem to imply, however. Already by the ninth century the text of the *Consolatio* had undergone a variety of lexical changes from Boethius's putative sixth-century original, and by the fourteenth, when Chaucer was writing, an entirely distinct tradition had developed. This tradition, known as the vulgate,[51] is materially not very different from what Boethius probably wrote in the prison at Pavia, though there are pervasive (if minor) lexical differences: pronouns are inserted, syntax is modernized to that of late-medieval Latin, unfamiliar idioms are normalized, and Greek quotations are almost uniformly translated into Latin or garbled beyond intelligibility. The vulgate tradition was not, however, a pure one, for a number of texts combine readings from it with those from the original tradition. Moreover, texts from both traditions were so extensively subjected to glossing that it is a rare *Consolatio* manuscript that does not have marginal or interlinear glosses. These glosses on occasion were incorporated directly into the text, so that the text of Boethius's *Consolatio* ultimately was lexically displaced by the vulgate text with glosses and conceptually by this text with commentary apparatus.

Late-medieval translations of the *Consolatio,* then, are really translations of the Latin work as it had developed in the Middle Ages. Around 1300, for example, Jean de Meung composed an all-prose translation of a vulgate text and selections from William of Conche's commentary on the *Consolatio*. Given the stress on interpretation in medieval positions on translation and given the way the text of the *Consolatio* in particular had come to be conceived, it is not surprising that Jean does not typically distinguish among translations from the Latin, translations from the commentary, and his own interpretive additions. Jean's translation enjoyed its own thriving transmission, which in some ways mirrored the transmission of the *Consolatio*. The *Livres de Confort de la Philosophie* survives in twenty-two manuscripts representing two distinct traditions,[52] with the texts of some of these manuscripts departing radically from Jean's text. For example, the text of Besançon, Municipal Library MS 434, in addition to embodying several large omissions and lexical differences from Jean's putative original, does not always divide the books and sections in the way the rest of the French (or Latin) tradition does. In another vein, the preface that Jean translated from William of Aragon and presented as his own was attached to an entirely different, verse-and-prose French translation.

Chaucer's method of composition was even more eclectic than Jean's. He utilized a vulgate text that nonetheless had some readings of the older tradition, the commentary of Nicholas Trevet, a few of the short glosses associated with Remigius of Auxerre, and a text of Jean's translation—incorporating, again, selections from William of Conche's commentary—that had some affinities with the eccentric tradition of Besançon 434. In view of the predominant *mise-en-page* of extant *Consolatio* manuscripts, the Remigian glosses probably appeared interlinearly in the Latin text, to which the Trevet text in its entirety may have been appended. Since in the other common commentary format the entire Latin text is broken up into lemmata with adjoining commentary, it is entirely possible that Chaucer did not have a discrete text of the *Consolatio* but a text that, like the French text, ran the "original" and its explanation together. In any case, Chaucer does not overtly distinguish among these sources, but sometimes translates the French in place of the Latin, sometimes uses it as a gloss, sometimes translates both, sometimes glosses with Trevet, and sometimes apparently glosses on his own initiative. Sometimes he will follow one method for several sentences, and sometimes he will change methods several times within a sentence, though throughout the composition he follows Jean's lead of rendering proses and meters alike in prose. As important as the eclectic character of his sources and methods, however, is the fact that no Latin or

French manuscript displays this particular combination of these particular sources. Chaucer rarely departs very far from at least one of his source texts, but the decision to combine them in the way he did was entirely his own. In effect, Chaucer created his source in the very act of translating it.[53]

When the *Boece* was transmitted, Chaucer's text was diversified in a number of ways. In one textual subgroup of manuscripts, for example, every direct quotation is prefaced with a *B* or *P* to specify whether Boethius or Lady Philosophy is speaking, and in one late manuscript of this subgroup the procedure is refined through the elimination of the now redundant "quod I" and "quod she."[54] Because Chaucer's original text apparently did not have the rubrics that appear before each prose and meter in modern editions, moreover, several strategies were developed to improve the work's *ordinatio*. One manuscript uses English rubrics,[55] three others use Latin ones,[56] and one numbers all the proses and meters of each book sequentially.[57] Most manuscripts preface each section with the brief extracts from the *Consolatio* found in modern editions, but in one subgroup these extracts are substantially extended; in two other manuscripts, proses and meters of the English text alternate with those of the entire Latin text.[58]

In terms of the *Boece* text itself, a thriving gloss tradition developed and was supplemented in several manuscripts by independent traditions. Some of these glosses, moreover, were incorporated into the *Boece* text, as were independent translations from the French, Latin, and Trevet's commentary. The manuscripts suggest two distinct textual traditions, and while the differences between them are not as great as those between the manuscripts of, say, *Sir Beues of Hamtoun* (assuming all of the latter represent one work), there is pervasive lexical and syntactic variation both between traditions and among manuscripts of a given tradition. The text of one manuscript in particular—Oxford, Bodleian Library MS Bodley 797—embodies extensive modernization. In the case of Oxford, Bodleian Library MS Auct F.3.5, which contains book 1 only, the *Boece* text is both radically altered and, in the manner of an academic commentary, divided into lemmata with interpretations. This text contains a preface that offers a life of Boethius but nowhere mentions Chaucer or the *Boece,* and, as in Jean's and Chaucer's procedures, no rhetorical or graphic distinction is made between "text" and "gloss." For example, the beginning of the second meter in both the standard *Riverside* edition and Auct F.3.5 is as follows:

"Allas! How the thought of this man, dreynt in overthrowynge depnesse,
dulleth and forleteth his propre clernesse" (1–3)
Allas sche sais now the thou3t of man drownyth and ou*er*thrawen with
worldely besynes dulles the soule and lettis it fro his owne propir clernes
that is the bry3tnes of wisdam and of vndurstandynge (f. 204r)

The differences between this text and other *Boece* texts are so great that
the unique work in Auct. F.3.5 cannot really be judged the *Boece* at
all. Similarly, even though John Walton drew extensively on Chaucer's
composition, his all-verse production of the early fifteenth century is
generally considered a translation of the *Consolatio* and not an adaptation of the *Boece*, much less the *Boece* itself.

In a tradition like this the linguistic codes through which textual
negotiation takes place and the correlations between the discourse of
late Middle English manuscripts and that of Latin literary criticism
again imply conceptions of work and text that differ markedly from
those of humanist textual criticism. To make historical sense of this tradition, one needs to understand the work that Boethius composed to be
the *res and* the interpretations that lie behind the *verba* of all the Latin
texts—including the commentaries. Specific lexicon and syntax—Latin
or vernacular—must be neither necessary nor absolute indicators of
what this *res* is. Moreover, inasmuch as Chaucer was attempting to recuperate Boethius's *res* from the *Consolation* tradition—the *Consolatio*,
the commentaries, and Jean's translation—the *Boece* cannot be said to
have its own *res*, even though Chaucer's composite source was his own
invention. What Chaucer did produce were specific lexical items, but
these were evidently not presumed to construct an autonomous *Boece*,
for they were processed and transmitted in terms of their appositeness
to Boethius's *res*. In purely lexical terms, there are a great many cumulative differences between what are typically regarded as Boethius's
text, the vulgate text, the vulgate text with commentary, Jean's text,
Chaucer's text, the texts of the "*Boece* manuscripts," Auct F.3.5, and
Walton's translation. But these same differences suggest, therefore, that
the medieval framework of evaluation was not lexical but conceptual,
since all these texts were understood to reflect the same work. In other
words, the work—Boethius's or, for the sake of argument, Jean's or
Chaucer's—is not largely or evenly significantly lexical. Discrimination
among the documents on the basis of text is thus quite alien to the character of the transmission, for the isolation of Jean's text, or Chaucer's,

or Walton's—however much it is *possible* to isolate them—depends on the elision of the tradition before and after their texts in order to define the *res* of the work.

As disparate as Harley MS 2253 and the *Boece* are, they provide a detailed and consistent framework of the linguistic codes of late Middle English literature and of the attendant relationships between words and text and text and work. Within this framework, words and their layout are not integral to a given text, which in turn is not integral to a given work. Lexical changes in transmission reveal that the works of both Boethius and Chaucer are inadequately and unreliably realized in texts, though these same changes reflect the necessity and importance of texts. Similarly, individual Harley lyrics require realization in a text if they are to be read by a reader, but the text's subjection to the demands of production underscores how imperfectly and, perhaps, inconsequentially it represents the work. As in the discourse of Latin literary criticism, the act of reading supplements both text and work by actualizing meter and invoking an interpretive background, even though the insubstantial *res* of a lyric like *De Clerico et Puella* is scarcely commensurate with that of Scripture or even the *Aeneid* as it was traditionally allegorized.

Conceptions of work and text that inform the Harley lyrics and the *Boece* are not aberrant in the later medieval period, for this same consistent framework can be constructed from a number of late Middle English compositional methods and rhetorical strategies. From the way it prefigures the discursive field, humanist textual criticism inescapably recuperates such methods and strategies as textual alterations, even degenerations or contaminations. Seen from within (in Foucault's sense), they rather circumscribe the transmission of works and their *res* as they mediate medieval cultural practices.

The fact that the same portion of text can function in a number of apparently different compositions, for example, reflects the limited role a text played in the constitution of a work. The same passage might appear in a long narrative poem and circulate independently as a lyric, as was frequently the case with stanzas found in Lydgate's *Fall of Princes*.[59] In turn, the same lyric passage often figures in a number of distinct poems,[60] so that in such cases critics' judgments about the integrity of some verse in a manuscript depend on their familiarity with longer Middle English compositions and other lyrics. Perhaps the most radical example of this kind of appropriation is Henry Scogan's *A Moral Balade,* wherein he incorporates the whole of Chaucer's *Gentillesse.* Scogan acknowledges that the passage is by Chaucer, but this is rare with lyrics, if only because they are characteristically anonymous.[61] Whether or not such compositions were read intertextually, with readers interpreting an "extract" against the context in which it "originally" appeared, they suggest that the conditions of existence for Middle English literature excluded identification of specific words with specific texts and did not limit the number of works that the same text could construct. But ideas as well as words could be appropriated, as in Lydgate's *Siege of Thebes* or the anonymous *Tale of Beryn,* both of which extend Chaucer's *Canterbury Tales* and thereby undermine the latter's integrity as a work.

A view of a work as not determined by *verba* but as an intangible yet definable *res* is rhetorically negotiated in several ways, most generally in conceptions of the work itself. No other Middle English writers figure the *text* as strongly in this regard as does Chaucer, whose cataloging of his compositions by name nonetheless also demonstrates the influence traditional perspectives had on even him.[62] Indeed, within the discourse of late Middle English manuscripts, works are typically conceived as thematic composites or entities, not as sequences of specific words. Robert Mannyng's self-referential remarks in *Handlyng Synne,* for example, relate only to large sections of the work, as at the end of his account of the ninth commandment, where he abbreviates and cross-references "covetise":

> And for hyt haþ þe same assyse
> Þat lonyþ vnto coueytyse,
> Y wyle now ouerlepe hyt here
> And afterward ȝe mowe hyt lere.   (2911–14)[63]

Similarly, Margery Kempe refers only generally to preceding or succeeding passages, while Thomas Usk displays pride in the *Testament of Love* as a whole, even explaining its title and providing a rationale for its structure and contents.[64] In the same vein, the propriety the author of *Mum and the Sothsegger* feels for his work is directed not at its *verba* but its *res.* In the Prologue to Richard II he observes:

> And if ȝe fynde fables / or foly þer amonge,
> Or ony fantasie yffeyned / þat no frute is in,

Lete ȝoure conceill corette it / and clerkis to-gedyr,
And amende þat ys amysse / and make it more better:
For ȝit it is secrette / and so it shall lenger,
Tyll wyser wittis / han waytid it ouere,
That it be lore laweffull / and lusty to here.

(57–63)

Even Hoccleve's sequence of poems known as the *Series,* which John Burrow describes as "to an unusual degree preoccupied with the business of its own composition," focuses on a broad scale; the work's metacritical narration concerns the acquisition and ordering of the individual pieces that make up the *Series* as a whole, not specific textual passages in this whole.[65]

The character of these sections within longer works and of the relationships between them implies no intrinsic restrictions on the content and further suggests, therefore, the limited ways in which words construct a text or a text, in turn, constructs a Middle English work. While the same lyric passage could appear in part or entirety in various texts, longer poems are typically assembled in what might be called a mode of infinite expandability. The broad contours of a work might be outlined in any number of ways, including the cycle of the liturgical year, Christian morality, world history, or the education of a prince, and this outline might be stabilized either by rubrics or by textual transitions.[66] But development by exempla meant that any work could be expanded or contracted at any point. Such is the case with the *South English Legendary,* the *Mirror of Man,* the *Troy Book, Handlyng Synne, Cursor Mundi,* and *Confessio Amantis.* In *Piers Plowman* both the dreams and the passus divisions offer structural determinants within which— as Langland's own revisions alone show—there was great stylistic and compositional latitude. The organizational principle for Lydgate's *Fall of Princes* and Caxton's *Aesop's Fables* is little more than structural similarity among individual stories, while the introduction of the *Canon's Yeoman's Tale* to the *Canterbury Tales* shows that even explicit indications of a work's structure did not restrict alteration. On a more localized stylistic level, the type scenes through which romances, saints' lives, and chronicles were constructed enabled almost unrestricted narrative contraction or expansion. Similarly, reliance on formulaic diction in lyrics and romances facilitated and obscured both the alteration of a text and the exportation of lines from it into another text, procedures that help to account for the widely differing texts of "works" like *Sir Orfeo* and *Sir Beuis of Hamtoun*. Significantly, the more individually distinctive aureate diction of the fifteenth century came about among the writers with the strongest sense of their own authority and at a time when the status of vernacular writing in general was being elevated. The result of all these compositional techniques was that the most characteristic writers in the discourse of late Middle English manuscripts were those who *lacked* the distinctive authorial voice that has been valorized since the Renaissance.[67] Not coincidentally, though in the late-medieval period the writers with such a voice form a small minority— Chaucer, Gower, Langland, the *Gawain* poet, and Margery Kempe— they are the writers who have been most prized in modern criticism.

In the discourse of late Middle English manuscripts, manuscript transmission manifests the same conception of a work apparent in composition: a nonlexical, not self-contained *res* inseparable from the supplements of others. On the most general level, the manuscript context of any text could contribute to its relation to a work in ways I can only briefly allude to here. If they are to be read, all texts must necessarily exist in material forms, but the striking aspect of medieval texts in comparison to modern ones is the diversity of textual and non-textual ways for generating meaning, for the pragmatics through which a work was articulated included highly expressive features of layout and design that manuscript producers could consciously manipulate. For example, the presence or absence of illuminations, decorative flourishes, historiated initials, and marginalia could accent or counterpoint a text in any number of ways and thereby contribute to the reader's perception— even construction—of the *res* behind the *verba*.[68] Equally striking is the variability of medieval documents. Though as in manuscripts of the *Confessio* layout features could be transmitted along with a text, they could also be changed, adapted, or deleted in any copy by any scribe, and these alterations, as much as the "original" text, might affect the character of the work a reader encountered. The texts of the Hengwrt and Ellesmere manuscripts of the *Canterbury Tales* may be fairly similar, for example, but the former document is an unremarkable vernacular manuscript that imputes nothing out of the ordinary to Chaucer's poem, while the latter is a lavish production, packaging the *Tales* as a distinctive, superior composition. As works themselves, then, Hengwrt could thus be regarded as a normative Middle English piece, Ellesmere as the progenitor of English literary tradition.

Since medieval manuscripts regularly contain a number of different texts (and, by implication, works), the texts with which a Middle English text was bound would also contribute to the work it was understood to reflect.[69] When the *Boece* appears with a complete text of the *Consolatio,* the commentary of William of Aragon, and other interpretive aids in Cambridge, University Library MS Ii.3.21, for instance, it becomes in effect a commentary itself, unlike in Cambridge, Pembroke College MS 215, where it appears alone and therefore as a nominally independent work. Similarly, poems like *Truth* or *The Complaint of Venus* assume strikingly different qualities whether they appear as scattered occasional verse or in Chaucerian anthologies like Oxford, Bodleian Library MS Fairfax 16 or Cambridge, Magdalene College MS Pepys 2006. This textual context might be determined by the selections of a patron, by the requirements of a bespoke trade, by individual preference, or simply by fortuitous availability of texts. But in any of these situations, the generation of manuscripts through smaller sections of text meant that the character of the manuscript and its relation to a given text were always subject to change as a condition of existence for both manuscripts and texts. As Ralph Hanna has noted, "The use of the booklet in production forestalls or delays quite indefinitely any very absolute decisions about the form of the final product."[70] Economics and aesthetics thus overlapped significantly and inevitably in manuscript composition, a conjunction that has been particularly determinative throughout English literary history. A similar overlap early in the printed age, for instance, fostered the transformation of vernacular works through layout features like title-page format and pagination, both of which helped to stabilize the text physically and conceptually.

More narrowly, numerous Middle English texts display attitudes toward lexical constitution, arrangement, and transmission that are similarly fluid to the ones evident in Harley 2253 and in the *Boece* tradition. Sometimes specifically theological or political motivations characterize a work's transmission. Such is the case with Julian of Norwich's *Showings,* where the two surviving manuscript texts differ in their presentation of the dynamics of religious experience, and with Wynkyn de Worde's 1501 printing of *The Book of Margery Kempe,* which in comparison with the unique London, British Library MS Add. 61823 offers only passages displaying doctrinally unproblematic patience.[71] The manuscripts of *Piers Plowman* in particular reflect this type of motivation: Contentious views are regularly mitigated or emphasized.

But stylistic preference or the very process of production might also motivate the conception of a work and its textual transmission, and at times this casual attitude toward lexis simply cannot be accommodated in traditional textual criticism. Parallel-text editions of works like *Sir Orfeo* and *Lybeaus Desconsus* reveal that the distinction between work and version is particularly tenuous in the romance genre, where faulty copying, lapse of memory, and conscious alteration by a *disour* are determinants of the text.[72] Large-scale manipulations of a work on a different order appear in the *ordinatio* of Middle English manuscripts; in Lydgate's *Lyf of Our Lady,* for instance, the development of chapter divisions and manuscript layout recuperated a distinctly meditative work and facilitated reading accordingly. The transmission of the *Clerk's Tale* in San Marino, Huntington Library MS HM 140 defines the work through a combination of textual and design features. There, the poem appears anonymously without the Prologue or any of the other *Canterbury Tales* and surrounded by didactic, religious poetry. After the envoy, moreover, Chaucer's *Truth* appears, so that rather than the modern editions' problematic *Canterbury Tale* that responds in part to the Wife of Bath, this *Clerk's Tale* offers its readers a stark, exemplary tale squarely within the tradition of the ethical poetic.[73] Similarly, in Oxford, Christ Church MS 152 Hoccleve's *Miracle of the Virgin* ("Who so desireth to gete and conquere") is incorporated as the *Ploughman's Tale.* This example is doubly striking, since Hoccleve's poem itself is reminiscent of Chaucer's *Prioress's Prologue and Tale.*

Stylistic preference can also characterize the transmission of specific lexical features typically considered integral to a composition, such as meter. Works can appear in different metrical formats in different manuscripts, alternate meter within a given text, or betray the remnants of another, apparently earlier metrical patterning. Such metrical variation occurs in the lyric *Miracles of Oure Lady* in the Vernon manuscript and in the manuscripts of the romances *Sir Beues of Hamtoun, Guy of Warwick, Richard Coer de Lion,* and *Sir Ferumbras.* In a related vein, the scribes transmitting the text of John Hardyng's fifteenth-century *Chronicle* perceived to varying degrees the fact that Hardyng, who was over eighty when he wrote the work, completed the sense but not the meter of his rhyme-royal stanzas, for which he apparently never added the often difficult fifth line. Some scribes simply produced the unusual six-line stanzas, some supplied a number of fifth lines on their own, and others skipped a line at the appropriate place.[74] In this variety of response, we again see the limited ways in which lexical items were understood to define the text and in which texts were understood to reflect works.

Scribes, of course, are central to manuscript transmission and perhaps most directly responsible for absolute variation between manuscript texts. The detection and interpretation of such variation rests, however, on specific assumptions about the character of a work and a text. For the occurrence of variation as it is traditionally understood, one must assume that a text is a significant and inseparable aspect of a work and that a variety of texts represent the same work. Yet agreement or disagreement between specific readings in specific texts does not by itself validate these larger assumptions, for it is the larger assumptions that give meaning to the readings: Theoretically (at least) ideological tools necessarily confirm their ideology.[75] To attempt to view these tools from within, one needs to utilize the theoretical, compositional, and transmissional contexts in which such absolute variations occurred in order to identify them and their meaning in their discourse. Seen from this perspective, Middle English scribal transmission is not, in fact, congruent with traditional textual criticism's conception of variation.

It is certainly possible, for example, to locate and collate all extant copies of what is regarded as the same work and thereby to find any number of lexical variations between the texts. However, a common (and indeed reliable) scholarly tool like this has become possible only through developments in the past two centuries in paleography, cataloging, printing, and reproduction, and the view of transmission that it enables is inherently a retrospective one: Manuscript traditions are identifiable only after they have been completed. Such a tool is accurate and valuable, moreover, only in the discursive field as traditional textual criticism has prefigured it. Before humanism and the modern period— in the late Middle Ages—scribes and readers, lacking the technological and methodological developments of modern textual criticism, would have had vastly more restricted opportunities for identifying, much less evaluating, the "inauthenticity" of the texts in front of them as well as their relations to other texts of the same "work." And, as I have argued in this and the preceding chapter, they would have located the texts within a discursive field vastly different from that of humanist textual criticism. If one seeks to judge variation in medieval terms—to assess how well scribes performed the task of copying the texts in front of them and how authentic the texts they produced are—one needs to determine not only what the scribes' exemplars were but also how the scribes understood fidelity and whether they saw it as one of their primary objectives.

The medieval conception of a work as something outside of a text, as something that was supplemented mentally by readers and literally by writers, affects every one of these determinations. An exemplar, accordingly, would not necessarily be a text but a conception of a work, and it is this conception that might determine the objective of copying fidelity. Theoretically, such a perspective could justify the complete remaking of any text, though this clearly was not the case for many medieval works. What, then, did define the scribal task and constrain scribes from unregulated textual change? How does such a definition figure as a condition of existence for texts within the discourse of late Middle English manuscripts?

The institutions that sanctioned the scribal enterprise constitute some of the practical and ideological constraints on it and its treatment of texts. Foremost among these institutions early in the Middle Ages was monasticism, which both overtly sustained text production and determined its character. Since from the time of the Benedictine Rule copying was considered an act of prayer, doctrinal orthodoxy would have exerted consistent if covert pressure on scribes. After the development of the universities in the twelfth and thirteenth centuries, this conceptual pressure would have remained and in fact, during the fourteenth-century controversies surrounding nominalism, perhaps increased. At the same time, the transmission of manuscripts by means of the *pecia* system, whereby copies were executed of portions of approved and corrected exemplars borrowed from a centralized bookmaker, provided practical restraint on lexical changes in a text.[76] Such a system produced radial transmission from a single exemplar, as did the process of *reportatio,* whereby several individuals simultaneously copied a dictated text. Similar practical restraint governed the production of ecclesiastical legislation in England. In the thirteenth century, for instance, archdeacons possessed the exemplar from which priests throughout a diocese copied decrees; periodically, the priests brought their copies to a convocation in order to be corrected and updated.[77]

But ideological pressures also informed and determined scribal copying to the end of the Middle Ages. As late as 1492 the German Benedictine Johannes Trithemius, in his *De laude scriptorum,* still saw copying as fundamentally a moral act of devotion to God and scripture, as evidenced in the following story he tells:

> There once lived in a Benedictine monastery with which I am well acquainted a pious brother who zealously supplied their library with copied books. After performing his choir duties he regularly retired to the solitude of his cell and gave himself to this sacred labor. With boundless devotion he copied a great number of books of the saints. When many years after his death his remains were exhumed, it was discovered that the three fingers of his right hand, with which he had written so many books, were as preserved and fresh as if buried the day before. Of the rest of his body nothing remained but bones. This proves how sacred the task of the scribe is in the eyes of God who so honored even in death the limbs of the scribe to demonstrate to the living the merits of his work.[78]

Production of the Wycliffite sermons of the fourteenth and fifteenth centuries was also ideologically determined. Theoretically emerging from and reflecting a body of heterodox and potentially explosive doctrines, the sermons were produced within a centralized location around 1400 in the East Midlands, where a great deal of collation and correction took place. In effect, *because* of the controversial character of the works, the texts of the sermons do indeed display a remarkable amount of agreement, even in an absolute sense. One might similarly cite the context of theoretical and ideological coherence for a similar interpretation of the texts of the thirteenth-century works in the Katherine Group and of the early sixteenth-century annotations and collations of the *Cloud of Unknowning* and the *Scale of Perfection* by James Grenehalgh. All three cases, significantly, correlate with the authorizing influence of the church and theology.[79]

By the fifteenth century, however, the status of copying as a craft and moneymaking profession also exerted pressure on the scribal enterprise for vernacular texts. Already in 1357 book artisans were formally recognized in London records, and by the end of the century, due to increasing demands for vernacular books, an extensive group of binders, writers, and limners is identifiable. Working primarily independently but clustered in the environs of St. Paul's Cathedral, these were recognizable professionals with guild representation and with close ties among them. In the context of their professionalism, whatever *res* might underlie the *verba* of a text being copied, it had in part to be accommodated to the demands a bespoke trade made on the design, layout, and contents of a manuscript. This professionalism eventually influenced monastic copying as well, when monasteries, due to the decline in monastic scriptoria, participated in the bespoke trade by hiring professional scribes. As the Middle English period went on, furthermore, scribes came to anticipate and in fact prescribe public demand by producing set combinations of texts and standardized formatting.[80] When such procedures were technologically reinforced by the printing press, economics and public demand further cooperated with cultural change in the promulgation of fixed texts.

Even as these ecclesiastical and secular institutions sanctioned the scribal enterprise, however, they were consistently ambivalent about its success, and this ambivalence both implies the complex character of the enterprise and responds to the textual latitude inherent in late-medieval conceptions of the work. It is true enough that the scribal task is regularly figured as one of exact textual duplication. For example, within monastic scriptoria, which were the primary sources of manuscript production in the low and high Middle Ages, there is a great deal of evidence that scribes were instructed to copy the texts in front of them exactly.[81] In both this period and later, moreover, there is ample evidence of scribes and correctors rectifying their texts. In the legal discourse contemporaneous with that of late Middle English manuscripts, there are also indications that the scribal task was understood to be textual duplication. Notary publics of the period, for instance, swore an oath that they would effect the accurate production of texts: "The oath binds the notary to draw up contracts and instruments according to the wishes of the parties or party, adding and subtracting nothing; nor shall he prepare instruments recording enforced or fraudulent contracts."[82]

Presumption of scribal exactitude is witnessed in the discourse of late Middle English manuscripts itself. In the *Franklin's Tale,* for instance, the Latin manuscripts that the wily clerk uses to construct the illusion that the Brittany rocks have disappeared contain "tables Tolletanes . . . Ful wel corrected" (*Canterbury Tales,* 5.1273–74) for the appropriate latitude. And in *The Complaint of the Black Knight* Lydgate describes the scribe's task as one of textual subservience to what his master desires:

> But euen-like as doth a skryuener,
> That can no more what that he shal write,
> But as his maister beside doth endyte
>
> (194–96)

To Hoccleve, the difficulty of the scribal task is underestimated by those who have not directly experienced it:

> Many men, fadir, wenen þat writynge
> No trauaile is; þei hold it but a game . . .
> It is wel gretter labour þan it seemeth;
> Þe blynde man of coloures al wrong demeth.
>
> (*Regement of Princes,* 988–89, 993–94)

This difficulty arises both from physical demands on eye and hand and also from mental demands on scribal concentration, which must exclude *all other language and texts.* Though other artificers "Talken and syng, and make game and play," scribes

> labour in trauaillous stilnesse;
> We stowpe and stare vp-on þe shepes skyn,
> And keepe muste our song and wordes in.
>
> (1011, 1013–15)

On rare occasions, a vernacular scribe might even collate copies of the same work in order to improve the quality of his text, as is the case with San Marino, Huntington Library MS HM 114, where the collation is, however, inconsistent.[83]

But though the scribal task may have been figured as an attempt at exact textual reproduction, it is also regularly figured as one that repeatedly fails in this attempt. Indeed, in both monastic and vernacular discourses images of scribal failure in this regard perhaps predominate over those of scribal success. As early as the days of imperial Rome, scribal inexactitude, much like the humility topos, serves as a trope for book production that deflects criticism from the work and its auctor. Cicero uses the trope in a letter to Quintus, and Martial offers a particularly developed formulation in one of his epigrams: "If any poems in those sheets, reader, seem to you either too obscure or not quite good

Latin, not mine is the mistake: the copyist spoiled them in his haste to complete for you his tale of verses. But if you think that not he, but I am at fault, then I will believe that you have no intelligence. 'Yet, see, those *are* bad.' As if I denied what is plain! They *are* bad, but you don't make better."[84]

The trope was adopted in the early Christian era, as in St. Jerome's letter to Lucinius Boeticus, wherein he mentions scribes "who write not what they find, but what they understand; and while they strive to emend others' errors, they also display their own."[85] Throughout Latin ecclesiastical discourse of the Middle Ages the trope proliferates in complaints about texts that scribes have willfully or carelessly altered in the act of copying, as does the related trope of imploring the reader: "If the scribe has erred, you, reader, ought to make corrections."[86] The mention of biblical texts in particular seems almost inevitably to elicit recognition that the *verba* of scribes have obscured the divine *res,* as in Studie's observation in the *C* text of *Piers Plowman* that Clergie is "ouer Skripture þe skilfole and screueynes were trewe" (*Piers Plowman, C.*11.97). The trope of inexactitude in copying also pervades the academic discourse of the late Middle Ages. In his early fourteenth-century *Philobiblon,* for example, Richard de Bury, bishop of Durham, laments transcriptional damage, while the commentator Nicholas Lyre develops the trope at length in his *Literal Postill on the Bible:*

> One should moreover, bear in mind that the literal sense, which should be our starting-point, as I have said, seems to be greatly obscured in these modern times. This is partly through the fault of scribes who, misled by similarities between letters, have in many places written something which differs from the true reading of the text (*veritas textus*). Partly it is the fault of lack of skill of correctors, who in several places have punctuated where they should not, and have begun and ended verses where they should not begin or end, and for this reason the meaning of the text (*sententia literae*) is inconstant.[87]

And at the end of the late Middle English period, Trithemius, in a nostalgic if doomed attempt to advocate copying by hand over typographic reproduction, condemns those lazy and negligent scribes who spoil sacred texts through "faulty copying" and praises the conscientious ones who correct them: "As soon as the conscientious scribe has finished copying a book, he should once more compare original and copy and, in case of errors, make exact corrections. This procedure will prove his ability and care, and his work will duly meet with approval."[88]

For much of the modern period, it was customary for scholars to reconcile these conflicting images of the scribal task by taking them at face value and concluding that though scribes generally aspired to textual exactitude, being human they necessarily failed to varying degrees.[89] Recently this perspective has been joined by one that misappropriates Bédier's arguments about best-text editing and that sees scribes as co-operating completely and unrestrictedly in the texts they produce: Each manuscript is imputed with a claim to be a distinctive work. To be sure, there are clear examples of nominal scribes participating fully in the texts they are copying and thereby producing new compositions. In the fourteenth and fifteenth centuries vernacular manuscripts were primarily produced by scattered, independent craftsmen;[90] when the sections of text they produced were then assembled by another craftsman who, as in the case of the Auchinleck manuscript of the early fourteenth century, had editorial responsibilities for layout and arrangement, this craftsman's duties went a long way toward determining the character of a work as it was embodied in a given manuscript.[91] Such elision between writer and scribe seems even more apparent in *The Book of Margery Kempe,* which was the collaborative effort of the illiterate Margery and two scribes,[92] or in the case of Richard Sellyng, who explicitly requests the scribe and bibliophile John Shirley to improve his text if he can:

> Sellyng makithe / þis in hes manere
> And to John Shirley . nowe sent it is
> ffor to amende where it is a misse.[93]

However, to disregard the incommensurability among medieval conceptions of the scribal task—to suppress the diversity and discontinuity of manuscript discourse—is to mute the poignancy of figuring the task as an ideal that always fails. Such a view erases the tension that defined all writing in the preprint era and that, at least for the later Middle Ages, emerged specifically from the difficulties of representing the intangible *res* of medieval conceptions of a work in tangible *verba*. As the ubiquity of the scribal tropes indicates, these difficulties are ultimately among the conditions of existence for medieval works. The one late Middle English writer to deploy the trope in detail is, significantly, Chaucer, whose importance for the appropriation of literary authority by vernacular writers I have discussed in the previous chapter.[94] Chaucer's petition at the end of *Troilus and Criseyde*—that "non myswrite" the poem (5.1795)—elliptically expresses the idea, while the short poem *Chaucers Wordes unto Adam* is essentially an amplification of the trope. In terms of the discourse of late Middle English manuscripts, what is important about these passages is not their utterly conventional content; it is the fact that in using the trope Chaucer co-opts one of the traditional methods of Antique and medieval authorial self-definition.[95] To lament scribal depredations, in other words, is implicitly to assume elevated status as a writer, and it is therefore no coincidence that throughout his letters Petrarch, one of Chaucer's theoretical and practical models, himself repeatedly complains of his inability to locate good and reliable scribes. When Caxton adopts the trope in the introduction to the second edition of the *Canterbury Tales,* he confirms the significance of both the trope and Chaucer's use of it.

Similarly, to absolve scribes of any responsibility for the duplication of the texts in front of them—to elide any distinction between vernacular "author" and "scribe"—is to overlook the evidence of traditions with little textual variation as well as the cultural and ideological restraints that scribal institutions and medieval understandings of a work would have exercised upon copying. As the institutional means for the production of medieval literature, the church, theology, the universities, and the marketplace all delimited medieval conceptions of works and their transmission. It is true enough that the linguistic codes through which late Middle English texts were negotiated can result in individual texts in which the traces of transmission are not easily distinguishable from those of composition: Expansion by exempla or the use of formulaic diction can be utilized either by an "author" writing a new work or a "scribe" bringing the *verba* of a text into harmony with their putative *res.* To the extent that the abstract work governs the activities of both "authors" and "scribes," moreover, the distinction between the two can seem to dissolve or at least become insignificant.

But socially and institutionally the distinction between individual composition (*dictare*) and scribal production (*scribere*) is maintained throughout the Middle English period. In the *Regement of Princes,* for example, Hoccleve presents the one occupation as materially useful for—yet distinct from—the other; the beggar tells him to make a complaint to Henry V about the loss of his annuity and to compose this *literary* work in Latin, French, or English, since his *scribal* experience has trained him in all three.[96] Moreover, literary roles, as much as literary works, are not autonomously produced; as I suggested in chapter 3, the development of authorship in the eighteenth and nineteenth centuries shows just how clearly they are constructed by and help to constitute a number of social and cultural networks. One example of these interconnections from the Middle Ages is the fact that medieval writers' habit of extracting and adapting in their own compositions texts created by others was in part enabled by the absence of legal discourse in the construction of Middle English authors, works, and texts. Since the role of "author" or "scribe" is finally determined more by social contract than by aesthetic principle, there is thus every reason to distinguish the two roles at least conceptually.

To return to my initial example: Is the punctuation poem or the carol on ivy informed by the more representative conceptions of work and text in the discourse of late Middle English manuscripts? The evidence assembled in this chapter suggests the latter. The text of the carol is an inherently imperfect realization of a work that requires writer and reader to supplement through graphic correspondence and mystical signification. As the graphs of "ivy" must be likened to symbolic truths, so the text of the carol must be—can *only* be—likened to the work. The punctuation poem, on the other hand, is a novelty, for it requires that the conceit be somehow out of the ordinary, just as the once-popular pictures that imaged fish swimming if looked at from one angle and birds flying if looked at from another.[97] When a novelty catches on, it loses both purpose and effectiveness. The novelty of the punctuation poem is in part the fixity of the text as a concretization of the work, which eventually became not a novelty but a condition of existence for English literature. In the preface to his edition of Sir David Lindsay's Middle Scots works, Henry Charteris accepts textual fixity as the unassailable horizon of his complaint that earlier editions were compromised by false orthography, transpositions of words and lines, omissions of lines, and textual changes to make Lindsay's language approximate the southern dialect—"quhairfor ye natiue grace and first mynd of ye writer, is often tymes peruertit."[98] But this complaint was written in 1568, well after technological, social, and cultural changes had transformed the factors that enabled the production and transmission of vernacular literature. Much like granting authority to Middle English writers, crediting Middle English literature with modern textual criticism's conception of texts and works supplies it with a quality whose absence was one of its conditions of existence.

❦

CHAPTER SIX

Middle English Textual Criticism

THEORIES ABOUT CONCEPTS like author, work, and text can never be finally validated. A hypothesis in the hard sciences can be tested through repeated experimentation under controlled laboratory conditions, but this option is scarcely available in textual criticism. We cannot ingenuously write new Middle English literature and observe whether it manifests certain theoretical suppositions; we cannot summon authentic Middle English readers to ask them their views or to examine their reading strategies; and we cannot simulate Middle English culture and wait for it to generate literary works. It is possible to follow the explanatory model of philology, which evaluates all available evidence not in order to predict what linguistic changes will or must happen under certain circumstances but to suggest which specific factors coalesced in a specific situation to produce a specific result; a combination of London's social prestige and a drag-chain mechanism, for instance, probably led to the Great Vowel Shift, though such a combination will not necessarily produce a similar shift whenever it occurs. This is largely the model that I have followed in my examination of the discourse of late Middle English manuscripts from within.

I began by exploring the origins of textual criticism in the humanist period. For a variety of specific ideological reasons the humanists created a textual criticism that valorized the idealist, lexical works of individuals. As part of the humanist project, this textual criticism responded to the theoretical and practical characteristics of Antique literature as well as to the cultural suppositions of the Renaissance, among which were the fundamental cultural, intellectual, and social distinctions drawn between the modern period and the *medium aevum* that separated it from the classical world whose values it embraced. Consequently, this was a textual criticism that by design was theoretically and practically unresponsive to Middle English literature. Humanist textual criticism has nonetheless come to define the perimeters of textual criticism in general and the discursive field of Middle English in particular, largely because its totalizing positions, in a maneuver entirely consistent with humanist ideology, were articulated and institutionalized in such a way that subsequent critics have taken them at face value. Though embracing differing cultural imperatives and advocating varying methodological assumptions, Eichhorn, Wolf, Lachmann, Bédier, and Greg all relied on fundamentally humanist notions of author, work, and text that therefore, in the editions so produced, have remained influential, even primary, in the construction of the historical textual record that subsequent epochs have recuperated to varying ends. The history of textual criticism, indeed, is a remarkably fissureless history, one in which continuities such as Bédier's work have been conveniently conceived as (minor) ruptures, in which discontinuities such as McGann's work (which is in fact only partially discontinuous) have been recuperated *within* traditional positions, and in which potentially disruptive traditions such as Middle English have been reformulated in a fashion that consolidates humanist assumptions.

Because of the way textual criticism has prefigured the discursive field, to be edited at all Middle English works have had to assume the characteristics of the very works that were in part composed and defined through their differences from medieval vernacular compositions. The ideological and institutional power of humanism initially necessitated such an assumption, though in the nineteenth century this imperative was joined by that of philology. While strengthening humanist textual criticism, philology also furthered the accommodation of Middle English: It motivated the recovery of a lexical work without awkwardly imputing aesthetic value to the work, and its methodological advancements facilitated the objectives of traditional textual criticism. For these reasons, perhaps, concentration on an authorial text has often been seen as originating in the nineteenth century. Such a view, however, obscures the fact that in dating to the humanist period, this concentration recapitulates the antagonism toward Middle English literature that is inherent in traditional textual criticism.

Antagonism, in fact, aptly characterizes the historical situation not only of the humanist reception of works in the discourse of late Middle English manuscripts but also of their medieval production. Developed within a network of institutions, practices, theories, and ideologies that overtly and covertly repressed vernacular language and literature, Middle English conceptions of author, work, and text are characteristically definable through their opposition to authorized views. If an auctor was a named individual who produced institutionally authorized works in the authorized language, Middle English makers, expressly denied access to authorized discourse and to the venues in which this discourse occurred, could share none of these qualities, so that their works could not be recognized as authorized by the literary community. In mediating larger cultural concerns, the authorial, narrative, and stylistic anonymity that characterizes Middle English writing and that traditional textual criticism seeks to individualize is thus in part predicated on an antagonistic relationship between makers and the auctores who did participate in authorized discourse, an antagonism that emerges even more clearly in the fifteenth-century contest over authority played out by writers like Hoccleve, Lydgate, and Henryson. Conceptually, it is possible to distinguish further a vernacular "author" from a vernacular "scribe." But a Middle English definition of the former remains vague, even contradictory, and shows how significant aspects of the Middle English author function emerge from what the discourse of late Middle English manuscripts excludes: a nonprofessionalized, unindividualized individual whose text is neither a necessary nor precise reflection of his or her work, over which he or she has no cultural or literary authority. In contrast, a scribe was socially defined as a professional or institutional position devoted to the reproduction of prior compositions but similarly constrained by prevailing understandings of author, work, and text.

Some of the contradictions involving vernacular authorship can be clarified against conceptions of work and text in the discourse of late Middle English manuscripts. The antagonism that helped to shape these concepts was less between vernacular writers and authorized theory and more between vernacular discourse and authorized culture, which excluded Middle English from the institutions and discursive practices that not only conveyed social power and literary prestige but also contributed to the medieval perception of regularized, potentially correct texts. Beyond this antagonism, Middle English literature was negotiated through linguistic and bibliographical codes that it shared with other preprint literatures and that framed the constitution of a work most generally by the *res* underlying it and more narrowly by the supplements of the reader, tradition, and documentary realization. Thus, not only were the works of Middle English "authors" neither authorized nor authoritative, they were literally authored as much traditionally as by the "authors" themselves. The Middle English text, in turn, had no autonomous status of its own but merely reflected an underlying *res,* which, rather than a textual exemplar, provides the best historical standard for evaluating authenticity. The valorization of scribal contributions to a Middle English text—or, simply, of "scribal" texts—thus disregards the institutional distinction between vernacular "scribes" and "authors," the theoretical priority of the work over both, and the discursive and nondiscursive practices through which Middle English works were produced.

The methods and theoretical principles of humanist textual criticism, even in the permutations of socialization or versioning, therefore, do not respond well to the historical character of Middle English literature.[1] Not only are they unable to represent this character, they in fact obscure if not obliterate it through resolution of the tensions that motivated the production and transmission of the literature. Humanist textual criticism was designed to foreclose the very compositional, stylistic, and documentary variation that characterizes the enunciation of Middle English literature. While the edited Middle English texts produced through traditional procedures and attitudes can be empirically justified and aesthetically valid, they are not framed by the recognition that historical works exist and mean through a variety of social, political, cultural, and institutional networks, *as well as* through literary ones. Just as the advent of print, linguistic standardization, Renaissance valorization of the self and language, and the sixteenth-century expansion of England's political and economic influence mutually reinforced one another in the development of humanist conceptions of author, work, and text, so manuscript production, the church and the universities, medieval views of authority, and the medieval archive of discursive practices (including, for example, literary criticism, the law, and other linguistic traditions) together constructed Middle English conceptions. Briefly stated: Middle English texts are less lexical than those of traditional textual criticism, even while its documents are more physical. Its authors are defined as much by their works as the other way around, and its works are not constituted even in part by texts but only reflected—and necessarily inadequately—in them. The very conceptions of author, work, and text that are inherited from humanism and with which I necessarily began this study are thus subverted and replaced.

The sense of work underlying *textual production* in the Middle English period—depending as it does on supplementation and implying the almost infinite deferral of the work itself—in fact parallels that underlying *literary interpretation* in the modern era; in the space framed by the parallel of these senses lies the cultural distance separating the Middle Ages from the present. Within the discourse of late Middle English manuscripts, there are no preeminent motivations for valorizing the text or work of an individual, or the words, meter, orthography, or punctuation of a text. To attempt to recreate the text of an individual that lexically precedes that in an extant manuscript is thus especially problematic. In any number of places in poems of the alliterative revival, for example, editors can (and do) replace nonalliterating staves with alliterating synonyms. Empirically, such a procedure is well justified, but it does not take into account the clearest implication of such breakdowns in alliteration: that even in a poetics as dependent on surface realizations as the alliterative revival, scribes sometimes copied for—and, presumably, readers read for—*sense,* not specific lexical markers. Restoring alliteration in such cases imputes a priority to words that the manuscripts and their cultural contexts do not support.

Chaucer's works offer a particularly clear—because controversial—example in this regard. All of the modern editions of Chaucer's complete works contain carefully presented, artistically pleasing poetry, but none of them offer genuine examples of works produced within the discourse of Middle English manuscripts, since the Chaucer they imply can only be a projection of postmedieval thinking. The very idea of an authoritative canon or authoritative texts, for example, is an inherently retrospective idea that is possible only after a tradition of documents, texts, and works has been identified. It is thus an idea that was not available to an individual possessing or reading a single manuscript copy of the works or texts in that tradition; in the fifteenth century, such an individual would have had neither the technology for identifying the tradition in its entirety nor a cultural context in which such an identification would be meaningful. To the extent that Chaucer (and perhaps Gower) did himself evince an interest in valorizing his own words, there is historical justification for recovering them. But since writers do not autonomously define themselves and their compositions, the recovered *works* are less broadly medieval ones and more private curiosities, like diaries. Once Chaucer's compositions became available to the medieval reading public—in effect, published—they were subject to and defined by the same discursive and institutional forces as any other Middle English compositions, regardless of Chaucer's own attitudes toward himself and his works.

In strictly literary terms, perhaps the most relevant of these forces are authorized Latin discourse, the medieval ideology of authority, and the priority of the work over the author and the text. Together these indicate not only that isolation of an individual vernacular writer's specific words is unmotivated but that the particular, expressed desires of such individuals are subservient to the social negotiation of the work. Indeed, the transmission of the *Canterbury Tales* in particular shows the negligible effect Chaucer's auctorial aspirations had on the reception (hence conception) of his texts and of the works they reflect, and what Hoccleve and early editors championed was less Chaucer's actual works than an *idea* of Chaucer. While Shelley, thus, lived in a culture that *would* countenance and give meaning to the self-expression and individuality he desired even in the physical appearance of *Queen Mab,* Chaucer did not. The latter's authorial self-consciousness, accordingly and despite the intrinsic merits of his poetry, provides no broadly historical reason for valorizing his particular texts in the face of overwhelming contextual evidence to the contrary, though by the same token it does offer a number of ahistorical reasons for doing so.

I want to reiterate here that I am not arguing that individual Middle English textual qualities should never be represented in an edition. I am saying that since their representation is not historical, editions that employ strategies to recover them are themselves misrepresented if they are understood as historical recuperations of Middle English works. The key point, again, is that despite the systemizing, totalizing orientation that textual criticism has inherited from its humanist origins, the answer to the question How should this work be edited? ought to be For whom and for what purposes? For an edition that emerges from nonhistorical aesthetic principles or allegedly transhistorical ones—as I understand the vast majority of Middle English editions to do—there is every reason to focus on the specific words of specific individuals. Depending on where editors situate themselves on the theoretical hierarchy of textual criticism—or, perhaps, can be shown to be situated, since the theoretical underpinnings of modern editing are so little examined—such editions can of course be coherent, interesting, and valuable. But they are not therefore historically sensitive to the discourse of late Middle English manuscripts, and their empirical achievement does not validate the theoretical propositions motivating them to the exclusion of other conceptual frameworks.

I also want to underscore that my intention in this book has not been to demonize humanism or traditional textual criticism. To state the obvious, the humanists were vital in the transmission of English and classical literature, and while they did presume to construct a transcendent textual criticism, they alone were not responsible for the fact that their successors so rarely interrogated this presumption or any of the other theoretical principles of textual criticism. Since textual criticism is largely a humanist invention, moreover, there is clearly a sense in which it is invalid to criticize it for being what it is and not something else: As a construction of the humanist project, it *does* exclude the sorts of issues I have talked about in the last two chapters.

Yet interest in history and literature and a reliance on written or printed texts are scarcely specific to Renaissance humanism, so that even though traditional textual criticism is a humanist invention, the need for such criticism is endemic to literate societies. The difficulty of traditional approaches is that in a fundamental way they theoretically close off any other kinds of textual criticism. Even this principle, however, should not be considered insidious. While a reconceptualization of textual criticism is possible, as is the manifestation of such a criticism in specific editions, it will inevitably be the case that as a hermeneutic gesture any textual criticism will mediate something of its own cultural context and will foreclose some interpretive options through the way it prefigures the discursive field. This is as true of my own attempt to describe the discourse of late Middle English manuscripts as it is of the Anglo-American tradition associated with Greg and Bowers or of the socialization perspective of McGann and McKenzie. None of these approaches, furthermore, is a culmination in textual critical history. Despite the totalizing present at the discipline's formation and often characteristic of its subsequent practice, a historical endeavor like textual criticism can never be an ahistorical praxis: It is always both an ideological discourse and a dialogue between a past and a present that dialectically form and reform each other.

At the outset I stressed that this was a theoretical study, that I had not written an editorial manual. I think it appropriate to conclude, however, by underscoring the salient practical issues and suggesting how an edition predicated on the historical determinants of the discourse of late Middle English manuscripts would begin to emerge from the conceptions of author, work, and text that I have here traced. The most general objective in such an edition would be to recover not an authorized text behind a number of documentary ones—as is the case in traditional textual criticism—but the work behind a document. The character of this work would depend on the physical and textual evidence of the manuscript, on the literary and cultural traditions that frame it and on which it draws, and on its relationship to other manuscripts of what might be considered, *within these contexts,* the same work. It is thus not true, as is often maintained through a misapplication of Bédier's work, that a diplomatic edition of one manuscript text has the advantage of offering what at least one medieval reader read. Medieval readers read by supplementing the text in front of them from a variety of cultural and literary networks; in turn, the texts themselves were circumscribed by a number of social and institutional frameworks. Specific texts remained only a part of both the writing and reading experiences in the late Middle Ages, and the fact that texts can be recovered with apparently more empirical rigor than can contexts should not be allowed to exaggerate their significance.

Given Middle English views, material realization is not an essential quality of a work, so that the simple reproduction of the physicality of a document that many materialist textual critics advocate does not seem to recuperate completely or, perhaps, even largely the original work. The *implications* of this physicality, however, may well be important, though they are also often ambiguous for works of any historical period. The fact that all literary works necessarily exist in material realizations, for example, does not manifestly reveal which (if any) qualities of these realizations figured in historical conceptions of the work. If traditional textual criticism errs in dissociating all aspects of material realization from the character of a work, I believe it is equally erroneous to assume without discursive and cultural confirmation that all of these same aspects figure in the work. It is clear enough that modern writers like Blake, Morris, and Pound did in various ways consciously incorporate material realization in the conception of their works, but as exceptions in this regard they reveal little about the documentary significance of nonexceptional writing. The problem here is how to define *normative* strategies of production and reading, and this is a problem even for contemporary works. Put simply: How do modern writers utilize and modern readers process basic bibliographic codes like running heads, pagination, spacing, type font, and illustration? Is there anywhere one can look up this information, the way one can look up representative modern views on a word's meaning, on the legal status of a text, or on the procedures authors undertake to get their works published? Or can the information be obtained only by asking individual readers their individual opinions, in which case there may in fact be no consensus or normative position?

If we are uncertain about the hermeneutic effects and ontological significance of contemporary bibliographic codes, this uncertainty is compounded for medieval texts: Not only do we not have definitive reference works explaining the pragmatics of medieval bibliographic codes, the codes themselves—such as marginalia, illumination, historiated initials, variable handwriting, abbreviations, and (sporadic) running heads—seem to be visually more demonstrative than their modern counterparts. Lavish illustration programs such as those in many manuscripts of the *Confessio,* or isolated layout accommodations such as those in Harley 2253, furthermore, contrast sharply with unillustrated manuscripts and presumably unaccommodated layouts by the ways in which they collaborate with other documentary features (e.g., the texts themselves) in the constitution of the literary work. In light of this variability and demonstrativeness, and also of Middle English views of work and text, it does indeed seem appropriate in an edition of a medieval work to represent—or at least acknowledge—the implications of material realization. The basic tools of traditional textual criticism are inapplicable in this area, however, for they are essentially lexical, such as the principle of *difficilior lectio,* which is itself of questionable validity for Middle English works. Though the array of lexical tools and absence of nonlexical ones attest to the achievement of humanism, they also underscore how theoretically close to its origins traditional textual criticism remains. Repeated calls to get more Middle English texts into print emerge from this closeness and, if realized, would not necessarily offer modern readers a better sense of Middle English works. If there is one area in Middle English textual criticism that needs particular work, therefore, I believe it is the determination of the meaning and relevance of medieval bibliographic codes. And if there is one area in Middle English editing in need of particular work, in turn, it is the representation of these codes.

It is important to recognize, too, that even within the constraints of historically sensitive reconstruction there are editorial options. As I suggested in chapter 5, for example, one historically valid option for Chaucer's *Boece* would be a refusal to edit the translation at all, since the tradition through which it emerges defines the *res* of the work as what Boethius intended; from this perspective, Chaucer's actual words, while possibly recoverable, have no historical value or autonomy, and only an edition of the *Consolation* could be prepared. It is this option, I maintained, that is most consistent with the discourse of late Middle English manuscripts. Another historical option would be to edit the *Boece* so as to recover *for historical interest* the actual text Chaucer wrote, regardless of how this text was received and processed in the Middle Ages. Such an edition would be of *Chaucer's Boece,* not of the *Boece* itself.[2] Yet a third historical option, then, would be to recover the *Middle English Boece* isolated from the largest traditions that informed and determined it but nonetheless consonant with Middle English notions of author, work, and text.

This recovery would itself produce more than one *Boece.* Textually, the twelve extant authorities fall into two general groupings (α and β), though the textual is but one of the indicators of the *res* that a manuscript text presumes to represent. Other reflections include reception, layout, presentation, and the texts with which the *Boece* texts are bound, and these features align individual manuscripts variously and often differently from the way the texts alone do. For example, Salisbury, Cathedral MS 113 is textually part of the β grouping and has particular affinities with London, British Library MS Add. 10340, with which it shared an exemplar. But while the latter manuscript binds the *Boece* with *Truth* and a portion of the *General Prologue* in a mini-Chaucerian anthology—thus grouping it with Thynne's edition and, to an extent, London, British Library MS Add. 16165, both of the α branch—Salisbury 113 binds it with three Latin theological works: Pierre de Blois's *De XII utilitatibus tribulationis,* St. Bonaventure's *De passione Christi,* and the anonymous *Carmen Lugubre.* The only other manuscript to present the *Boece* with this theological bent is Oxford, Bodleian MS Bodley 797, a textually eccentric, heavily glossed manuscript of the α grouping whose presentation also differentiates it from Salisbury 113: The latter, like Add. 10340, is in double columns in a neat, professional hand and accompanied by a restrained program of illumination,[3] while the former appears in single columns with rudimentary decorations and is in an awkward hand that does not seem to be that of a professional scribe. The roughness of the production, in turn, associates Bodley 797 with Cambridge, Pembroke College MS 215, which, as a manuscript devoted exclusively to the *Boece,* can itself also be aligned with four other authorities;[4] but the heavy glossing of Bodley 797 links it with Cambridge, University Library MS Ii.3.21. This, however, is a β manuscript that, like Columbia, University of Missouri MS Fragmenta manuscripta No. 150 (containing another β text), alternates sections of the *Boece* with those of the Latin original. These two β manuscripts— particularly Cambridge Ii.3.21, which includes an alphabetized list of topoi, a brief summary of each prose and meter, and the commentary of William of Aragon—thus present the English text as in effect a gloss on the Latin one and as part of an elaborate academic production. In their overt valorization of Boethius and his Latin work, they in turn link themselves with Oxford, Bodleian MS Auct. F.3.5, which begins with an elaborate *accessus ad auctorem* for Boethius (not Chaucer). But this is a far less textually elaborate (though still physically polished) manuscript that transforms Chaucer's composition into lemmata and attendant commentary, so that textually the manuscript cannot be considered to contain the *Boece,* as modern critics understand the work, at all. Finally, in a different vein and as I noted in chapter 5, the *Boece* manuscripts display several different programs of *ordinatio,* which align the manuscripts in still other ways.

To define a work or works among these authorities and their shifting affiliations, *any* edition must cut across categories like layout, manuscript contents, presentation, and reception as well as text, prioritizing some factors, suppressing others.[5] Traditional editions, in their lexical and idealist conception of the work, of course suppress everything but the text. A work constructed in recognition of the breadth of social, documentary, and literary factors, however, might be theological and institutional, or private and casual, or academic, or "Chaucerian," or Boethian, or any combination thereof. All of these works would be broadly and authentically medieval, far more consistent with the discourse of late Middle English manuscripts, in fact, than one based solely on textual criteria.

At least three related practical constraints circumscribe any edition intended to reflect the discourse of late Middle English manuscripts, and they should be mentioned here, too. These are the limitations of typography, the fact that an edition is a site of interpretation, and the conjoined demands of cost and pedagogical utility. At present, many features of medieval manuscripts, particularly color and graph shape, can only be approximated, even at great expense. Furthermore, such approximations, like all features of any edition, make necessary if ambiguous contributions to the character of the edition both as itself a work subject to interpretation and, since in most cases access to original documents is difficult if not impossible, as the historical text and work it presumes to recover. Though these two works—the editorial and the historical—are ontologically distinct, within the ambivalent sense of historicity of traditional textual criticism it is possible for editors and critics alike to overlook the distinction: There can be the implicit presumption that in producing (and reading) the critical edition one is attempting to reproduce (and is reading) the original work.

The edited text, however, signifies in complex and sometimes contradictory ways quite different from those in which a medieval text or work does, and I think it is worth pausing for a moment to recollect (or expose) them. The final page of the *Franklin's Tale* in Pratt's edition of the *Canterbury Tales* can again serve as a focus. To the reader uninitiated in the techniques of critical editing, this page immediately announces itself as something alien to the more familiar presentations of written language in novels or newspapers. The narrow column of type with an unjustified right margin unmistakably indicates poetry and therefore, since prose is today the normative medium for most kinds of written communication, marks the text as "artistic" and in fact unusual. Indeed, for many modern readers, including the very well educated, the fact that the text is poetry immediately elicits disinterest and conjures up unpleasant images of schools and racks of greeting cards, the forums where poetry is most often encountered today.

To the reader familiar with critical apparatus, the page from Pratt's edition signifies in different, though still complex, ways. The marginal lexical glosses and longer glosses at the bottom of the page on history, literature, and mythology reassuringly imply the intervention of a scholarly editor and apparently serve to make the work more accessible. A reader who knows something of the physical appearance of late Middle English manuscripts would likewise recognize the punctuation, capitalization, paragraphing, and regularized orthography—features inherent in modern notions of printed language—as editorial. While the familiarity of these features also seems to make the text user-friendly, the unfamiliarity of so much of the page—the glosses, language, and content—ironically defamiliarizes them. In fact, the page as a symbolic object offers a curiously ambivalent message. If the various reader aids constitute a way for the reader to circumvent the linguistic barriers of an alien form of English and appreciate a historical poem, at the same time they emphasize just how far the modern reader is from this historical work, since their very existence designates the poem and reader as alien to each other. They invite and simultaneously repulse the reader, and this is even more so the case in a major scholarly edition like the *Riverside Chaucer*. On the one hand, the very size and bulk of the volume, as well as the hundreds of pages of notes, commentary, bibliography, and glossary, proclaim the scholarly thoroughness with which it was prepared and offer the reader between two covers many of the requisites for gaining a broadly based historical sense of Chaucer's works. On the other hand, this same material seems forbiddingly to say, "Abandon all hope, ye who enter here," since if this material is necessary for the modern reader to understand and appreciate Chaucer, then Chaucer by implication is very far indeed from the modern reader and the modern world.

More constraining than either the limitations of typography or the dual ontology of an edition are the conjoined demands of cost and pedagogical utility. Because of production costs and limited classroom and public use, medieval literature, more so than English literature of any other period, is caught in a cycle whereby publishers print what will be used in courses and instructors teach from what publishers make available, thereby guaranteeing the production of only those books that are already in use. In this way, for example, the poems of London, British Library MS Cotton Nero A.x and Chaucer's works—far less representative of Middle English literature than the works of, say, Minot or Lydgate—stay in print. Occasionally the works of a Hoccleve or Henryson might reappear in an affordable format, only to disappear when the initial press run is sold out, and some lesser known works do appear in anthologies—the contemporary format that perhaps most radically alters their Middle English character. Much Middle English literature thus remains restricted to "scholarly" editions, which typically share the theoretical orientation of students' editions; in part because of their greater thoroughness and more restricted audience, however, they are often prohibitively expensive, sometimes even for libraries. Once out of print, they are also not typically reissued, so that they may be accessible only in large research libraries or through interlibrary loan. The Middle English canon, thus, is very much a canon shaped by economics.

Within these practical constraints and the increasing theoretical marginalization of medieval literature since the advent of the New Criticism, there is nonetheless room for editorial maneuverability. Hypertext already offers the technology to construct editions that respond to some of the documentary and textual diversity of Middle English works. In linking blocks of electronic text and allowing for their assembly in any number of sequential orders, hypertext subverts not only the linearity of conventional texts but, when joined by hypermedia with nontextual blocks like pictures and charts, their very textuality as well. In pedagogical uses, such as *The Dickens Web,* hypertext can join a literary work with a nexus of modern and historical texts on the social issues informing the work, including Victorian history, health, religion, and the like; cross-indexing between these social texts and the literary work enables a user to move back and forth at will within the entire hypertext network. In creative uses like Michael Joyce's hypertext fiction *Afternoon,* on the other hand, the technology requires readers to create their own literary works by assembling any or all of the 538 lexias that make up *Afternoon* in whatever order they please.[6]

For editing, hypertext offers the possibilities of editions that are simultaneously responsive to the various ways a literary work might have been historically constituted. It would be possible, for example, to have in one electronic edition *all* the varieties of the *Boece* that I outlined above. Hypertext could also produce editions of a given work that enabled the reader to put that work in all the textual contexts in which it appeared, to substitute alternate readings at any point in that work, or sequentially to examine all extant texts of that work. A hypertext edition of a lyric, thus, might connect the text of the lyric not only with texts containing different readings but also with other literary works, say a romance, in which that lyric might be incorporated. With hypermedia, this textual variability could be linked to illustrations that occur with the lyric or in comparable manuscripts. Hypertext, like any textual critical theory or practice, by no means offers unambiguous solutions to all editorial issues; hypertext and hypermedia cannot, for instance, forestall interpretive closure of medieval documents and texts, since they are themselves hermeneutic gestures that, in fact, assemble a broadly historical work that first became identifiable and accessible only with postmedieval developments in paleography and bibliography. As technologies, they thus mediate the modern era perhaps far better than the medieval one. Even so, for the historical representation of Middle English works, hypertext and hypermedia do unarguably transcend the technology of print, a technology that emerged with humanist textual criticism and is thus perhaps most responsive to it.[7]

Hypertext, as well as computerized typesetting and production on disk, not only extends the capabilities of typographic representation but does so at less cost, so that editions thus produced might break or at least expand the cycle of pedagogy and marketability. Even should this happen in only a restricted way, the fixed demand of libraries guarantees some accessibility to all kinds of editions. If research libraries will continue to buy scholarly editions, in other words, production costs become less consequential: There is as great (or as little) an audience for historically sensitive editions as there is for traditionally constructed ones. Developments in hermeneutics and iconographic interpretation bode well, moreover, for improved understanding of the historicity of all editing and of editions as themselves sites of interpretation. It requires only imagination to respond to the problems of defining the *res* of a Middle English work, of representing medieval bibliographic codes, and of reconciling what a historical work was with what a modern edition of it is. We can of course never—should never—cross the chasms of print and romanticism to gain unmediated access to Middle English literature, but editions constructed according to the discourse of late

Middle English manuscripts can offer a far better view of the chasms themselves as well as of what lies on *both* sides than has readily been available until now.

At present, on this side of the chasms, disinterest in editions and editorial theory prevails in Middle English studies. A provocative index of this disinterest is the fact that for a long time an edition has been regarded as the ideal dissertation topic, one that will instruct the student in areas as disparate as literary interpretation, paleography, and linguistics, as well as textual criticism. Ten of the thirty-five dissertations on Middle English subjects that Dissertation Abstracts International records from 1954 to 1957 were in fact editions. For the years 1980 through 1990, the percentage of editions dropped from nearly one-third to approximately one-ninth, but the presence of thirty-two editions among the total of 277 Middle English dissertations recorded during the period indicates that many directors still consider textual criticism and editing to be useful practice for the business of the profession. The irony of this view of textual criticism—that it is simply a praxis that one acquires rather than a discourse sustained by theoretical propositions—is compounded by the fact that these editions are often then published in revised forms and come to define the canon of Middle English by being the only ones available for a great many compositions. By no means do I mean to suggest that such editions are a priori inadequate. But they do almost inevitably sustain the inherited positions of humanism at the same time they push the theoretical horizon of editing even further into the interpretive backgound: Textual criticism is so well-defined and unproblematic, the implication goes, that it is primarily appropriate for the education of graduate students.

The horizon is similarly recessed through arguments that attempt to hold theory in abeyance until more texts are in print; such arguments consolidate even more the humanists' idealist, lexical conception of the work. My position is that for the presentation and understanding of Middle English works according to presumed historical principles, we do not necessarily need more *texts*. At this point, moreover, I do not see that the argument that any edition is better than none at all—an argument that was inherent in the formation of the Early English Text Society—is in any way compelling. We have ample indications of the strengths and weaknesses of traditional methods and theories; it would be valuable to see the capabilities of other kinds of editions. Indeed, the longer the production of humanist editions prefigures the discursive field, the less likely Middle English textual criticism will ever expose and get beyond their theoretical horizon.

It remains at best imprecise, in any case, to call the editions produced according to traditional textual criticism historical, since they do not respond to all the demands of the discourse of late Middle English manuscripts. Like all editions, moreover, they emerge from clear if unrecognized theoretical positions and generate definite if unacknowledged interpretive consequences. Most generally, I am urging editorial and interpretive self-consciousness; more particularly, greater historical sensibility in an activity that is inherently historical. It may well be that there simply is no longer any reason for studying Middle English literature as Middle English literature, in which case the inherited tradition of textual criticism, since it responds to the imperative of marketability, is entirely adequate. But recent calls for new philology and new medievalism suggest that to many critics the medievalness of medieval literature is indeed important, and this is obviously a sentiment I share.[8] The positions of traditional textual criticism confirm the continuing demand for and fact of the accommodation of Middle English literature. For historical representation, the theoretical tensions, cultural restraints, and practical constraints of Middle English need to be not accommodated but affirmed, not resolved but disclosed.

NOTES

BIBLIOGRAPHY

INDEX

Introduction

1. Shillingsburg, *Scholarly Editing*, p. 173. Also see Tanselle, *Rationale*, pp. 11–38.

2. Shillingsburg, *Scholarly Editing*, p. 46.

3. Ibid., p. 47.

4. Ibid., p. 49.

5. Ibid., p. 51. The whole of Shillingsburg's discussion on pp. 44–55 is valuable.

Chapter One, Humanism and Textual Criticism

1. Pratt's edition is based on that by F. N. Robinson and, consequently, San Marino, MS EL 26.C.9 (Ellesmere) rather than the Hengwrt manuscript. As my present purpose is to discuss the general assumptions involved in transforming the text of a medieval manuscript into that of a printed edition, this difference is immaterial. My discussion of the hands on f. 165r draws on that by Doyle and Parkes, "Paleographical Introduction," pp. xlvii–xlviii.

2. Ibid., p. xxxii.

3. Ibid., pp. xxxi–xxxii.

4. See Hanna, "Hengwrt Manuscript."

5. See Beeson, *Lupus of Ferrières*. For discussion of textual criticism in the Antique and medieval periods, see Prete, *Observations*. More general surveys appear in Timpanaro, *Entstehung;* Pasquali, *Storia;* and Kenney, *Classical Text*. In his considerations of textual-critical history, D. C. Greetham suggests a continuity that extends back through the Renaissance and Middle Ages to the Alexandrians. While there are indeed similarities of outlook in all periods, several ideological and technological features distinctive of humanism lead me (as I argue here) to interpret modern textual criticism as essentially a humanist construction. See Greetham, "Textual Scholarship," pp. 105–13, and *Textual Scholarship*.

6. D'Amico, *Theory and Practice,* p. 8.

7. For a useful discussion of humanist views on language, see Elsky, *Authorizing Words,* pp. 35–69.

8. Schoeck, *Erasmus,* p. 66.

9. Timpanaro, *Entstehung,* p. 14.

10. Kenney, *Classical Text,* p. 21.

11. Also see Grafton, *Joseph Scaliger,* p. 14.

12. D'Amico, *Theory and Practice,* p. 27.

13. On the disjunction between the moral claims of humanism and its actual achievements in this regard, see Grafton and Jardine, *From Humanism.* They discuss in detail the tenuousness of the humanist "tacit assumption . . . that the two things *necessarily* go together: that successful drilling in *copia* and *methodus* will guarantee a classroom product of moral uprightness and good character" (pp. 148–49).

14. Italian textual criticism tended to be the most sophisticated in manuscript studies. See Grafton, *Joseph Scaliger.* Even in the early eighteenth century Bentley still put far more emphasis on what had been called *emendatio ope ingenii,* as two of his most famous sayings suggest: "Do not therefore think it enough to worship scribes, but venture to think for yourself" and "We prefer reason and sense to a hundred codices" (Brink, *English Classical Scholarship,* pp. 66 and 71; the translations are Brink's).

15. D'Amico, *Theory and Practice,* pp. 11–12.

16. Grafton, *Joseph Scaliger,* p. 20.

17. D'Amico, *Theory and Practice,* pp. 30 and 28. For an instance of Erasmus's concern about attention to manuscripts and the preparation of an accurate text, see his letter to Martin Dorp (*Epistola,* 337), in *Opus Epistolarum,* 2:90–114.

18. Brink, *English Classical Scholarship,* p. 20.

19. Grafton and Jardine, *From Humanism,* point out that humanist education was directed at the upper classes and in part encouraged docility and support of the status quo: "The individual humanist is defined in terms of his relations to the power structure, and he is praised or blamed, promoted or ignored, to just the extent that he fulfils or fails to fulfil those terms" (p. 44).

20. See his letter requesting an accurate copy of Dante in Ullman, *Collucio Salutati,* p. 104.

21. Williams and Abott, *Introduction,* p. 10.

22. Bowers, "Multiple Authority," p. 447. The equation of authoritative texts with authorial ones is now commonplace. See, e.g., Bowers, "Principle and Practice," p. 123; Thorpe, *Principles,* pp. 47–48; Tanselle, "Editorial Problem," p. 172, and "Recent Editorial Discussion," p. 54; and Kenney, "Textual Criticism," p. 616.

23. E.g., Aarsleff, "Scholarship and Ideology"; Patterson, *Negotiating the Past,* pp. 77–113; Cerquiglini, *Éloge de la variante;* Frantzen, *Desire for Origins,* pp. 62–95; and Sturges, "Textual Scholarship."

24. See the quotation in Ullman, *Collucio Salutati,* pp. 100–101. Salutati, Witt points out, "basically assumed that the poets did not make mistakes in quantities" (*Hercules at the Crossroads,* p. 234).

25. Salutati had indicated his intention to compose a manual of sorts: "to expound a tract *De Gloria,* in which writing I should elaborate with unrestricted language beyond letters; or, so that I might speak more properly, we aim to define the practice [of textual criticism]" (*De Laboribus Herculis,* 1:282.) He evidently never wrote this "gloria."

26. Robortello, *De arte* p. 44. A brief discussion of some of the other early theorists appears in Kenney, *Classical Text,* pp. 21–46.

27. Robortello, *De arte,* p. 40.

28. Eichhorn, *Einleitung,* 1:183–88, 55, and 375 (in error for 275).

29. For Wolf's debt to Eichhorn see Grafton, "*Prolegomena* to Friedrich August Wolf."

30. Wolf, *Prolegomena,* p. 131.

31. Ibid., p. 57.

32. Timpanaro, *Entstehung,* p. 72. On pp. 69–72 Timpanaro summarizes the origins of many of Lachmann's ideas and the nature of his original contributions to textual criticism.

33. Lachmann, ed., *De rerum natura,* pp. 1 and 11–15.

34. Lachmann, ed., *Nouum Testamentum,* p. v.

35. On Bentley's recognition that the original form of certain works cannot be recovered, see Brink, *English Classical Scholarship,* p. 73.

36. Kenney, *Classical Text,* p. 102.

37. Lachmann, ed., *Nouum Testamentum,* p. v.

38. Quoted in Novick, *That Noble Dream,* p. 31.

39. Darwin, *Origin of the Species,* p. 6.

40. Timpanaro, *Entstehung,* p. 81.

41. Lachmann, ed., *Nouum Testamentum,* p. v.

42. Grafton, *Joseph Scaliger,* pp. 175–76.

43. Speer, in a discussion of how Zumthor's theory of "mouvance" has affected the editing of Old French literature, also notes a fundamental similarity between the procedures of Lachmann and Bédier: "Both methods, in the final analysis, reduce the work to just one version" ("Wrestling with Change," p. 314.) For a typical statement of the antithesis of Lachmann's and Bédier's positions, see Hult, "Reading It Right."

44. Aarsleff, "Scholarship and Ideology," p. 101.

45. Bédier, "Tradition manuscrit . . . premier article," p. 175.

46. Ibid., p. 172.

47. Ibid., p. 175.

48. Bédier, "De L'Édition princeps . . . troisième article," pp. 501 and 518.

49. Ibid., p. 520.

50. Ibid., and Bédier, "De L'Édition princeps . . . deuxième article."

51. Quentin, *Essais,* pp. 162–63.

52. "Bédier, "Tradition manuscrit . . . deuxiéme article," p. 329.

53. Ibid., p. 325.

54. Ibid., p. 350.

55. Ibid., pp. 346 and 348.

56. Bédier, ed., *Lai de L'Ombre,* pp. vii–xxii.

57. Cf. Speer, "Wrestling with Change," pp. 313–14.

58. Aarsleff, "Scholarship and Ideology," p. 107.

59. Bédier, "De L'Édition princeps . . . troisième article," p. 492.

60. Robortello, *De arte,* pp. 39–40.

61. From a letter quoted in Ullman, *Collucio Salutati,* p. 104.

62. Grafton, *Joseph Scaliger,* p. 56.

63. Valla, *Donation of Constantine,* p. 139. The translation is Coleman's.

64. Ibid., p. 85. The translation is Coleman's.

65. Ibid., p. 105. The translation is Coleman's.

66. Erasmus, *Apologia respondens,* p. 238.

67. Ibid., p. 252, and Valla, *Antitodum in Facium,* p. 332.

68. Valla, *Antitodum in Facium,* p. 345, and Erasmus, *Apologia respondens,* p. 168.

69. Eichhorn, *Einleitung,* 1:48–51 and 137–66, and vols. 2 and 3.

70. Wolf, *Prolegomena,* pp. 56–57.

71. Lachmann, ed., *Nouum Testatmentum,* pp. viii and xxxix–li.

72. Havet, *Manual,* p. 25.

73. Greg, "Rationale," p. 26.

74. Robortello, *De arte,* p. 44.

75. Brink, *English Classical Scholarship,* pp. 49–58.

76. Eichhorn, *Einleitung,* p. v.

77. Wolf, *Prolegomena,* p. 72.

78. Quoted in Ullman, *Collucio Salutati,* p. 104.

79. Valla, *Epistole,* p. 201.

80. Eichhorn, *Einleitung,* p. vi.

81. Lachmann, ed., *Nouum Testamentum,* p. v.

82. Havet, *Manual,* p. 35.

83. See, for example, Bowers, "Some Relations," "Bibliographical Way," and "Textual Criticism," and Kristeller, "Textual Scholarship."

84. Tanselle, "Greg's Theory," pp. 295–96.

85. Greetham, "Challenges," pp. 73–75.
86. Eichhorn, *Einleitung,* 2:208.
87. Lachmann, ed., *Nouum Testamentum,* pp. v–vi.
88. See, e.g., Kristeller, "Lachmann Method"; Boyle, "Optimist and Recensionist"; and Reeve, "Stemmatic Method."
89. See, e.g., Bowers, "Multiple Authority" and "Mixed Texts"; Tanselle, "Greg's Theory"; Dane, "Copy-Text"; and, by extension to Bowers's devlopments of Greg's theories, Greetham, "Fredson Bowers."
90. Greg, "Rationale," p. 23. I want to stress, however, that Greg could be far more flexible in his thinking than this quotation might imply. He maintains elsewhere, for instance, that "in some limited sense, every scribe is a subsidiary author, even when he is doing his best to be a faithful copyist, still more when he indulges in emendations and improvements of his own" ("Bibliography," p. 259).
91. See, e.g., Peckham, "Reflections"; Zeller, "New Approach"; Timpanaro, *Freudian Slip;* McLaverty, "Concept"; Greetham, "Textual and Literary Theory" and "[Textual] Criticism"; and Tanselle, "Editorial Problem," "Classical," "Historicism," *Rationale,* and "Textual Criticism."
92. Quoted in Novick, *That Noble Dream,* p. 135.
93. Quoted ibid., p. 254.
94. Whorf, *Language,* p. 16.

Chapter Two, Accommodating Middle English

1. See, e.g., West, *Textual Criticism.*
2. Ullman, *Collucio Salutati,* p. 104.
3. See Timpanaro, *Entstehung,* pp. 32–33, and Ganz, "Lachmann as an Editor." But even in these vernacular studies, it should be noted, the overriding concerns of editorial theory for the author's authoritative text regardless of historical context are apparent. In his dismantling of the *lieder* of the *Niebelungenlied,* for example, as in his treatment of Hartman von Aue's poetry, Lachmann's concern was "the poet's own words" (Ganz, "Lachmann as an Editor," p. 23).
4. See, for example, Speer, "In Defense of Philology," "Wrestling with Change," and "Textual Criticism Redivivus"; Foulet and Speer, *On Editing;* Foulet and Uitti, "Chrétien's 'Laudine'"; Uitti, ed., "Poetics of Textual Criticism"; and Bennett and Runnalls, eds., *The Editor and the Text.*
5. Edwards, "Observations," p. 36.
6. Ibid., p. 35.

7. Thompson, *Shakespeare's Chaucer,* p. 17.

8. For discussion of these and other adaptations of Chaucer during the period, see Berry, "Chaucer Transformed," pp. 1–80, and Bowden, *Eighteenth-Century Modernizations.*

9. See Wright, *A Seventeenth-Century Modernisation,* pp. 14–15.

10. Caxton, *Prologues,* p. 91.

11. See Blake, *Caxton and His World,* pp. 101–6; Hellinga, "Manuscripts"; and Pearsall, *Canterbury Tales,* p. 304.

12. See Hench, "Printer's Copy."

13. Edwards, "Observations," p. 42.

14. Caxton, *Prologues,* p. 37.

15. Ibid., p. 94.

16. Urry, *The Works,* sigs. I4 and M2.

17. Kynaston, *Amorum,* sig. 1r.

18. Ibid., no sig.

19. Ibid., sig. †1r. Chaucer's contemporary Hoccleve was quick to label him the Vergil of English, an epithet that, along with the Homer of English, was often bestowed on Chaucer in the sixteenth and seventeenth centuries. See *Regement of Princes,* 2087–90. For more examples see Miskimin, *Renaissance Chaucer,* pp. 225 and 241.

20. Kynaston, *Amorum,* sig. *r.

21. Ibid., sig †1v.

22. Ibid., sig. A3v.

23. Ibid., no sig.

24. Ibid., sig. †1v.

25. Ibid.

26. Ibid., sig. *3r.

27. Ibid., sig. **r (by Guilford Cartwright) and no sig. (by Edward Foulis).

28. Ritson, ed., *Poems,* p. xiii.

29. Percy, *Reliques,* 1:8.

30. For further discussion of the historical significance of *Amorum Troili et Creseidae,* see Machan, "Kynaston's *Troilus.*"

31. Cf. Edwards, "Observations," p. 46.

32. See Wright, "Dispersion"; Hudson, "Middle English," p. 35; and Frantzen, *Desire for Origins,* pp. 35–45. Matthew Parker, one of the foremost Anglo-Saxonists of the period, was the first Anglican archbishop of Canterbury.

33. The *C* text of *Piers Plowman,* however, was printed in 1813. I base my conclusions on Jackson, Ferguson, and Pantzer, *A Short-Title Catalogue,* and Wing, *Short-title Catalogue.* I want to underscore that the works attributed to Rolle were not by him; none of his English compositions were in fact printed until the modern era (see Watson, *Richard Rolle,* p. 261). After Chaucer, Henry-

son may have been the most frequently reprinted vernacular medieval writer in the British Isles during the early modern period: In addition to the presence of the *Testament of Cresseid* in the various reprints of Thynne's *Workes,* there are eight extant printings of his individual works from the sixteenth and seventeenth centuries, some of which apparently had fairly large press runs, and there is reason to believe others once existed. See Fox, ed., *Poems,* pp. xxix–xxx.

34. On the latter see Hudson, "Middle English," p. 35.

35. See further Johnston, *Enchanted Ground.*

36. Some of Hoccleve's poems did appear in early Chaucer editions. The first independent edition dates to the very end of the eighteenth century, though it is short (113 pages and six poems) and probably had small circulation. See Mason, ed., *Poems.*

37. Manly and Rickert, *Canterbury Tales,* 2: 1–2.

38. Ibid., 2:22–23.

39. Ibid., 2:29–40.

40. Eagleton, *Literary Theory,* pp. 46–47.

41. Allen, *Ethical Poetic.*

42. See, e.g., Graff, *Professing Literature,* pp. 121–79, and Patterson, *Negotiating the Past,* pp. 3–39.

43. Wellek and Warren, *Theory of Literature,* pp. 59–60.

44. This first volume was entitled *Papers of the Bibliographical Society, University of Virginia.*

45. Patterson, *Negotiating the Past,* pp. 108.

46. See the discussion by Parker in *Flawed Texts,* pp. 213–43. For consideration of how poststructuralist theories and textual criticsm can reinforce one another, see Greetham, "Textual and Literary Theory" and "[Textual] Criticism."

47. Hult, "Lancelot's Two Steps," p. 851.

48. Parker, *Flawed Texts,* esp. pp. 1–16.

49. Ibid., pp. 115–79.

50. The controversial synoptic edition of Hans Walter Gabler is in part an attempt to accommodate this quality of *Ulysses.*

51. Hult speaks of "the hidden reason for the philological concentration upon—its basic need for—a unique authorial voice: Lacking that, what can be the justification for the modern critical stance? After all, since the implicit communication model is that of an unmediated dialogue involving an author's voice and a critical reader / listener's response, how can such multiplicity or ambiguity of intention be allowed? The avoidance of textual multiplicity is nothing other than the critic's attempt to safeguard his own imagined status within an otherwise murky situation of literary transmission" ("Lancelot's Two Steps," pp. 852–53).

52. One of the best discussions of recension is still *The A Version.* Also see Kane's "John M. Manly and Edith Rickert."

53. Kane, " 'Good' and 'Bad' Manuscripts," p. 137.

54. Kane, ed., *The A Version,* p. 59, and Kane and Donaldson, eds., *The B Version,* p. 62.

55. Kane, ed., *The A Version,* p. 154. For a rather different analysis of some of the New Critical underpinnings of Kane's formulations, see Patterson, *Negotiating the Past,* pp. 77–113. I do not mean to suggest, of course, that the New Criticism was the sole determinant of Kane's theories. Some of his positions he inherited from R. W. Chambers, who began what would become the Athlone editions and who was much influenced by the rigorous logic that late nineteenth-century classical textual criticism advocated. See Brewer, *"Piers Plowman:* The Poem and the Editors."

56. Kane, *Evidence for Authorship,* p. 24.

57. Kane and Donaldson, eds., *The B Version,* p. 73.

58. Kane, "The 'Z Version'" and " 'Good' and 'Bad' Manuscripts." This position and all of the other positions outlined here are also briefly stated in "The Text."

59. Kane, ed., *The A Version,* p. 37.

60. Kane and Donaldson, eds., *The B Version,* p. 130.

61. Kane, " 'Good' and 'Bad' Manuscripts," p. 139 n. 3. The observation with which Kane is disagreeing is from Pearsall, "Editing Medieval Texts," p. 103. Pearsall, of course, is the author of a book on Lydgate.

62. Kane and Donaldson, eds., *The B Version,* p. 71. Also see pp. 72–73 and 83–84.

63. See Parker, *Flawed Texts,* and Stillinger, *Multiple Authorship.* For a critique of Kane's position on this point, see Brewer, "Textual Principles."

64. Kane and Donaldson, eds., *The B Version,* p. 63; also see p. 128.

65. Kane, ed., *The A Version,* p. 115.

66. Kane and Donaldson, eds., *The B Version,* pp. 51 and 63.

67. Doyle and Parkes, "Production of Copies."

68. Kane, ed., *The A Version,* p. 43.

69. Kane, "John M. Manly and Edith Rickert," p. 220.

70. Kane, "The 'Z Version,'" p. 917 n. 16 and p. 927.

71. E.g., Gates, ed., *Awntyrs off Arthure;* Miskimin, ed., *Susannah;* Hanna, ed., *Awntyrs off Arthure;* Allen, ed., *King Horn.*

72. Tanselle, e.g., maintains that "editing ancient texts and editing modern ones are not simply related fields; they are essentially the same field. The differences between them are in details; the similarities are in fundamentals" ("Classical," p. 68.)

73. Hodgson, ed., *The Cloud of Unknowing,* p. xxiv.

74. D'Ardenne and Dobson, eds., *Seinte Katerine,* p. xli.

75. Furrow, ed., *Comic Poems,* pp. 69–70, 94, and 125.

76. In this regard, there have also been a number of insightful studies of Old English. See, e.g., Foley, "Editing Oral Epic Texts"; Stanley, "Unideal Principles"; and Mitchell, "Dangers of Disguise." As I noted earlier, there have been recent developments in textual criticism of Old French, and medieval Latin has also inspired specialized efforts. See Hödl and Wuttke, eds., *Probleme;* Asztalos, ed., *Theological and Philosophical Texts;* and Lapidge, "Textual Criticism."

77. See Iverson, "Problems"; Woods, "Editing Medieval Commentaries"; and Hamesse, " 'Reportatio.' "

78. Hanna, "Editing Middle English Prose Translations"; Mills, "Theories and Practices"; Johnston, ed., *Editing Early English Drama;* Thompson, "Textual Instability"; Fellows, "Editing Middle English Romances"; Beadle, "The York Cycle"; Boffey, "Middle English Lyrics"; and Edwards, "Middle English Romance."

79. See Greetham, "Models"; Machan, "Editorial Method"; Embree and Urquhart, *"The Simonie"*; Jacobs, "Processes"; Bowers, "Hoccleve's Two Copies"; Brewer, "Textual Principles" and "Authorial vs. Scribal Writing"; and Keiser, *"Ordinatio."*

80. See Pearsall, "Texts, Textual Criticism," "Middle English Romance," "Editing Medieval Texts," and "Chaucer's Meter."

81. Knight, "Textual Variants," pp. 48–49. See the responses of Love, "Sir Walter Greg," and of Trigg, "Politics."

82. Sturges, "Textual Scholarship."

83. See Patterson, *Negotiating the Past,* pp. 77–113.

84. E.g., Cowen, "Metrical Problems"; Jefferson, "Hoccleve Holographs"; Turville-Petre, "Editing *The Wars of Alexander*"; and Duggan, "Alliterative Patterning" and "Shape of the B-Verse."

85. Greetham, "Challenges" and "Normalisation."

86. Duggan, "Alliterative Patterning," pp. 82–83. Duggan's metrical theories are used as an editorial tool in Duggan and Turville-Petre, eds., *The Wars of Alexander.*

87. Greetham, "Challenges," p. 72.

Chapter Three, Editing, History, Discourse

1. E.g., Reid, "Right to Emend"; Hult, *Self-Fulfilling Prophecies,* p. 98; and Pearsall, *Old English,* p. 120, "Texts, Textual Criticism," and "Editing Medieval Texts."

2. Tanselle, *Rationale,* pp. 40 and 92.

3. Mailloux, *Interpretive Conventions,* p. 112.

4. See further Tanselle, "Editorial Problem" and "Recent Editorial Discussion," and McLaverty, "Concept."

5. McGann, "The Text, the Poem."

6. Also see, e.g., McGann, *Critique,* "The Monks and the Giants," and "Shall These Bones Live?"; McLaverty, "Mode of Existence"; McKenzie, *Bibliography;* Oliphant and Bradford, eds., *New Directions;* and Shillingsburg, "Text as Matter."

7. McGann, *Critique,* p. 84. Also see Thorpe, "Aesthetics" and *Principles;* Pizer, "Self-Censorship"; and Barnard, "Bibliographical Context."

8. Parker, *Flawed Texts,* pp. 17–51. Also see Parker, "Text Itself." In important respects, however, Parker should not be linked with McGann and the socialization approach in general. See note 13 below.

9. McGann, *Critique,* p. 121.

10. Shillingsburg, "Inquiry," p. 63. On p. 78 Shillingsburg offers some reservations about this shift.

11. Tanselle, "Historicism," pp. 15–16.

12. Tanselle, *Rationale,* pp. 84–85. Tanselle makes a similar distinction in "Historicism," p. 21, and "Textual Criticism," p. 127.

13. Parker, *Flawed Texts,* p. 221 n. 15.

14. Lass, *On Explaining,* pp. 51–52.

15. Owen, review, p. 186.

16. Patterson, *Negotiating the Past,* pp. 92–93.

17. For a discussion that does just this, see Brewer, "Authorial vs. Scribal Writing." Kidd's critique ("Inquiry") of Gabler's edition of *Ulysses* is occasionally weakened by a similar lack of discrimination among levels of the textual critical hierarchy: However many transcriptional errors Gabler may have made, their existence in no way undermines his overall theory, any more than the total absence of such errors would confirm it.

18. Cf. McGann, "Introduction," pp. 4–5; Hanna, "Problems," pp. 87–88; and Shillingsburg, "Autonomous Author."

19. See Nordloh, "Theory."

20. Greetham, *Textual Scholarship,* p. 335.

21. For a discussion of the spatial-temporal distinction, see Cohen and Jackson, "Notes."

22. Shanks and Tilley, *Social Theory,* p. 28. Also see Shanks and Tilley, *Re-Constructing Archaeology.* The differences between the traditional school of textual criticism and the socialization school are thus in some ways more apparent than real. Mailloux argues, e.g., that "the social model of authorship does not offer a real theoretical alternative to a focus on the individual

author because it is just as 'arbitrary' to draw your boundary of inquiry at the author-publisher collaboration as it is to draw it around only the author itself, for the publishing apparatus is just as enmeshed in material and ideological social formations and networks of power as the author is" ("Rhetorical Politics," p. 130).

23. The following discussion draws particularly on these studies: Collins, *Authorship* and *Profession of Letters;* Altick, *English Common Reader;* Barnes, *Free Trade in Books;* Hepburn, *Author's Empty Purse;* Griest, *Mudie's Circulating Library;* Patten, *Charles Dickens;* and Feltes, *Modes of Production.*

24. Quoted in Patten, *Charles Dickens,* p. 157.

25. Ibid., p. 45.

26. Professional writers existed, of course, before Dickens and his success made the position particularly attractive. Reiman has pointed to a 1755 letter that Samuel Johnson wrote to Chesterfield in which he stated that he had finished his *Dictionary* without the help of patronage: "This letter and the reality it represented marked Johnson as one of the first really distinguished professional authors; by means of his writings, he earned not only his livelihood, but also the friendship of the respectable part of society" ("Gentlemen Authors," p. 101).

27. Griest, *Mudie's Circulating Library,* pp. 36–37.

28. Feltes, *Modes of Production,* p. 7.

29. The account in this paragraph draws on Gatrell, *Hardy the Creator.*

30. Ibid., p. 118.

31. Cf. Howard-Hill, "Theory and Praxis": "The critical editor's text is subjected to the historical influences of its own period. All texts are historical and their transmission—even in critical editions—shows the inevitable interaction of historical agencies. However, acknowledgment of this fact (as I take it to be) does not warrant a conclusion that *all* historical agencies should be regarded as authorities or that, because they are authorities, a critical edition should attempt to record the different interplay of text and sequential transmissional processes" (p. 39).

32. Reiman has argued that since Samuel Johnson was rather less concerned than Cowper about accidentals, modern editors attempt more faithful reproduction of the latter's punctuation than of the former's. See "Gentlemen Authors."

33. Jones, ed., *Letters,* 1:361.

34. In Derridean terms, the issue here is the restriction of the iterability of any utterance. See Grigely, "Textual Event."

35. E.g., Sturges, "Textual Scholarship."

36. See, e.g., Zeller, "New Approach"; Shillingsburg, *Scholarly Editing;* and Reiman, " 'Versioning.' "

37. Grafton, "Introduction," p. 8.
38. Collingwood, *Idea of History,* p. 97.
39. Ibid., p. 218.
40. White, *Metahistory,* p. 30
41. Ibid., p. 21.
42. Ibid., p. 31.
43. Collingwood, *Idea of History,* p. 280.
44. White, *Metahistory,* p. 17. This type of historian is what Gallie calls a Realist, for whom "characteristic human actions are performed and interpreted as expressions of generally accepted institutions, beliefs, routines, and norms, quite as much as of personal feelings and dispositions" (*Philosophy,* p. 78).
45. White, *Metahistory,* pp. 17–18.
46. Foucault, *Archaeology of Knowledge,* pp. 131 and 130.
47. Ibid., p. 28.
48. Ibid., pp. 47–48.
49. Ibid., p. 203.
50. Ibid., p. 117.
51. See further Blake, *Textual Tradition.* Blake argues that the Hengwrt manuscript represents the first attempt to order the *Tales* after Chaucer's death and that it formed the basis for all subsequent orders.
52. See Fisher, "Language Policy."
53. See Doyle and Parkes, "Paleographical Introduction," pp. xix–xlix, and Ramsey, "Paleography."
54. Hawes, *Pastime of Pleasure,* 1373–74.
55. Thynne, *The Workes,* sig. A2v. For information on the early Chaucer editions see Hammond, *Bibliographical Manual.*
56. Ibid., sig. A3r.
57. Speght, *The Works,* sig. A2v.
58. Ibid., sig. A3r.
59. Urry, *The Works,* sig. E2v.
60. Ibid., sig. E2v.

Chapter Four, Authority

1. See Stillinger, *Multiple Authorship,* pp. 121–38 and 157–62.
2. See further Foucault, "What Is an Author?"
3. In the following chapter I take up the issue of the authority of individual Middle English documents.
4. See further Courtenay, *Schools & Scholars.*
5. The definitive discussion of authorship in the Middle Ages is Minnis,

Medieval Theory of Authorship. Also see Minnis and Scott, *Medieval Literary Theory and Criticism.*

6. Chenu, "Auctor."

7. Quoted from Parkes, "Influence," pp. 127–28.

8. See Copeland, *Rhetoric.*

9. Minnis, *Medieval Theory of Authorship,* p. 12.

10. E.g., Zumthor, *Essai,* p. 71.

11. Gower, *Confessio Amantis* 4.2395 ff. and 7.1439–92.

12. Goldschmidt *Medieval Texts,* p. 88, and Chaytor, *Script to Print,* p. 124.

13. Boffey, *Manuscripts,* p. 62.

14. *Secular Lyrics of the XIVth and XVth Centuries,* pp. 21–22 and 41–42.

15. See Woolf, *English Religious Lyrics.*

16. *English Lyrics of the XIIIth Century,* p. 62.

17. Minot, *Poems,* pp. 18 and 26.

18. Even if Girvan's contention (*Ratis Raving,* p. xxii) that the epilogue in which the identification occurs is by a scribe, the naming remains peripheral to the poem.

19. Also see Lydgate's naming of himself in *Guy of Warwick* and *Isopes Fabules.*

20. Audelay, *Poems,* p. 46.

21. Ibid., pp. 49 and 171. Also see pp. 94, 97, 101, 111, 123, 133, 149, 175, 195, 212, 214, and 224.

22. I certainly do not mean to suggest that Gower had no sense of authority, since the *Confessio,* in its blend of English text with Latin glosses, in fact displays a very sophisticated understanding of this concept. Here I am speaking only of Amans-Gower as named narrator, not of Gower as presumptive auctor.

23. Also see Lydgate, *Troy Book* 1.1823–2135, 3.4264–4388, and 5.2198–2203.

24. Lydgate, *Fall of Princes,* 1.4719–27.

25. Lydgate, *Troy Book,* Prologue 69–118, *Saint Albon* 1. 904–7, *The Legend of Seynt Margarete,* 69–74.

26. Audelay, *Poems,* pp. 148 and 145.

27. Chaucer, *Legend of Good Women,* Prologue F.475–97. The *Astrolabe* might be mentioned here as containing a possible comic inversion of this trope: If the translation was allegedly written for little Lowys, then he is to an extent the figure who authorizes the composition. On Lowys as rhetorical device in other ways, see Eisner, "Chaucer as a Technical Writer."

28. Gower, *Confessio Amantis,* Prologue 24–92 and 1.215–29.

29. For discussion of the credibility of Hoccleve's autobiographical passages, see Mitchell, *Thomas Hoccleve,* pp. 1–19; Burrow, "Autobiographical Poetry"; and Greetham, "Self-Referential Artifacts."

30. Rolle, *English Writings,* p. 7. On Rolle's writing career, see Watson,

Richard Rolle. Most of Rolle's struggle for authority takes place not in his English works but in the Latin ones.

31. Bowers, "Hoccleve's Huntington Holographs."

32. Pecock, *The Donet*, pp. 6–7.

33. Usk, *Testament*, p. 123.

34. Scogan, *Moral Balade*, 65–69 and 97–99.

35. E.g., *Fall of Princes* 1.287, 291, 308, and 337.

36. Hoccleve, *Regement of Princes*, 2079–99, and Lydgate, *Troy Book* 3.550–53.

37. Lydgate, *Fall of Princes* 3.3858–61.

38. Huot, *From Song to Book*, pp. 211–41.

39. Hult, *Self-Fulfilling Prophecies*, p. 102.

40. Foucault, "What Is An Author?" p. 271.

41. Gower, *English Works*, 1:37.

42. Gower, *Confessio Amantis*, Prologue 22–55*.

43. See further Yeager, "English"; Pearsall, "Gower's Latin"; and Minnis, *"De vulgari auctoritate."*

44. Elliott, *Chaucer's English*, pp. 173–74. Also see Palomo, "What Chaucer Really Did." Other scholars, of course, have argued just the opposite—that the *Melibee* is in fact a sensitive and artistically successful translation. See, e.g., Schlauch, "Chaucer's Prose." Ellis has suggested that Chaucer began the translation as a "stylistic experiment"—e.g., in patterns of word order—but that he "rapidly became aware of the limitations of a highly wrought surface as a cover for the original's own poor narrative façade, and the experiment lost most of its impetus within 40 lines of starting" (*Patterns*, p. 111). If the *Melibee* was not intended as the parody Elliott and Palomo argue it is but as an exercise in elevated style or as a stylistic experiment, then Chaucer's original contribution is still significant.

45. Reames, "Recent Discovery."

46. Machan, *Techniques of Translation*, pp. 125–31.

47. Pearsall, *Canterbury Tales*, p. 24.

48. Cf. Millett, "Chaucer." On Chaucer's conception of himself as a translator and original writer, see further Machan, "Chaucer as Translator."

49. It is entirely appropriate to speak of the portrait as part of Hoccleve's design for the poem. It survives only in London, British Library MS Harley 4866, where the figure points to line 4996, in London, B.L. MS Royal 17.D.6, where it points to lines 4997–98, and in Philadelphia, Rosenbach MS 1083/30, where the figure—apparently traced from the Harley manuscript as an afterthought, perhaps as recently as the nineteenth-century—points to the space between stanzas 712 and 713. The Royal picture, unlike those in Harley and Rosenbach, is not framed and gives a full frontal view of the poet standing. It

is nonetheless latent with some of the symbolic potential I note in Harley, for the Royal picture does show Chaucer pointing to the lines referring to him. Traces of the portrait appear in London, B.L. MS Harley 4826. The relevant leaf has been excised from London, B.L. MS Arundel 38, and the pertinent five stanzas are missing from Cambridge, University Library MS Gg.6.17; the Arundel manuscript suggests the picture had been present and was the reason the page was excised, and the Cambridge manuscript that something similar to this happened to the exemplar of the manuscript. Six manuscripts that never contained the picture nonetheless do have marginal notes referring to it. Thus, in the words of Brusendorff, though the majority of *Regement* manuscripts lacks the portrait, it is "beyond doubt that Hoccleve in the copies of his poem made under his direct supervision caused a portrait of Chaucer to be inserted here" (*Chaucer Tradition,* p. 14). Also see Mitchell, *Thomas Hoccleve,* pp. 110–15, and Anderson, *Sixty Bokes,* pp. 113–15.

50. Perhaps the "typical" author portrait of the fifteenth century was that of a writer presenting his book to a patron; such pictures exist, e.g., for both Hoccleve and Lydgate. See Seymour, "Manuscript Portraits." And marginal illustrations of Middle English works were certainly not unknown in the fifteenth century. See Scott, "Illustrations." The closest parallel to the marginal Chaucer illustration in the *Regement* may be the picture of Chaucer beside the *Tale of Melibee* in the Ellesmere manuscript of the *Canterbury Tales,* though the larger design of this manuscript indicates that the Chaucer depicted there is not so much the historical poet as the fictional pilgrim.

51. For a discussion of this function of the Chaucer portrait, see McGregor, "Iconography."

52. This is not to say, of course, that Lydgate had no theory of poetics. For an attempt to define his theory, see Ebin, *Illuminator,* pp. 19–48.

53. These references occur at lines 225, 427, 761, 1507, 1541, 1547, 1874, 1995, 2563, 2599, 2809, 3005, 3015, 3034, 3171, 3188, 3520, 3831, 3839, 3848, 3862, 4193, 4452, 4465, 4554, and 4622. Similar postcaesura rhyme-motivated references to authors and books frequently occur in Lydgate's *Saint Albon:* 1.38, 1.48, 1.619, 1.706, 1.708, 1.743, 1.818, 2.159, 2.1015, 2.1192, 2.1248, 2.1300, 2.1313, 2.1547, 3.128, 3.139, 3.325, 3.696. At 2.1316 an entire line is devoted to such a reference.

54. The relevant lines are 1059, 1266, 1660, 1679, 1716, 2144, 2612, 4235.

55. The other passages are at lines 199, 213, 307, 582, 874, 880, 1002, 1003, 1505, 1637, 2887, 3154, 3197, 4232, 4426, 4437, and 4611.

56. Other longer, though still self-contained, metatextual passages occur at lines 293, 1270, 3195, 3201, 3510, 3537, 3971, and 4541.

57. For a useful discussion, see the notes in Benson, ed., *Riverside Chaucer,* p. 1028.

58. Such beliefs seem to reflect Lydgate's view of the writing and reading of poetry, which he apparently saw as unambiguously moral activities. In Ebin's analysis: "Unlike Chaucer, who repeatedly questions the relation between appearance and reality, experience and authority in his writing and the limitations the poet's craft imposes on his effort to create a truthful vision, Lydgate neither doubts the inherent truthfulness of good poetry, nor does he question the master poet's intentions" (*Illuminator*, p. 32). Also see the rest of her discussion on pp. 32–39 and her comments in *John Lydgate*, pp. 16 and 42.

59. See Pearsall, *John Lydgate*, pp. 155–56, and Ebin, *John Lydgate*, pp. 56–57.

60. For discussion of Lydgate's treatment of metatextual topics in his minor poems and *Fall of Princes*, see Machan, "Textual Authority." For further consideration of the fifteenth-century response to Chaucer's authority and to the concept of literary authority in general, see Lerer, *Chaucer and His Readers*.

61. Spearing, *Medieval to Renaissance*, p. 34.

62. My discussion supports the arguments that assert that the order of the fables in the Bassandyne print is Henryson's. See Fox, *Poems*, pp. lxxv–lxxxi. A detailed discussion of the relevant issues lies outside the scope of my argument, though I would like to note that the "literary" evidence marshaled in support of the textual evidence of Bassandyne does not at all seem to me inadmissable or beside the point; indeed, such evidence has long been used in arguments about the intended order of the *Canterbury Tales*. The agreement of this evidence seems formidable: It is the Bassandyne order in which Roerecke has demonstrated thematic coherence and symmetrical patterning ("Integrity"), Gopen the aesthetic complexity of three "simultaneously functional symmetries" ("Essential Seriousness"), and Spearing an artful utilization of the sovereign midpoint. As Spearing notes, "It seems unlikely that an organization so ingenious in itself and so appropriate to the meaning of the central tale and of the whole series could have occurred by chance" ("Central and Displaced Sovereignty," p. 256). While it is possible that a later redactor and not Henyrson himself is responsible for the order, I would argue that such a redactor would had to have had a more sophisticated understanding of authorship and literary structure than Henryson. And then even if this were the case, this understanding remains a significant statement of vernacular medieval aesthetics.

63. On Aesop as an auctor, see Curtius, *European Literature*, pp. 49–50, and Minnis, *Medieval Theory of Authorship*, p. 161.

64. In Caxton's translation of Rinuccio's *Life*, e.g., Aesop "had a grete hede / large vysage / longe Iowes / sharp eyen / a short necke / corbe backed / grete bely / grete legges / and large feet" (Caxton, *Caxton's Aesop*, p. 27).

65. See *Beowulf*, 426–32, and *Sir Gawain*, 343–47.

66. In the *Inferno*, in what is perhaps the locus classicus of confrontations

between vernacular writers and auctores, Dante also demands the identity of the figure he meets. But there it is clear that Dante, unlike Henryson, does not in fact recognize the figure. It also may be noted that though Dante, like Henryson, is deferential to his auctor, he never challenges and overrules him the way the Scots poet does; when Vergil leaves Dante in the Earthly Paradise, it is because the Latin poet himself recognizes the limitations of his knowledge. See *Inferno* 1.61–87 and *Purgatorio* 27.127–43. Similarly, in the prologue to his translation of Mapheus Vegius's thirteenth book of the *Aeneid,* Gavin Douglas asks about the identity of the auctor he meets because he does not know who he is—"I saw ȝou nevir ayr." This meeting, however, is presented comically—Vegius beats the Scots poet "twenty rowtis apoun [his] rigging" because of Douglas's reluctance to translate the thirteenth book—though Douglas is nonetheless deferential to his auctor and acts according to his wishes.

67. Critics have interpreted Henryson's rendition of "The Lion and the Mouse" in a variety of ways, though they all agree on the political nature of the piece. See, for example, McDiarmid *Robert Henryson,* pp. 15–16; Spearing, "Central and Displaced Sovereignty," pp. 254–56; Fox, "Coherence," p. 277; Benson, "Moral Henryson," p. 227; and Gopen, ed., *Moral Fables,* p. 22.

68. So Kindrick asserts in *Robert Henryson,* p. 105.

69. See Green, *Poets and Princepleasers.*

70. See further Machan, "Robert Henryson."

71. See *Troilus and Criseyde* 1.740–42.

72. Minnis, *"De vulgari auctoritate,"* p. 62.

73. E.g., Douglas's *Palice of Honour,* 899–924.

Chapter Five, Work and Text

1. *Secular Lyrics of the XIVth and XVth Centuries,* p. 101. The designation "punctuation poem" is Robbins's, who offers two other examples on pp. 101–2.

2. See *OED,* s.v. *Ivy.* Though the spelling "iwen" is recorded in the fifteenth century, the most common pronunciation must still have been [ivi] or [ive], for spellings with *v* and *f* are by far the most common. In Scots dialects Old English [w] could develop into [v], but the typical spelling would then be with *v,* and this carol, in any case, shows no trace of Scots.

3. *The Early English Carols,* p. 84.

4. Shillingsburg, *Scholarly Editing,* pp. 173 and 49.

5. Already in the Middle Ages this displacement had begun to take place, as writers of the thirteenth century placed increasing influence on the contribution of the human auctores to the Bible. See Minnis, *Medieval Theory of Authorship,* pp. 118–59.

6. See Elsky, *Authorizing Words,* pp. 110–46. And cf. Lennard's contention that an interest in spatialization did not originate in printed texts but was facilitated by them (*But I Digress,* pp. 75–77). More generally see Watt, *Cheap Print,* and Hindman, ed., *Printing the Written Word.*

7. See Greetham, *Textual Scholarship,* pp. 77–151, and Dooley, *Author and Printer.*

8. *Patrologia Latina* 210, 579. In the following paragraphs I am of course abstracting what might be regarded as the official positions, which dominated authorized views in one form or another from Bede's typological reading of English history through scholasticism. Valuable (though differing) discussions of the metaphoric and cognitive uses of the image of the book in the Middle Ages are Curtius, *European Literature,* pp. 302–47, and Gellrich, *Idea of the Book.* These official views were challenged or subverted by more than one writer. In Irvine's opinion, for example, the *House of Fame* stresses the fact that all writing is in fact rewriting in order to foreground disruptively the textuality of authority and history and thereby deconstruct oppositions like fiction and history, or truth and falsehood. See "Medieval Grammatical Theory." It should go without saying that this "prelinguistic truth" was culturally and socially determined.

9. See further Colish, *Mirror of Language.*

10. Minnis, *Medieval Theory of Authorship,* p. 21.

11. Carruthers, *Book of Memory,* p. 190.

12. Morse, *Truth and Convention,* p. 104. An early example of these attitudes and procedures is Bede's incorporation of Sulpicius Severus's *Life of St. Martin* into his own *Life of St. Cuthbert,* which he utilized in book 4 of the *Ecclesiastical History.* Since St. Martin was the patron saint of the Merovingians, it could be presumed that the life of Cuthbert, the patron saint of Northumbria, would have many of the same significant events; the fact that they were not recorded simply attested to lapses in documentation.

13. See Clanchy, *From Memory,* and Morse, *Truth and Convention,* p. 104.

14. Carruthers, *Book of Memory,* pp. 189 ff. A still useful, if outdated, discussion is Lewis, "Genesis."

15. See further Copeland, *Rhetoric,* pp. 72 ff.

16. Carruthers, *Book of Memory,* pp. 164 and 169. On the psychological benefits of reading, see further Allen, *Ethical Poetic.* On the physiological benefits see Olson, *Literature as Recreation.*

17. Lydgate, *Minor Poems,* 1:35–43.

18. See Saenger and Heinlen, "Incunable Description."

19. Also see Morse, *Truth and Convention,* p. 32.

20. At least until the close of the fourteenth century, French also was more culturally prestigious than English.

21. Dante, *De vulgari eloquentia,* pp. 420–21.
22. Curtius, *European Literature,* p. 42.
23. See Saenger, "Silent Reading," and Kittay, "Utterance Unmoored."
24. Langland, *Piers Plowman,* B Prol. 128–32, 13.71–73, 3.332, and 5.415–21.
25. The colophon of Cambridge, University Library MS Ii.4.9, which contains Rolle's *Form of Living,* can also be mentioned here: "Translat out of Northarn tunge into Sutherne that it schulde be the bettir vnderstondyn of men that be of the selve countre" (Parkes and Beadle, eds., *Poetical Works,* 3:55).
26. See Thomson, ed., *An Edition.* Some grammars offer discussions of syntax that imply the word order of Middle English rather than Latin, though the pedagogical and descriptive focus is nonetheless on the latter. See Bland, *Teaching of Grammar.* Well through the Renaissance vernacular grammars in general were largely dependent on the categories of Latin, and it might be argued that English was not analyzed as a grammatically distinctive language until the twentieth century.
27. Petrarch, *Letters,* p. 244.
28. Fisher, Richardson, and Fisher, *Chancery English,* pp. xv–xvi.
29. On the characteristics of standardization and a standard language, see Hudson, *Sociolinguistics,* pp. 32–34, and James Milroy and Lesley Milroy, *Authority in Language.*
30. Hudson, *Premature Reformation,* p. 31. Also see Aston, "Wyclif and the Vernacular."
31. Pecock, *The Repressor,* p. 128, and *The Reule of Crysten Religioun,* pp. 17–22.
32. Usk, *The Testament of Love,* p. 2, and Lydgate, *Troy Book,* Prol. 111–18.
33. *Selections from English Wycliffite Writings,* pp. 69–71.
34. Ramus, *The Logike,* pp. 15–16.
35. Elton, *Tudor Constitution,* pp. 402–5.
36. See further Machan, "Editing, Orality."
37. See Minnis and Machan, "The *Boece* as Late-Medieval Translation."
38. Counts of the items in the manuscript in fact vary slightly, since some texts can stand alone or be considered part of adjoining ones.
39. For more information see Ker, ed., *Facsimile,* and Jones, "Harley Lyrics," pp. 26–110.
40. The standard edition of the religious and secular poems is Brook, ed., *The Harley Lyrics.* In Brook's edition I would designate the following poems as having the balladlike rhyme scheme: 5, 7, 9, 10, 11, 12, 13, 14, 15, 16, 17, 20, 27. I use Brook's titles throughout my discussion. All of the poems with which I am concerned are in the hand of the same scribe.
41. In Brook's edition I regard these as the poems numbered 1, 2, 3, 4, 6, 8,

18, 19, 21, 22, 23, 24, 25, 26, 28, 29, 30, 31, and 32. Distinction between the two forms (as in poems 1, 3, and 23) is not absolute.

42. I should note that the decisions about layout with which I am here concerned may have been made not by the scribe of Harley 2253 but by an editor or even by the scribe of the exemplar from which he was working. The differences are immaterial in a consideration of what layout reveals about text.

43. See, e.g., Revard, *"Gilote et Johane,"* which uses several Anglo-Norman texts to argue that the manuscript "is not a miscellany but a *miroir,* not merely assembled but structured, demonstrat[ing] both a principled *selection* of items and a principled *arrangement* of them" (p. 127). A more general account of how the poems are intentionally laid out in complementary ways is Jones, "Harley Lyrics," pp. 111–94. For an attempt at a reader-response approach to the manuscript, see Duncan, "Middle English Poems." Duncan maintains that "the poetics of these lyrics is intimately tied to their physical nature, and perhaps even to the question of physicality itself" (p. 23).

44. A similar situation obtains on f. 67r for *A Wayle Whyt ase Whalles Bon.*

45. This is true of Brook's edition and the following anthologies, each of which has a few of the Harley lyrics: Brown, ed., *English Lyrics of the XIIIth Century;* Davies, ed., *Medieval English Lyrics;* Luria and Hoffman, eds., *Middle English Lyrics;* and Wilhelm, ed., *Lyrics of the Middle Ages.*

46. Brook, ed., *The Harley Lyrics,* p. 18.

47. Numbers 24, 25, and 26 in Brook's edition. Brown prints the first two in long lines but does not include the third at all. Davies divides the first two into short lines but does not include the third, Hoffman divides all three into short lines, and Wilhelm includes none of the three.

48. These examples are, respectively, lines 21–24 of *De Clerico et Puella* and lines 1–4 of *When þe Nyhtegale Singes.* Since these three poems appear one after the other on f. 80v and f. 81r, they (and the apparent alteration of their rhyme schemes) may have originated together.

49. For *An Autumn Song* the procedure was to write the first six lines of the stanza as editors have printed them but then to write what modern editions show as the last four lines in two long ones. The scribe regularly had to double the latter back in the margin in order to fit them on the page. The meter of this poem is ambiguous, since the rhyme scheme (*a a b a a b c b c b*) embodies elements of both forms, while the layout suggests the couplet form alone.

50. An example like Harley 2253 would seem to counter or at least qualify McGann's assertion that "all poetry, even in its most traditional forms, asks the reader to decipher the text in spatial as well as linear terms. Stanzaic and generic forms, rhyme schemes, metrical orders: all of these deploy spatial functions in scripted texts, as their own roots in oral poetry's 'visual' arts of memory should remind us" (*Textual Condition,* p. 113). The reader may well necessarily

decipher the spatial arrangement of Harley 2253, but part of the decipered message is that the spatial arrangement does not require deciphering.

51. Kottler, "Chaucer's *Boece.*" For more discussion of the following points see Machan and Minnis, *The Boece.*

52. Dedeck-Héry, "Manuscripts." Since Dedeck-Héry's article, five more manuscripts have been identified.

53. Machan, *Techniques of Translation,* pp. 125–31.

54. These authorities are Oxford, Bodleian Library MS Bodley 797; London, B. L. MS Harley 2421; Caxton, [*Boece*]; and Thynne, *The Workes.* Bodley 797 is the manuscript in which "quod I" and "quod she" are eliminated.

55. Cambridge, University Library MS Ii.3.21.

56. Cambridge, University Library MS Ii.1.38; London, B.L. MS Add. 16165; Oxford, Bodleian Library MS Bodley 797.

57. London, B.L. MS Harley 2421.

58. The authorities with the extended headings are: London B.L. MS Harley 2421; Cambridge, Pembroke College MS 215; Caxton, [*Boece*], and Thynne, *The Workes.* The complete Latin and English texts are intercalcated in Cambridge, University Library MS Ii.3.21. Columbia, University of Missouri MS Fragmenta manuscripta no. 150, containing only a fragment of Latin and some of the corresponding English from book 2, presumably also once had both texts in their entirety.

59. Pearsall, *John Lydgate,* p. 251.

60. Boffey, *Manuscripts* and "Middle English Lyrics."

61. And Chaucer's poetry, of course, was not always thus recognized. In the mid-fifteenth century, e.g., three stanzas of the *Troilus* (3.302–22) were adapted without acknowledgment in an anonymous seven-stanza poem on loose talk in Cambridge, University Library MS Ff.1.6. See *Odd Texts of Chaucer's Minor Poems,* part 2, pp. xi–xii.

62. See *Canterbury Tales* 2.57–76 and 10.1086–88, and the Prologue to the *Legend of Good Women* G.405–20. Pecock catalogs his works several times, e.g., *The Donet,* pp. 1–3.

63. Also see Mannyng's remarks at the end of his account of the tenth commandment (2981–87).

64. Kempe, *The Book of Margery Kempe,* pp. 12 and 38, and Usk, *Testament of Love,* pp. 3 and 101–6.

65. Burrow, "Hoccleve's *Series,*" p. 260. See further Burrow, "The Poet and the Book," and Machan, "Textual Authority." An exception that tests and confirms the rule I have suggested here is *The Pilgrim's Tale* as it appears in the *Courte of Venus.* When the priest mentions the "blak flet of norwey," the narrator notes that the priest would not explain the allusion but bade him "to reyd the 'romant of the rose,' / the thred leafe, Iust from the end / to the

secund page" (Furnivall and Kingsley, eds., *Animadversions,* p. 97). Though the specificity here seems to refer to a particular copy of the *Roman,* even it is undermined when shortly after this passage the poet in fact quotes six stanzas from Chaucer's translation.

66. E.g., Mannyng, *Handlyng Synne,* Kempe, *The Book of Margery Kempe* (pp. 220–21), and Pecock, *The Reule of Crysten Religioun* (pp. 13–16).

67. Cf. Chaytor, *From Script,* p. 82.

68. E.g., Dahood, "Coloured Initials." On the role of illumination as a mnemonic aid, see Carruthers, *Book of Memory,* pp. 221–57.

69. A number of recent studies have significantly advanced understanding of manuscript context and its relation to individual texts. See, e.g., Boffey, *Manuscripts;* Thompson, *Robert Thornton;* Griffiths and Pearsall, eds., *Book Production;* and Pearsall, ed., *Vernon Manuscript.*

70. Hanna, "Booklets," pp. 102–3.

71. Glasscoe, "Visions and Revisions," and Holbrook, "Margery Kempe."

72. See Edwards, "Middle English Romance," and Pearsall, "Texts, Textual Criticism," "Middle English Romance," and "Editing Medieval Texts."

73. Keiser, "*Ordinatio,*" and Lerer, "Rewriting Chaucer."

74. Edwards, "Manuscripts and Texts."

75. See, e.g., Hamel, "Scribal Self-Corrections"; Jacobs, "Processes"; and Kane, ed., *The 'A' Version,* pp. 115–72. Cf. Machan, "Late Middle English Texts."

76. The *pecia* system was never as formal and well established in Oxford as in Paris, though the copying of booklets from centrally held exemplars exerted similar pressure in textual transmission. See Parkes, "Book Provision."

77. Gillespie, "Vernacular Books," p. 317.

78. Trithemius, *In Praise of Scribes,* pp. 61 and 63. The translation is Behrendt's.

79. See Hudson, ed., *English Wycliffite Sermons,* 1:189–202, and Sargent, *James Grenehalgh.*

80. For the formal recognition of book artisans, see Christianson, *Directory,* p. 22. On the professional workings of scribes in late-medieval London, see further Christianson, *Memorials* and "Community," and Edwards and Pearsall, "Manuscripts." On monastic hiring of professional scribes, see Doyle, "Book Production," and on the production of texts in standardized formatting, see Meale, "Patrons," p. 220.

81. For examples and discussion, see de Roover, "The Scriptorium."

82. Cheney, *Notaries Public,* p. 75.

83. Hanna, "Scribe of Huntington HM 114."

84. Martial, *Epigrams,* 1:115. The translation is Ker's. Also see Cicero, Epistola III.5.

85. *Patrologia Latina* 22, 671.

86. See further Wattenbach, *Scriftwesen,* pp. 317–44. For examples from the later Middle Ages, see Bühler, *Fifteenth-Century Book,* pp. 96–97.

87. Quoted in Minnis and Scott, eds., *Medieval Literary Theory and Criticism,* pp. 268–69. Also see de Bury, *The Philobiblon,* pp. 26–27.

88. Trithemius, *In Praise of Scribes,* p. 69. The translation is Behrendt's.

89. E.g., Sandys, *History,* 1:624. For Middle English texts, the conception has been stated most forcefully and articulately in the various works of Kane.

90. Doyle and Parkes, "Production."

91. Shonk, "Study." Also see the role of Robert Thornton in the manuscripts he copied as discussed by Keiser, "Lincoln Cathedral Library MS. 91," and Thompson, *Robert Thornton,* pp. 35–55.

92. See *The Book of Margery Kempe,* pp. 3–6. Also see Hirsh, "Author and Scribe."

93. The passage, which occurs in London, B.L. MS Harley 7333, is quoted from Greenberg, "John Shirley," p. 377n. Such "collaboration" might also be unintentional. Kane sees the *G* Prologue to the *Legend of Good Women,* e.g., as a fortuitous combination of Chaucer's revisions and scribal alterations ("The Text of *The Legend of Good Women*"). A much more limited kind of collaboration is scribal production of various "rolling revisions" of a work in progress. See Hanna, "Authorial Versions."

94. Indeed, I am aware of only one other passage—from Henry Daniel's *Liber uricrisiarum*—suggesting special concern with the words of a Middle English text subject to manuscript transmission. See Hanna, "Presenting Chaucer," p. 19.

95. Cf. Johnson's discussion of medieval women writers' use of the trope of scribal reference as a way of legitimizing their work ("Trope").

96. Hoccleve, *Regement of Princes,* 1779–1862.

97. A comparable example might be the copy of *Ihesu for thy Holy Name* (*IMEV* 1703) in Oxford, Bodleian Library MS Douce 54, where the lyric is accompanied by a brief commentary that explains that the thirty-three words of the poem (including the colophon "Swere Ihesu Amen") represent the thirty-three years of Christ's life. See Hirsh, "Fifteenth-Century." But also compare a 1425 court case in which an objection was raised over the variant spellings Banester and Benester for the same place; in overruling the objection, the judge noted that pronunciation varied throughout England and that one " 'is just as good as the other' " (Ballard, *Manual,* p. 105).

98. Quoted in *The Works of David Lindsay,* p. 403.

Chapter Six, Middle English Textual Criticism

1. See Zeller, "New Approach," and Reiman, " 'Versioning.' "

2. Minnis and I have attempted just such a recovery in *The Boece.*

3. MS Add. 10340 is significantly more elaborate in this regard.

4. These are Caxton's edition, London, B.L. MS Harley 2421, Aberystwyth, National Library of Wales MS Peniarth 393D, and Cambridge, University Library MS Ii.1.38. The *Boece* text in the latter is now bound with the Latin orations of Demosthenes by Leonardus Aretinus, though this is a separate and unrelated manuscript of the fifteenth century. Within this grouping there is still significant variation in areas that affect determination of the work. Harley 2421, e.g., is a small volume, neatly but casually written and containing a unique system of rubrication that numbers the proses and meters of each book consecutively. The bigger Peniarth 393D, however, is the more professional production and contains illuminations, paragraph markings, and the placement in banners of the rubrics and the attributions "Boece" and "Philosophie."

5. An adaptation of reader-response criticism might help in defining the *res* that manuscripts project. See the discussion of reader-response criticism and editing in Mailloux, *Interpretive Conventions,* pp. 93–125.

6. See Landow, *Hypertext.* The examples I mention are discussed, respectively, on pp. 96–100 and 113–19. Also see McGann's discussion of the Rossetti archive in *Textual Condition,* pp. 19–47.

7. Even as I write, hypertext editions of the sort I describe are being planned. On the e-mail Chaucernet, for instance, Kellogg relayed an announcement of the formation of the Society for Early English and Norse Electronic Texts, which "will combine the full capacities of computer technology with the highest standards of traditional scholarly editing to publish machine-readable texts with reliable introductory materials, annotations, and apparatus." See Kellogg, "E-Text Society."

8. E.g., Nichols, guest ed., "New Philology," and Brownlee, et al., eds., *New Medievalism.*

BIBLIOGRAPHY

Primary Works

Ashby, George. *George Ashby's Poems*. Ed. Mary Bateson. EETS e.s. 76. London: Kegan Paul, 1899.

Audelay, John. *The Poems of John Audelay*. Ed. Ella Keats Whiting. EETS o.s. 184. London: Oxford Univ. Press, 1931.

Bokenahm, Osbern. *Mappula Angliae*. Ed. Carl Horstmann. *Englische Studien* 10 (1887): 1–34.

Caxton, William. *Caxton's Aesop*. Ed. R. T. Lenaghan. Cambridge: Harvard Univ. Press, 1967.

———. *The Prologues and Epilogues of William Caxton*. Ed. W. J. B. Crotch. 1928. Rpt. New York: Burt Franklin, 1971.

Chaucer, Geoffrey. *The Riverside Chaucer*. Ed. Larry D. Benson. 3d. ed. Boston: Houghton Mifflin, 1987.

The Cloud of Unknowing and the Book of Privy Counselling. Ed. Phyllis Hodgson. EETS o.s. 218. Oxford: Oxford Univ. Press, 1944.

The Court of Sapience. Ed. E. Ruth Harvey. Toronto: Univ. of Toronto Press, 1984.

Douglas, Gavin. *Selections from Gavin Douglas*. Ed. David F. C. Coldwell. Oxford: Clarendon Press, 1964.

———. *The Shorter Poems of Gavin Douglas*. Ed. Priscilla J. Bawcutt. STS 4th ser., 3. Edinburgh: William Blackwood, 1967.

———. *Threttene Buik of Eneados*. In *Maphaeus Vegius and His Thirteenth Book of the Aeneid*. Ed. Anne Cox Brinton. Stanford: Stanford Univ. Press, 1930.

Dunbar, William. *The Poems of William Dunbar*. Ed. James Kinsley. Oxford: Oxford Univ. Press, 1979.

The Early English Carols. Ed. Richard Leighton Greene. 2d. ed. Oxford: Clarendon Press, 1977.

English Lyrics of the XIIIth Century. Ed. Carleton Brown. Oxford: Clarendon Press, 1932.

Gower, John. *The English Works of John Gower*. Ed. G. C. Macaulay. EETS e.s. 81. 2 vols. London: Kegan Paul, 1900.

Handlyng Synne. Ed. Idelle Sullens. Binghamton, N.Y.: Medieval and Renaissance Texts and Studies, 1983.

The Harley Lyrics: The Middle English Lyrics of MS. Harley 2253. Ed. G. L. Brook. 4th ed. Manchester: Manchester Univ. Press, 1968.

Hawes, Stephen. *The Pastime of Pleasure.* Ed. William Edward Mead. EETS o.s. 173. London: Oxford Univ. Press, 1928.

Henryson, Robert. *The Poems of Robert Henryson.* Ed. Denton Fox. Oxford: Clarendon Press, 1981.

Hoccleve, Thomas. *Hoccleve's Works: The Minor Poems.* Ed. Frederick J. Furnivall and I. Gollancz. Rev. Jerome Mitchell and A. I. Doyle. EETS e.s. 61 and 73. Oxford: Oxford Univ. Press, 1970.

——— . *A New Ploughman's Tale.* Ed. Arthur Beatty. Chaucer Society Publications, 2d ser., 34. London: Kegan Paul, 1902.

——— . *The Regement of Princes.* Ed. Frederick J. Furnivall. EETS e.s. 72. London: Kegan Paul, 1897.

James I. *The Kingis Quair.* Ed. John Norton-Smith. Oxford: Clarendon Press, 1971.

Kempe, Margery. *The Book of Margery Kempe.* Ed. Sanford Brown Meech. EETS o.s. 212. London: Oxford Univ. Press, 1940.

Langland, William. *Piers Plowman by William Langland: An Edition of the C-Text.* Ed. Derek Pearsall. Berkeley and Los Angeles: Univ. of California Press, 1979.

——— . *Piers Plowman: The A Version.* Ed. George Kane. Rev. ed. Berkeley and Los Angeles: Univ. of California Press, 1988.

——— . *Piers Plowman: The B Version.* Ed. George Kane and E. Talbot Donaldson. Rev. ed. Berkeley and Los Angeles: Univ. of California Press, 1988.

Lydgate, John. *Lydgate's Fall of Princes.* Ed. Henry Bergen. EETS e.s. 121, 122, 123, 124. 4 vols. London: Oxford Univ. Press, 1924–27.

——— . *Lydgate's Siege of Thebes.* Ed. Axel Erdmann. EETS e.s. 108. 1911. Rpt. London: Oxford Univ. Press, 1960.

——— . *Lydgate's Troy Book.* Ed. Henry Bergen. EETS e.s. 97, 103, 106, 126. 4 vols. London: Kegan Paul, 1906, 1908, 1910, 1935.

——— . *The Minor Poems.* Ed. Henry W. MacCracken. EETS e.s. 107 and o.s. 192. 1911 and 1934. 2 vols. Rpt. Oxford: Oxford Univ. Press, 1961, 1962.

——— . *Saint Albon and Saint Amphibalus.* Ed. George F. Reinecke. New York: Garland, 1985.

Minot, Laurence. *Poems Written Anno MCCCLII.* Ed. Joseph Ritson. London: J. H. Burn, 1825.

"Morte Arthure": A Critical Edition. Ed. Mary Hamel. New York: Garland, 1984.

Mum and the Sothsegger. Ed. Mabel Day and Robert Steele. EETS o.s. 199. London: Oxford Univ. Press, 1936.

Odd Texts of Chaucer's Minor Poems. Ed. Frederick J. Furnivall. Chaucer Society, 1st ser. 23 and 60. 1871. Rpt. Oxford: Oxford Univ. Press, 1934.

Pearl. Ed. E. V. Gordon. Oxford: Clarendon Press, 1953.

Pecock, Reginald. *The Donet.* Ed. Elsie Vaughan Hitchcock. EETS o.s. 156. London: Oxford Univ. Press, 1921.

———. *The Repressor of Over Much Blaming of the Clergy.* Ed. Churchill Babington. Rolls Series 19. 2 vols. London: Longman, 1860.

———. *The Reule of Crysten Religioun.* Ed. William Cabell Greet. EETS o.s. 171. London: Oxford Univ. Press, 1927.

Ratis Raving and Other Early Scots Poems on Morals. Ed. R. Girvan. STS, 3d ser., 11. Edinburgh: William Blackwood, 1939.

Rolle, Richard. *English Writings of Richard Rolle, Hermit of Hampole.* Ed. Hope Emily Allen. 1931. Rpt. Oxford: Clarendon Press, 1963.

Scogan, Henry. *A Moral Balade.* In *Chaucerian and Other Pieces.* Vol. 7 of *Complete Works of Geoffrey Chaucer.* Ed. W. W. Skeat. Oxford: Oxford Univ. Press, 1897.

Secular Lyrics of the XIVth and XVth Centuries. Ed. Rossell Hope Robbins. Oxford: Clarendon Press, 1952.

Seinte Katerine. Ed. S. R. T. O. d'Ardenne and E. J. Dobson. EETS s.s. 7. Oxford: Oxford Univ. Press, 1981.

Selections from English Wycliffite Writings. Ed. Anne Hudson. Cambridge: Cambridge Univ. Press, 1978.

Sir Gawain and the Green Knight. Ed. J. R. R. Tolkien and E. V. Gordon. 2d ed. Rev. Norman Davis. Oxford: Oxford Univ. Press, 1967.

Skelton, John. *The Complete English Poems.* Ed. John Scattergood. Harmondsworth: Penguin, 1983.

Ten Fifteenth-Century Comic Poems. Ed. Melissa M. Furrow. New York: Garland, 1985.

Usk, Thomas. *Testament of Love.* In *Chaucerian and Other Pieces.* Vol. 7 of *Complete Works of Geoffrey Chaucer.* Ed. W. W. Skeat. Oxford: Oxford Univ. Press, 1897.

Walton, John. *Boethius: De consolatione philosophiae.* Ed. Mark Science. EETS o.s. 170. London: Oxford Univ. Press, 1927.

The Wars of Alexander. Ed. Hoyt N. Duggan and Thorlac Turville-Petre. EETS s.s. 10. Oxford: Oxford Univ. Press, 1989.

The Works of David Lindsay of the Mount 1490–1555. Ed. Douglas Hamer. STS 3d ser., 1. 4 vols. Edinburgh: William Blackwood, 1931.

Secondary Works

Aarsleff, Hans. "Scholarship and Ideology: Joseph Bedier's Critique of Romantic Medievalism." In McGann, ed., *Historical Studies and Literary Criticism,* pp. 93–113.

Allen, Judson Boyce. *The Ethical Poetic of the Later Middle Ages: A Decorum of Convenient Distinction.* Toronto: Univ. of Toronto Press, 1982.

Allen, Rosamund, ed. *King Horn: An Edition based on Cambridge University Library MS Gg.4.27 (2).* New York: Garland, 1984.

Altick, Richard D. *The English Common Reader: A Social History of the Mass Reading Public 1800–1900.* Chicago: Univ. of Chicago Press, 1957.

Anderson, David. *Sixty Bokes Olde and Newe.* Knoxville: New Chaucer Society, 1986.

Aston, Margaret. "Wyclif and the Vernacular." In *From Ockham to Wyclif,* ed. Anne Hudson and Michael Wilks, pp. 281–330. Studies in Church History, Subsidia 5. Oxford: Blackwell, 1987.

Asztalos, Monika, ed. *The Editing of Theological and Philosophical Texts from the Middle Ages.* Stockholm: Almqvist and Wiksell, 1986.

Ballard, W. C. *A Manual of Year Book Studies.* Cambridge: Cambridge Univ. Press, 1925.

Barnard, John. "Bibliographical Context and the Critic." *Text* 3 (1987): 47–54.

Barnes, James J. *Free Trade in Books: A Study of the London Book Trade since 1800.* Oxford: Clarendon Press, 1964.

Barthes, Roland. *Le Bruissement de la langue.* Paris: Seuil, 1984.

Bédier, Joseph. "De L'Édition princeps de la *Chanson de Roland* aux éditions les plus récentes . . . premier article." *Romania* 63 (1937): 433–69.

———. "De L'Édition princeps de la *Chanson de Roland* aux éditions les plus récentes . . . deuxiéme article." *Romania* 64 (1938): 145–244.

———. "De L'Édition princeps de la *Chanson de Roland* aux éditions les plus récentes . . . troisième article." *Romania* 64 (1938): 489–521.

———. "La Tradition manuscrit du *Lai de L'Ombre:* Réflexions sur l'art d'éditer les anciens textes, premier article." *Romania* 54 (1928): 161–96.

———. "La Tradition manuscrit du *Lai de L'Ombre:* Réflexions sur l'art d'éditer les anciens textes, deuxiéme article." *Romania* 54 (1928): 321–56.

———, ed. *Le Lai de L'Ombre par Jean Renart.* Paris: Librairie de Firmin-Didot, 1913.

Beeson, Charles Henry. *Lupus of Ferrières as Scribe and Text Critic: A Study of His Autograph Copy of Cicero's "De Oratore."* Cambridge: Medieval Academy of America, 1930.

Bennett, Philip E., and Graham A. Runnalls, eds. *The Editor and the Text.* Edinburgh: Edinburgh Univ. Press, 1990.

Benson, C. David. "O Moral Henryson." In Yeager, ed., *Fifteenth-Century Studies,* pp. 215–35.

Benson, Larry D., ed. *The Riverside Chaucer.* 3d. ed. Boston: Houghton Mifflin, 1987.

Berry, Reginald John. "Chaucer Transformed, 1700–[17]21." Diss. Univ. of Toronto, 1978.

Blake, N. F. *Caxton and His World.* New York: Andre Deutsch, 1969.

———. *The Textual Tradition of The Canterbury Tales.* London: Edward Arnold, 1985.

Bland, Cynthia Renée. *The Teaching of Grammar in Late Medieval England: An Edition, with Commentary, of Oxford, Lincoln College MS Lat. 130.* East Lansing, Mich.: Colleagues Press, 1991.

Boffey, Julia. *Manuscripts of English Courtly Love Lyrics in the Later Middle Ages.* Woodbridge, England: D. S. Brewer, 1985.

———. "Middle English Lyrics: Texts and Interpretation." In Machan, ed., *Medieval Literature,* pp. 105–19.

Bowden, Betsy, ed. *Eighteenth-Century Modernizations from the Canterbury Tales.* Woodbridge, England: D. S. Brewer, 1991.

Bowers, Fredson. "The Bibliographical Way." In Bowers, Fredson, *Essays in Bibliography, Text, and Editing,* pp. 54–74.

———. *Essays in Bibliography, Text, and Editing.* Charlottesville: Univ. Press of Virginia, 1975.

———. "Mixed Texts and Multiple Authority." *Text* 3 (1987): 63–90.

———. "Multiple Authority: New Problems and Concepts of Copy-Text." In Bowers, Fredson, *Essays in Bibliography, Text, and Editing,* pp. 447–87.

———. "Principle and Practice in the Editing of Early Dramatic Texts." In Bowers, Fredson, *Textual and Literary Criticism,* pp. 117–50.

———. "Some Relations of Bibliography to Editorial Problems." In Bowers, Fredson, *Essays in Bibliography, Text, and Editing,* pp. 15–36.

———. *Textual and Literary Criticism.* Cambridge: Cambridge Univ. Press, 1959.

———. "Textual Criticism and the Literary Critic." In Bowers, Fredson, *Textual and Literary Criticism,* pp. 1–34.

Bowers, John M. "Hoccleve's Huntington Holographs: The First 'Collected Poems' in English." *Fifteenth Century Studies* 15 (1989): 27–51.

———. "Hoccleve's Two Copies of *Lerne to Dye:* Implications for Textual Critics." *Papers of the Bibliographical Society of America* 83 (1989): 437–72.

Boyle, Leonard E. "Optimist and Recensionist: 'Common Errors' or 'Common Variations'?" In *Latin Script and Letters: A.D. 400–900,* ed. John J. O'Meara and Bernd Naumann, pp. 264–74. Leiden: E. J. Brill, 1976.

Brewer, Charlotte. "Authorial vs. Scribal Writing in *Piers Plowman.*" In Machan, ed., *Medieval Literature,* pp. 59–89.

————. *"Piers Plowman:* The Poem and the Editors." In *The Medieval Text: Editors and Critics: A Symposium,* ed. Marianne Børch, Andreas Haarder, and Julia McGrew, pp. 45–63. Odense: Odense Univ. Press, 1990.

————. "The Textual Principles of Kane's A Text." *Yearbook of Langland Studies* 3 (1989): 67–90.

Brink, C. O. *English Classical Scholarship: Historical Reflections on Bentley, Porson, and Housman.* Cambridge: James Clarke, 1986.

Brook, G. L., ed. *The Harley Lyrics: The Middle English Lyrics of MS Harley 2253.* 4th ed. Manchester: Manchester Univ. Press, 1968.

Brownlee, Marina S., Kevin Brownlee, and Stephen G. Nichols, eds. *The New Medievalism.* Baltimore: Johns Hopkins Univ. Press, 1991.

Brusendorff, Aage. *The Chaucer Tradition.* 1925. Rpt. Oxford: Clarendon Press, 1967.

Bühler, Curt F. *The Fifteenth-Century Book: The Scribes, the Printers, the Decorators.* Philadelphia: Univ. of Pennsylvania Press, 1960.

Burrow, John. "Autobiographical Poetry in the Middle Ages: The Case of Thomas Hoccleve." In *Middle English Literature: British Academy Gollancz Lectures,* sel. Burrow, pp. 223–46. Oxford: Oxford Univ. Press, 1989.

————. "Hoccleve's *Series:* Experience and Books." In Yeager, ed., *Fifteenth-Century Studies,* pp. 259–73.

————. "The Poet and the Book." In *Genres, Themes and Images in English Literature: From the Fourteenth to the Fifteenth Century,* ed. Piero Boitani and Anna Torti, pp. 230–45. Tübinger Beiträge zur Anglistik 11. Tübingen: Gunter Narr Verlag, 1988.

Carew, Richard. *The Excellencie of the English Tongue.* In *Remaines, concerning Britaine,* William Camden. London: F. Legatt, 1614.

Carruthers, Mary J. *The Book of Memory: A Study of Memory in Medieval Culture.* Cambridge: Cambridge Univ. Press, 1990.

Caxton, William, ed. *[Boece],* c. 1478.

Cerquiglini, Bernard. *Éloge de la variante: Histoire critique de la philologie.* Paris: Seuil, 1989.

Chalmers, Alexander, ed. *The Works of the English Poets: From Chaucer to Cowper.* 21 vols. London: Whittingham, 1810.

Chaytor, Harold. *From Script to Print: An Introduction to Medieval Vernacular Literature.* Cambridge: W. Heffer, 1945.

Cheney, C. R. *Notaries Public in England in the Thirteenth and Fourteenth Centuries.* Oxford: Clarendon Press, 1975.

Chenu, Marie-Dominique. "Auctor, actor, autor." *Bulletin du Cange-Archivum Latinitatis Medii Aevii* 3 (1927): 81–86.

Christianson, C. Paul. "A Community of Book Artisans in Chaucer's London." *Viator* 20 (1989): 207–19.

————. *A Directory of London Stationers and Book Artisans 1300–1500.* New York: Bibliographical Society of America, 1990.

————. *Memorials of the Book Trade in Medieval London: The Archives of Old London Bridge.* Cambridge: D. S. Brewer, 1987.

Clanchy, M. T. *From Memory to Written Record: England, 1066–1307.* Cambridge: Harvard Univ. Press, 1979.

Cohen, Philip, ed. *Devils and Angels: Textual Editing and Literary Theory.* Charlottesville: Univ. Press of Virginia, 1991.

Cohen, Philip, and David H. Jackson. "Notes on Emerging Paradigms in Editorial Theory." In Cohen, ed., *Devils and Angels,* pp. 103–23.

Colish, Marcia L. *The Mirror of Language: A Study in the Medieval Theory of Knowledge.* Rev. ed. Lincoln: Univ. of Nebraska Press, 1983.

Collingwood, R. G. *The Idea of History.* Oxford: Clarendon Press, 1946.

Collins, A. S. *Authorship in the Days of Johnson: Being a Study of the Relation between Author, Patron, Publisher and Public, 1726–1780.* London: Robert Holden, 1927.

————. *The Profession of Letters: A Study of the Relation of Author to Patron, Publisher, and Public, 1780–1832.* London: George Routledge, 1928.

Cooper, Christopher. *Grammatica Linguae Anglicanae.* 1685. Rpt. Menston, England: Scolar Press, 1968.

Copeland, Rita. *Rhetoric, Hermeneutics, and Translation in the Middle Ages: Academic Traditions and Vernacular Texts.* Cambridge: Cambridge Univ. Press, 1991.

Courtenay, William J. *Schools & Scholars in Fourteenth-Century England.* Princeton: Princeton Univ. Press, 1987.

Cowen, Janet M. "Metrical Problems in Editing *The Legend of Good Women.*" In Pearsall, ed., *Manuscripts and Texts,* pp. 26–33.

Crowley, Robert, ed. *The Vision of Pierce Plowman.* London: Robert Crowley, 1550.

Curtius, Ernst Robert. *European Literature and the Latin Middle Ages.* Trans. Willard R. Trask. Bollingen Series 36. New York: Pantheon, 1953.

Dahood, Roger. "The Use of Colored Initials and Other Division Markers in Early Versions of *Ancrene Riwle.*" In *Medieval English Studies Presented to George Kane,* ed. Edward Donald Kennedy, Ronald Waldron, and Joseph S. Wittig, pp. 79–97. Cambridge: D. S. Brewer, 1988.

D'Amico, John F. *Theory and Practice in Renaissance Textual Criticism.* Berkeley and Los Angeles: Univ. of California Press, 1988.

Dane, Joseph A. "Copy-Text and Its Variants in Some Recent Chaucer Editions." *Studies in Bibliography* 44 (1991): 164–83.

Dante (Dante Alighieri). *De vulgari eloquentia.* In *Classical and Medieval Literary Criticism: Translations and Interpretations,* ed. and trans. Alex Preminger et al., pp. 412–46. New York: Frederick Ungar, 1974.

d'Ardenne, S. R. T. O., and E. J. Dobson, eds. *Seinte Katerine.* EETS s.s. 7. Oxford: Oxford Univ. Press, 1981.

Darwin, Charles. *The Origin of the Species by Means of Natural Selection, The Descent of Man and Selection in Relation to Sex.* Chicago: Encyclopedia Britannica, 1952.

Davies, R. T., ed. *Medieval English Lyrics.* London: Faber and Faber, 1963.

Day, Mabel, ed. *The English Text of the Ancrene Riwle.* EETS o.s. 225. London: Oxford Univ. Press, 1952.

de Bury, Richard. *The Philobiblon.* Trans. Archer Taylor. Berkeley and Los Angeles: Univ. of California Press, 1948.

Dedeck-Héry, V. L. "The Manuscripts of the Translation of Boethius' *Consolatio* by Jean de Meung." *Speculum* 15 (1940): 432–43.

de Roover, Florence Edler. "The Scriptorium." In *The Medieval Library,* ed. James Westfall Thompson, pp. 594–612. Chicago: Univ. of Chicago Press, 1939.

Dooley, Allan C. *Author and Printer in Victorian England.* Charlottesville: Univ. Press of Virginia, 1992.

Doyle, A. I. "Book Production by the Monastic Orders in England (c. 1375–1530): Assessing the Evidence." In *Medieval Book Production, Assessing the Evidence,* ed. Linda L. Brownrigg, pp. 1–19. Los Altos Hills, Calif.: Anderson-Lovelace, 1990.

Doyle, A. I., and M. B. Parkes. "A Paleographical Introduction." In *The Canterbury Tales: A Facsimile and Transcription of the Hengwrt Manuscript with Variants from the Ellesmere Manuscript,* ed. Paul G. Ruggiers, pp. xix–xlix. Norman: Univ. of Oklahoma Press, 1979.

———. "The Production of Copies of the *Canterbury Tales* and the *Confessio Amantis* in the Early Fifteenth Century." In *Medieval Scribes, Manuscripts and Libraries: Essays Presented to N. R. Ker,* ed. Parkes and A. G. Watson, pp. 163–210. London: Scolar Press, 1978.

Duggan, Hoyt N. "Alliterative Patterning as a Basis for Emendation in Middle English Alliterative Poetry." *Studies in the Age of Chaucer* 8 (1986): 73–105.

———. "The Shape of the B-Verse in Middle English Alliterative Poetry." *Speculum* 61 (1986): 564–92.

Duggan, Hoyt, and Thorlac Turville-Petre, eds. *The Wars of Alexander.* EETS s.s. 10. Oxford: Oxford Univ. Press, 1989.

Duncan, Bonnie Israel. "Middle English Poems in Harley MS. 2253: Semiosis and Reading Scribes." Diss. Univ. of Iowa, 1988.

Eagleton, Terry. *Literary Theory: An Introduction.* Minneapolis: Univ. of Minnesota Press, 1983.

Ebin, Lois A. *John Lydgate.* Boston: Twayne, 1985.

———. *Illuminator, Makar, Vates: Visions of Poetry in the Fifteenth Century.* Lincoln: Univ. of Nebraska Press, 1988.

Edwards, A. S. G. "The Manuscripts and Texts of the Second Version of John Hardyng's *Chronicle.*" In *England in the Fifteenth Century,* ed. Daniel Williams, pp. 75–84. Cambridge: Boydell, 1987.

———. "Middle English Romance: The Limits of Editing, the Limits of Criticism." In Machan, ed., *Medieval Literature,* pp. 91–104.

———. "Observations on the History of Middle English Editing." In Pearsall, ed., *Manuscripts and Texts,* pp. 34–48.

Edwards, A. S. G., and Derek Pearsall. "The Manuscripts of the Major English Poetic Texts." In Griffiths and Pearsall, eds., *Book Production,* pp. 257–78.

Eichhorn, Johann Gottfried. *Einleitung ins Alte Testament.* 2d. ed. 3 vols. Reutlingen: Johannes Grözinger, 1790.

Eisner, Sigmund. "Chaucer as a Technical Writer." *Chaucer Review* 19 (1985): 179–201.

Elliott, Ralph W. V. *Chaucer's English.* London: Andre Deutsch, 1974.

Ellis, Roger. *Patterns of Religious Narrative in the Canterbury Tales.* Totowa, N.J.: Barnes and Noble, 1986.

Elsky, Martin. *Authorizing Words: Speech, Writing, and Print in the English Renaissance.* Ithaca: Cornell Univ. Press, 1989.

Elton, G. R. *The Tudor Constitution: Documents and Commentary.* 2d ed. Cambridge: Cambridge Univ. Press, 1982.

Embree, Dan, and Elizabeth Urquhart. "*The Simonie:* The Case for a Parallel-Text Edition." In Pearsall, ed., *Manuscripts and Texts,* pp. 49–59.

Erasmus, Desideratus. *Apologia respondens ad ea quae Iacobus Lopis Stunica taxaverat in prima duntaxat Novi Testamenti aeditione.* Vol.9, pt. 2 of *Opera Omnia Desiderii Erasmi Roterodami.* Ed. H. J. de Jonge. Amsterdam: North Holland Publishing Co., 1983.

———. *Opus Epistolarum Des Erasmi Roterodami.* Ed. P. S. Allen. Oxford: Clarendon Press, 1910.

Fellows, Jennifer. "Editing Middle English Romances." In *Romance in Medieval England,* ed. Maldwyn Mills, Jennifer Fellows, and Carol M. Meale, pp. 5–16. Cambridge: D. S. Brewer, 1991.

Feltes, N. N. *Modes of Production of Victorian Novels.* Chicago: Univ. of Chicago Press, 1986.

Fisher, John H. "A Language Policy for Lancastrian England." *PMLA* 107 (1992): 1168–80.

Fisher, John H., Malcolm Richardson, and Jane L. Fisher, eds. *An Anthology of Chancery English.* Knoxville: Univ. of Tennessee Press, 1984.

Foley, John Miles. "Editing Oral Epic Texts: Theory and Practice." *Text* 1 (1981): 75–94.

Foucault, Michel. *The Archaeology of Knowledge and The Discourse on Language.* Trans. A. M. Sheridan Smith. New York: Pantheon Books, 1972.

———. "What Is an Author?" Trans. Donald F. Bouchard and Sherry Simon.

In *Contemporary Literary Criticism: Literary and Cultural Studies,* ed. Robert Con Davis and Ronald Schleifer, pp. 263–75. 2d ed. New York: Longman, 1989.

Foulet, Alfred, and Mary Blakely Speer. *On Editing Old French Texts.* Lawrence: Regents Press of Kansas, 1979.

Foulet, Alfred, and Karl D. Uitti. "Chrétien's 'Laudine': *Yvain,* vv. 2148–55." *Romance Philology* 37 (1984): 293–302.

Fox, Denton. "The Coherence of Henryson's Work." In Yeager, ed., *Fifteenth-Century Studies,* pp. 275–81.

———, ed. *The Poems of Robert Henryson.* Oxford: Clarendon Press, 1981.

Frantzen, Allen J. *Desire for Origins: New Language, Old English, and Teaching the Tradition.* New Brunswick, N.J.: Rutgers Univ. Press, 1990.

Furnivall, F. J., and G. H. Kingsley, eds. *Animadversions.* London: Oxford Univ. Press, 1875.

Furrow, Melissa M., ed. *Ten Fifteenth-Century Comic Poems.* New York: Garland, 1985.

Gabler, Hans Walter, ed. *Ulysses: The Corrected Text.* New York: Random House, 1986.

Gallie, W. B. *Philosophy and the Historical Understanding.* New York: Schocken Books, 1964.

Ganz, Peter F. "Lachmann as an Editor of Middle High German Texts." In *Probleme Mittelalterlicher Überlieferung und Textkritik,* ed. Peter Ganz and Werner Schröder, pp. 12–30. Berlin: Erich Schmidt Verlag, 1968.

Gascoigne, George. "Certayne Notes of Instruction concerning the Making of Verse or Ryme in English." In *Complete Works of George Gascoigne,* ed. John W. Cunliffe, 1:465–73. 2 vols. Cambridge: Cambridge Univ. Press, 1907, 1910.

Gaskell, Philip. *A New Introduction to Bibliography.* Oxford: Oxford Univ. Press, 1972.

Gates, Robert J., ed. *The Awntyrs off Arthure at the Terne Wathelyne: A Critical Edition.* Philadelphia: Univ. of Pennsylvania Press, 1969.

Gatrell, Simon. *Hardy the Creator: A Textual Biography.* Oxford: Clarendon Press, 1988.

Gellrich, Jesse M. *The Idea of the Book in the Middle Ages: Language Theory, Mythology, and Fiction.* Ithaca: Cornell Univ. Press, 1985.

Gillespie, Vincent. "Vernacular Books of Religion." In Griffiths and Pearsall, eds., *Book Production,* pp. 317–44.

Girvan, R., ed. *Ratis Raving and Other Early Scots Poems on Morals.* STS, 3d ser., 11. Edinburgh: William Blackwood, 1939.

Glascoe, Marion. "Visions and Revisions: A Further Look at the Manuscripts of Julian of Norwich." *Studies in Bibliography* 42 (1989): 103–20.

Goldschmidt, E. P. *Medieval Texts and Their First Appearance in Print.* Supplement to the Bibliographical Society's Transactions no. 16. Oxford: Oxford Univ. Press, 1943.

Gopen, George D. "The Essential Seriousness of Robert Henryson's *Moral Fables:* A Study in Structure." *Studies in Philology* 82 (1985): 42–59.

――――, ed. and trans. *The Moral Fables of Aesop.* Notre Dame: Univ. of Notre Dame Press, 1987.

Graff, Gerald. *Professing Literature: An Institutional History.* Chicago: Univ. of Chicago Press, 1987.

Grafton, Anthony. "Introduction: The Humanists Reassessed." In *Defenders of the Text: The Traditions of Scholarship in an Age of Science, 1450–1800,* ed. Grafton, pp. 1–22. Cambridge: Harvard Univ. Press, 1991.

――――. *Joseph Scaliger: A Study in the History of Classical Scholarship.* Oxford: Clarendon Press, 1983.

――――. "*Prolegomena* to Friedrich August Wolf." *Journal of the Warburg and Courtauld Institutes* 44 (1981): 101–29.

Grafton, Anthony, and Lisa Jardine. *From Humanism to the Humanities: Education and the Liberal Arts in Fifteenth- and Sixteenth-Century Europe.* Cambridge: Harvard Univ. Press, 1986.

Green, Richard Firth. *Poets and Princepleasers: Literature in the English Court in the Middle Ages.* Toronto: Univ. of Toronto Press, 1980.

Greenberg, Cheryl. "John Shirley and the English Book Trade." *The Library,* 6th ser. 4 (1982): 369–80.

Greetham, D. C. "Challenges of Theory and Practice in the Editing of Hoccleve's *Regement of Princes.*" In Pearsall, ed., *Manuscripts and Texts,* pp. 60–86.

――――. "Models for the Textual Transmission of Translation: The Case of John Trevisa." *Studies in Bibliography* 37 (1984): 131–55.

――――. "Normalisation of Accidentals in Middle English Texts: The Paradox of Thomas Hoccleve." *Studies in Bibliography* 38 (1985): 121–50.

――――. "The Place of Fredson Bowers in Medieval Editing." *Papers of the Bibliographical Society of America* 82 (1988): 53–69.

――――. "Self-Referential Artifacts: Hoccleve's Persona as a Literary Device." *Modern Philology* 86 (1989): 242–51.

――――. "[Textual] Criticism and Deconstruction." *Studies in Bibliography* 44 (1991): 1–30.

――――. "Textual and Literary Theory: Redrawing the Matrix." *Studies in Bibliography* 42 (1989): 1–24.

――――. "Textual Scholarship." In *Introduction to Scholarship in Modern Languages and Literatures,* 2d ed., ed. Joseph Gibaldi, pp. 103–37. New York: MLA, 1992.

———. *Textual Scholarship: An Introduction.* New York: Garland, 1992.

Greg, W. W. "Bibliography—an Apologia." In *Collected Papers,* ed. J. C. Maxwell, pp. 239–66. Oxford: Clarendon Press, 1966.

———. "The Rationale of Copy-Text." *Studies in Bibliography* 3 (1950): 19–36.

Griest, Guinevere L. *Mudie's Circulating Library and the Victorian Novel.* Bloomington: Indiana Univ. Press, 1970.

Griffiths, Jeremy, and Derek Pearsall, eds. *Book Production and Publishing in Britain 1375–1475.* Cambridge: Cambridge Univ. Press, 1989.

Grigely, Joseph. "The Textual Event." In Cohen, ed., *Devils and Angels,* pp. 167–94.

Hamel, Mary. "Scribal Self-Corrections in the Thornton *Morte Arthure.*" *Studies in Bibliography* 36 (1983): 119–37.

Hamesse, Jacqueline. " 'Reportatio' et transmission de textes." In Asztalos, ed., *The Editing of Theological and Philosophical Texts,* pp. 11–34.

Hammond, Eleanor. *Chaucer: A Bibliographical Manual.* New York: Macmillan, 1908.

Hanna, Ralph, III. "Authorial Versions, Rolling Revision, Scribal Error? Or, The Truth about *Truth.*" *Studies in the Age of Chaucer* 10 (1988): 23–40.

———. "Booklets in Medieval Manuscripts: Further Considerations." *Studies in Bibliography* 39 (1986): 100–11.

———. "Editing Middle English Prose Translations: How Prior Is the Source?" *Text* 4 (1988): 207–16.

———. "The Hengwrt Manuscript and the Canon of *The Canterbury Tales.*" In *English Manuscript Studies 1100–1700,* ed. Peter Beal and Jeremy Griffiths, pp. 64–84. Oxford: Blackwell, 1989.

———. "Presenting Chaucer as Author." In Machan, ed., *Medieval Literature,* pp. 17–39.

———. "Problems of 'Best Text' Editing and the Hengwrt Manuscript of *The Canterbury Tales.*" In Pearsall, ed., *Manuscripts and Texts,* pp. 87–94.

———. "The Scribe of Huntington HM 114." *Studies in Bibliography* 42 (1989): 120–33.

———, ed. *The Awntyrs off Arthure at the Terne Wathelyne: An Edition Based on Bodleian Library MS Douce 324.* Manchester: Manchester Univ. Press, 1974.

Havet, Louis. *Manuel de critique verbale appliquée aux textes latins.* Paris: Librairie Hachette, 1911.

Hellinga, Lotte. "Manuscripts in the Hands of Printers." In *Manuscripts in the Fifty Years after the Invention of Printing,* ed. J. B. Trapp, pp. 3–11. London: Warburg Institute, 1983.

Hench, Atcheson L. "Printer's Copy for Tyrwhitt's Chaucer." *Studies in Bibliography* 3 (1950): 265–66.

Hepburn, James. *The Author's Empty Purse and the Rise of the Literary Agent.* London: Oxford Univ. Press, 1968.

Hindman, Sandra, ed. *Printing the Written Word: The Social History of Books circa 1450–1520.* Ithaca: Cornell Univ. Press, 1991.

Hirsh, John C. "Author and Scribe in *The Book of Margery Kempe.*" *Medium Aevum* 44 (1970): 145–50.

———. "A Fifteenth-Century Commentary on 'Ihesu for Thy Holy Name.'" *Notes and Queries* n.s. 17 (1970): 44–45.

Hodgson, Phyllis, ed. *The Cloud of Unknowing and the Book of Privy Counselling.* EETS o.s. 218. Oxford: Oxford Univ. Press, 1944.

Hödl, Ludwig, and Dieter Wuttke, eds. *Probleme der Edition mittel- und neulateinischer Texte.* Boppard: Harald Boldt, 1978.

Holbrook, Sue Ellen. "Margery Kempe and Wynkyn de Worde." In *The Medieval Mystical Tradition in England: Exeter Symposium IV,* ed. Marion Glascoe, pp. 27–46. Cambridge: D. S. Brewer, 1987.

Howard-Hill, T. H. "Theory and Praxis in the Social Approach to Editing." *Text* 5 (1991): 31–46.

Hudson, Anne, ed. *English Wycliffite Sermons.* 3 vols. Oxford: Clarendon Press, 1983.

———. "Middle English." In *Editing Medieval Texts: English, French and Latin, Written in England,* ed. A. G. Rigg, pp. 34–57. New York: Garland, 1977.

———. *The Premature Reformation: Wycliffite Texts and Lollard History.* Oxford: Clarendon Press, 1988.

Hudson, R. A. *Sociolinguistics.* Cambridge: Cambridge Univ. Press, 1980.

Hult, David F. "Lancelot's Two Steps: A Problem in Textual Criticism." *Speculum* 61 (1986): 836–58.

———. "Reading It Right: The Ideology of Text Editing." In Brownlee et. al., eds., *The New Medievalism,* pp. 113–30.

———. *Self-Fulfilling Prophecies: Readership and Authority in the First "Roman de la Rose".* Cambridge: Cambridge Univ. Press, 1986.

Huot, Sylvia. *From Song to Book: The Poetics of Writing in Old French Lyric and Lyrical Narrative Poetry.* Ithaca: Cornell Univ. Press, 1987.

Irvine, Martin. "Medieval Grammatical Theory and Chaucer's *House of Fame.*" *Speculum* 60 (1985): 850–76.

Iverson, Gunilla. "Problems in the Editing of Tropes." *Text* 1 (1981): 95–132.

Jackson, W. A., F. S. Ferguson, and Katherine F. Pantzer. *A Short-Title Catalogue of Books Printed in England, Scotland, & Ireland and of English Books Printed Abroad, 1475–1640.* 2d ed. 2 vols. London: Bibliographical Society, 1986.

Jacobs, Nicolas. "The Processes of Scribal Substitution and Redaction: A Study of the Cambridge Fragment of *Sir Degarré.*" *Medium Aevum* 53 (1984): 26–48.

Jefferson, Judith A. "The Hoccleve Holographs and Hoccleve's Metrical Practice." In Pearsall, ed., *Manuscripts and Texts,* pp. 95–109.

Johnson, Lynn Staley. "The Trope of the Scribe and the Question of Literary Authority in the Works of Julian of Norwich and Margery Kempe." *Speculum* 66 (1991): 820–38.

Johnson, Thomas H., ed. *The Poems of Emily Dickinson.* 3 vols. Cambridge: Belknap Press of Harvard Univ. Press, 1955.

Johnston, A. F., ed. *Editing Early English Drama: Special Problems and New Directions.* New York: AMS Press, 1987.

Johnston, Arthur. *Enchanted Ground: The Study of Medieval Romance in the Eighteenth Century.* London: Athlone Press, 1964.

Jones, Frederick L., ed. *The Letters of Percy Bysshe Shelley.* 2 vols. Oxford: Clarendon Press, 1964.

Jones, Meredith Joy. "The Harley Lyrics in Context: The Structure and Organization of MS. Harley 2253." Diss. Univ. of Michigan, 1985.

Kane, George. " 'Good' and 'Bad' Manuscripts: Texts and Critics." In *Studies in the Age of Chaucer, Proceedings No. 2, 1986 Fifth International Congress 20–23 March 1986 Philadelphia, Pennsylvania,* ed. John V. Fleming and Thomas J. Heffernan, pp. 137–45. Knoxville: New Chaucer Society, 1987.

————. "John M. Manly and Edith Rickert." In *Editing Chaucer: The Great Tradition,* ed. Paul G. Ruggiers, pp. 207–29. Norman, Okla.: Pilgrim Books, 1984.

————. *Piers Plowman: The Evidence for Authorship.* London: Athlone Press, 1965.

————. "The Text." In *A Companion to "Piers Plowman,"* ed. John A. Alford, pp. 175–200. Berkeley and Los Angeles: Univ. of California Press, 1988.

————. "The Text of *The Legend of Good Women* in CUL MS Gg.4.27." In *Middle English Studies Presented to Norman Davis in Honour of His Seventieth Birthday,* ed. E. G. Stanley, pp. 39–58. Oxford: Clarendon, 1983.

————. "The 'Z Version' of *Piers Plowman.*" *Speculum* 60 (1985): 910–30.

————, ed. *Piers Plowman: The A Version.* Rev. ed. Berkeley and Los Angeles: Univ. of California Press, 1988.

Kane, George, and E. Talbot Donaldson, eds. *Piers Plowman: The B Version.* Rev. ed. Berkeley and Los Angeles: Univ. of California Press, 1988.

Keiser, George R. "Lincoln Cathedral Library MS. 91: Life and Milieu of the Scribe." *Studies in Bibliography* 32 (1987): 158–79.

————. "*Ordinatio* in the Manuscripts of John Lydgates's *Lyf of Our Lady:* Its Value for the Reader, Its Challenge for the Modern Editor." In Machan, ed., *Medieval Literature,* pp. 139–58.

Kellogg, Robert L. "E-Text Society." Chaucernet, May 12, 1993.

Kenney, Edward J. *The Classical Text: Aspects of Editing in the Age of the Printed Book.* Berkeley and Los Angeles: Univ. of California Press, 1974.

———. "Textual Criticism." *New Encyclopedia Britannica,* 15th ed.

Ker, N. R., ed. *Facsimile of British Museum MS. Harley 2253.* EETS o.s. 255. Oxford: Oxford Univ. Press, 1965.

Kidd, John. "An Inquiry into *Ulysses: The Corrected Text.*" *Papers of the Bibliographical Society of America* 82 (1988): 411–584.

Kindrick, Robert L. *Robert Henryson.* Boston: Twayne, 1979.

Kittay, Jeffrey. "Utterance Unmoored: The Changing Interpretation of the Act of Writing in the European Middle Ages." *Language in Society* 17 (1988): 209–30.

Knight, Stephen. "Textual Variants: Textual Variance." *Southern Review* (Adelaide) 16 (1983): 44–54.

Kottler, Barnet. "Chaucer's *Boece* and the Late Medieval Textual Tradition of the *Consolatio Philosophiae.*" Diss. Yale Univ., 1953.

Kristeller, Paul Oskar. "The Lachmann Method: Merits and Limitations." *Text* 1 (1981): 11–20.

———. "Textual Scholarship and General Theories of History and Literature." *Text* 3 (1987): 1–9.

Kynaston, Francis, ed. and trans. *Amorum Troili et Creseidae Libri duo priores Anglico-Latini.* Oxford: Johannes Lichfield, 1635.

Lachmann, Karl, ed. *In T. Lucretii Cari De rerum natura libros commentarius.* 1855. Rpt. New York: Garland, 1979.

———, ed. *Nouum Testamentum Graece et Latine.* Berlin: George Reimer, 1842.

Landon, Richard, ed. *Editing and Editors: A Retrospect.* New York: AMS Press, 1988.

Landow, George P. *Hypertext: The Convergence of Contemporary Critical Theory and Technology.* Baltimore: Johns Hopkins Univ. Press, 1992.

Lapidge, Michael. "Textual Criticism and the Literature of Anglo-Saxon England." *Bulletin of the John Rylands Library* 73 (1991): 17–45.

Lass, Roger. *On Explaining Language Change.* Cambridge: Cambridge Univ. 1980.

Lennard, John. *But I Digress: The Exploitation of Parentheses in English Printed Verse.* Oxford: Clarendon Press, 1991.

Lerer, Seth. *Chaucer and His Readers: Imagining the Author in Late-Medieval England.* Princeton: Princeton Univ. Press, 1993.

———. "Rewriting Chaucer: Two Fifteenth-Century Readings of the Canterbury Tales." *Viator* 19 (1988): 311–26.

Lewis, C. S. "The Genesis of a Medieval Book." In *Studies in Medieval and*

Renaissance Literature, ed. Walter Hooper, pp. 18–40. Cambridge: Cambridge Univ. Press, 1966.

Love, Harold. "Sir Walter Greg and the Chaucerian Force Field." *Bibliographical Society of Australia and New Zealand Bulletin* 8 (1984): 73–81.

Luria, Maxwell S., and Richard L. Hoffman, eds. *Middle English Lyrics.* New York: W. W. Norton, 1974.

McDiarmid, Matthew P. *Robert Henryson.* Edinburgh: Scottish Academic Press, 1981.

McGann, Jerome J. *A Critique of Modern Textual Criticism.* Chicago: Univ. of Chicago Press, 1983.

———. "Introduction: A Point of Reference." In McGann, ed., *Historical Studies and Literary Criticism,* pp. 3–21.

———. "The Monks and the Giants." In McGann, ed., *Textual Criticism and Literary Interpretation,* pp. 180–99.

———. "Shall These Bones Live?" *Text* 1 (1981): 21–40.

———. "The Text, the Poem, and the Problem of Historical Method." In *The Beauty of Inflections: Literary Investigations in Historical Method and Theory,* ed. McGann, pp. 111–32. Oxford: Clarendon Press, 1985.

———. *The Textual Condition.* Princeton: Princeton Univ. Press, 1991.

———, ed. *Historical Studies and Literary Criticism.* Madison: Univ. of Wisconsin Press, 1985.

———, ed. *Textual Criticism and Literary Interpretation.* Chicago: Univ. of Chicago Press, 1985.

McGregor, James H. "The Iconography of Chaucer in Hoccleve's *De Regimine Principum* and in the *Troilus* Frontispiece." *Chaucer Review* 11 (1977): 228–50.

Machan, Tim William. "Chaucer as Translator." In *The Medieval Translator: The Theory and Practice of Translation in the Middle Ages,* ed. Roger Ellis, pp. 55–67. Cambridge: D. S. Brewer, 1989.

———. "Editing, Orality, and Late Middle English Texts." In *Vox Intexta: Orality and Textuality in the Middle Ages,* ed. A. N. Doane and Carol Braun Pasternack, pp. 229–45. Madison: Univ. of Wisconsin Press, 1991.

———. "Editorial Method and Medieval Translations: The Example of Chaucer's *Boece.*" *Studies in Bibliography* 41 (1988): 188–96.

———. "Kynaston's *Troilus,* Textual Criticism, and the Renaissance Reading of Chaucer." *Exemplaria* 5 (1993): 161–83.

———. "Late Middle English Texts and the Higher and Lower Criticisms." In Machan, ed., *Medieval Literature,* pp. 3–15.

———. "Middle English Text Production and Modern Textual Criticism." In *Crux and Controversy in Middle English Textual Criticism,* ed. A. J. Minnis and Charlotte Brewer, pp. 1–18. Cambridge: Boydell and Brewer, 1992.

————. "Robert Henryson and Father Aesop: Authority in the *Moral Fables.*" *Studies in the Age of Chaucer* 12 (1990): 193–214.

————. *Techniques of Translation: Chaucer's "Boece."* Norman, Okla.: Pilgrim Books, 1985.

————. "Textual Authority and the Works of Hoccleve, Lydgate, and Henryson." *Viator* 23 (1992): 281–99.

————, ed. *Medieval Literature: Texts and Interpretation.* Binghamton, N.Y.: Medieval and Renaissance Texts and Studies, 1991.

————, ed. *Vafþrúðnismál.* Durham, England: Durham Medieval Texts, 1988.

Machan, Tim William, and A. J. Minnis, eds. *The Boece: A Variorum Edition of the Works of Geoffrey Chaucer,* pt. 6, *The Prose Treatises.* Norman: Univ. of Oklahoma Press, forthcoming.

McKenzie, D. F. *Bibliography and the Sociology of Texts.* London: British Library, 1986.

McLaverty, James. "The Concept of Authorial Intention in Textual Criticism." *The Library,* 6th ser. 6 (1984): 121–38.

————. "The Mode of Existence of Literary Works of Art: The Case of the *Dunciad Variorum.*" *Studies in Bibliography* 37 (1984): 85–105.

Mailloux, Steven. *Interpretive Conventions: The Reader in the Study of American Fiction.* Ithaca: Cornell Univ. Press, 1982.

————. "The Rhetorical Politics of Editing: A Response to Eggert, Greetham, and Cohen and Jackson." In Cohen, ed., *Devils and Angels,* pp. 124–33.

Manly, John M., and Edith Rickert, eds. *The Text of the Canterbury Tales.* 8 vols. Chicago: Univ. of Chicago Press, 1940.

Martial (Marcus Valerius Martialis). *Martial Epigrams.* Ed. and trans. Walter C. A. Ker. 2 vols. London: William Heineman, 1919.

Mason, George, ed. *Poems by Thomas Hoccleve.* London: C. Rowerth, 1796.

Meale, Carol M. "Patrons, Buyers and Owners: Book Production and Social Status." In Griffiths and Pearsall, eds., *Book Production,* pp. 201–38.

Millett, Bella. "Chaucer, Lollius, and the Medieval Theory of Authorship." In *Studies in the Age of Chaucer, Proceedings, No. 1, 1984: Reconstructing Chaucer,* ed. Paul Strohm and Thomas J. Heffernan, pp. 93–103. Knoxville: New Chaucer Society, 1985.

Mills, David. "Theories and Practices in the Editing of the Chester Cycle Play-Manuscripts." In Pearsall, ed., *Manuscripts and Texts,* pp. 110–21.

Milroy, James, and Lesley Milroy. *Authority in Language: Investigating Language Prescription and Standardisation.* London: Routledge, 1985.

Minnis, A. J. "*De Vulgari auctoritate:* Chaucer, Gower and the Men of Great Authority." In *Chaucer and Gower: Difference, Mutuality, Exchange,* ed. R. F. Yeager, pp. 36–74. Victoria, B.C.: English Literary Studies, 1991.

————. *Medieval Theory of Authorship: Scholastic Literary Attitudes in the Later Middle Ages.* 2d. ed. Aldershot, England: Scolar Press, 1988.

Minnis, A. J., and T. W. Machan. "The *Boece* as Late-Medieval Translation." In *Chaucer's "Boece" and the Medieval Tradition of Boethius,* ed. Minnis, pp. 167–88. Cambridge: Boydell and Brewer, 1993.

Minnis, A. J., and A. B. Scott. *Medieval Literary Theory and Criticism, c. 1100-c. 1375: The Commentary Tradition.* Oxford: Clarendon Press, 1988.

Miskimin, Alice. *The Renaissance Chaucer.* New Haven: Yale Univ. Press, 1975.

————, ed. *Susannah: An Alliterative Poem of the Fourteenth Century.* New Haven: Yale Univ. Press, 1969.

Mitchell, Bruce. "The Dangers of Disguise: Old English Texts in Modern Punctuation." In *On Old English: Selected Papers,* ed. Mitchell, pp. 172–202. Oxford: Blackwell, 1988.

Mitchell, Jerome. *Thomas Hoccleve: A Study in Fifteenth-Century Poetic.* Urbana: Univ. of Illinois Press, 1968.

Moorman, Charles. *Editing the Middle English Manuscript.* Jackson: Univ. of Mississippi Press, 1975.

Morse, Ruth. *Truth and Convention in the Middle Ages: Rhetoric, Representation, and Reality.* Cambridge: Cambridge Univ. Press, 1991.

Nichols, Stephen G., guest ed. "The New Philology." *Speculum* 65 (1990): 1–108.

Nordloh, David J. "Theory, Funding, and Coincidence in the Editing of American Literature." In Landon, ed., *Editing and Editors,* pp. 136–55.

Novick, Peter. *That Noble Dream: The "Objectivity Question" and the American Historical Profession.* Cambridge: Cambridge Univ. Press, 1988.

O'Keeffee, Katherine O'Brien. *Visible Song: Transitional Literacy in Old English Verse.* Cambridge: Cambridge Univ. Press, 1990.

Oliphant, David, and Robin Bradford, eds. *New Directions in Textual Studies.* Austin, Tex.: Harry Ransom Humanities Research Center, 1990.

Olson, Glending. *Literature as Recreation in the Later Middle Ages.* Ithaca: Cornell Univ. Press, 1982.

Owen, Charles A., Jr. Review of *The Textual Tradition of the "Canterbury Tales,"* by N. F. Blake. *Studies in the Age of Chaucer* 9 (1985): 183–87.

Palomo, Dolores. "What Chaucer Really Did to *Le Livre de Mellibee.*" *Philological Quarterly* 53 (1974): 304–20.

Parker, Hershel. *Flawed Texts and Verbal Icons: Literary Authority in American Fiction.* Evanston: Northwestern Univ. Press, 1984.

————. " 'The Text Itself'—Whatever That Is." *Text* 3 (1987): 47–54.

Parkes, M. B. "Book Provision and Libraries at the Medieval University of Oxford." *University of Rochester Bulletin* 40 (1987): 28–43.

————. *English Cursive Book Hands 1250–1500.* Oxford: Oxford Univ. Press, 1969.

————. "The Influence of the Concepts of *Ordinatio* and *Compilatio* on the Development of the Book." In *Medieval Learning and Literature: Essays Presented to Richard William Hunt*, ed. J. J. G. Alexander and M. T. Gibson, pp. 115–41. Oxford: Clarendon Press, 1976.

Parkes, M. B., and Ricard Beadle, eds. *The Poetical Works of Geoffrey Chaucer: A Facsimile of Cambridge University Library MS Gg.4.27.* 3 vols. Norman, Okla.: Pilgrim Books, 1979–80.

Pasquali, Georgio. *Storia della tradizione e critica del testo.* 2d ed. Florence: Felice le Monnier, 1962.

Patten, Robert L. *Charles Dickens and His Publishers.* Oxford: Clarendon Press, 1978.

Patterson, Lee. *Negotiating the Past: The Historical Understanding of Medieval Literature.* Madison: Univ. of Wisconsin Press, 1987.

Pearsall, Derek. *The Canterbury Tales.* London: Allen and Unwin, 1985.

————. "Chaucer's Meter: The Evidence of the Manuscripts." In Machan, ed., *Medieval Literature*, pp. 41–57.

————. "Editing Medieval Texts: Some Developments and Some Problems." In McGann, ed., *Textual Criticism and Literary Interpretation*, pp. 92–106.

————. "Gower's Latin in the *Confessio Amantis*." In *Latin and Vernacular: Studies in Late-Medieval Texts and Manuscripts*, ed. A. J. Minnis, pp. 13–25. Cambridge: D. S. Brewer, 1989.

————. *John Lydgate.* Charlottesville: Univ. Press of Virginia, 1970.

————. "Middle English Romance and Its Audiences." In *Historical and Editorial Studies in Medieval and Early Modern English for Johann Gerritsen*, ed. Mary-Jo Arn et al., pp. 37–47. Groningen: Wolters-Noordhoff, 1985.

————. *Old English and Middle English Poetry.* London: Routledge and Kegan Paul, 1977.

————. "Texts, Textual Criticism, and Fifteenth Century Manuscript Production." In Yeager, ed., *Fifteenth-Century Studies*, pp. 121–36.

————, ed. *Manuscripts and Texts: Editorial Problems in Later Middle English Literature.* Cambridge: D. S. Brewer, 1987.

————, ed. *Studies in "The Vernon Manuscript."* Woodbridge, England: D.S. Brewer, 1990.

Peckham, Morse. "Reflections on the Foundations of Modern Textual Editing." *Proof* 1 (1971): 122–55.

Percy, Thomas. *Reliques of Ancient English Poetry.* 4th ed. 1794. Ed. Rev. Henry B. Wheatley. 3 vols. London: Swan Sonnenschein, 1889.

Petrarch (Francesco Petrarca). *Letters from Petrarch.* Sel. and trans. Morris Bishop. Bloomington: Indiana Univ. Press, 1966.

Pizer, Donald. "Self-Censorship and Textual Editing." In McGann, ed., *Textual Criticism and Literary Interpretation*, pp. 144–61.

Pratt, Robert A., ed. *The Tales of Canterbury Complete*. Boston: Houghton Mifflin, 1974.

Prete, Sesto. *Observations on the History of Textual Criticism in the Medieval and Renaissance Periods*. Collegeville, Minn.: St. John's Univ. Press, 1969.

Quentin, Dom Henri. *Essais de critique textuelle*. Paris: Libraire Auguste Picard, 1926.

Ramsey, R. Vance. "Paleography and Scribes of Shared Training." *Studies in the Age of Chaucer* 8 (1986): 107–44.

Ramus, Peter. *The Logike*. Trans. Roland Makilmenaeum. 1574. Rpt. Leeds: Scolar Press, 1966.

Reames, Sherry L. "A Recent Discovery concerning the Source of Chaucer's 'Second Nun's Tale.'" *Modern Philology* 87 (1990): 337–61.

Reeve, M. D. "Stemmatic Method: 'Qualcosa che non Funziona.'" In *The Role of the Book in Medieval Culture,* ed. Peter Ganz, 1:57–69. 2 vols. Turnholt: Brepols, 1986.

Reid, T. B. W. "The Right to Emend." In *Medieval French Textual Studies in Memory of T. B. W. Reid,* ed. Ian Short, pp. 1–32. ANTS Occasional Publication Series 1. London: Anglo-Norman Text Society, 1984.

Reiman, Donald H. "Gentlemen Authors and Professional Writers: Notes on the History of Editing Texts of the 18th and 19th Centuries." In Landon, ed., *Editing and Editors,* pp. 99–136.

———. "'Versioning': The Presentation of Multiple Texts." In *Romantic Texts and Contexts,* ed. Reiman, pp. 167–80. Columbia: Univ. of Missouri Press, 1987.

Revard, Carter. "*Gilote et Johanne:* An Interlude in B.L. MS. Harley 2253." *Studies in Philology* 79 (1982): 122–46.

Rigg, A. G., and Charlotte Brewer, eds. *Piers Plowman: The Z Version*. Toronto: Pontifical Institute of Medieval Studies, 1983.

Ritson, Joseph, ed. *Poems Written Anno MCCCLII*. London: J. H. Burn, 1825.

Robbins, R. H., ed. *Secular Lyrics of the XIVth and XVth Centuries*. Oxford: Clarendon Press, 1952.

Robinson, F. N., ed. *The Works of Geoffrey Chaucer*. 2d. ed. Boston: Houghton Mifflin, 1957.

Robortello, Francesco. *De arte sive ratione corrigendi antiquorum libros disputatio*. Ed. G. Pompella. Naples: Luigi Loffredo Editore, 1975.

Roerecke, Howard. "The Integrity and Symmetry of Robert Henryson's *Moral Fables*." Diss. Pennsylvania State Univ., 1969.

Saenger, Paul. "Silent Reading: Its Impact on Late Medieval Script and Society." *Viator* 13 (1982): 367–414.

Saenger, Paul, and Michael Heinlen. "Incunable Description and Its Implication for the Analysis of Fifteenth-Century Reading Habits." In Hindman, ed., *Printing the Written Word,* pp. 225–58.

Salutati, Collucio. *Colucii Salutati: De Laboribus Herculis.* Ed. Berthold Louis Ullman. 2 vols. Zurich: Societas Thesauri Mundi, 1951.

Sandys, John Edwin, ed. *A History of Classical Scholarship.* 1921. 2 vols. Rpt. New York: Hafner, 1958, 1964.

Sargent, Michael G. *James Grenehalgh as Textual Critic.* Analecta Cartusiana 85. 2 vols. Salzburg: Institüt für Anglistik und Amerikanistik, 1984.

Schlauch, Margaret. "The Art of Chaucer's Prose." In *Chaucer and Chaucerians: Critical Studies in Middle English Literature,* ed. D. S. Brewer, pp. 140–63. London: Thomas Nelson, 1966.

Schoeck, R. J. *Erasmus of Europe: The Making of a Humanist 1467–1500.* Savage, Md.: Barnes and Noble, 1990.

Scott, Kathleen L. "The Illustrations of *Piers Plowman* in Bodleian Library MS. Douce 104." *Yearbook of Langland Studies* 4 (1990): 1–86.

Seymour, Michael. "Manuscript Portraits of Chaucer and Hoccleve." *Burlington Magazine* 124 (1982): 618–23.

Shanks, Michael, and Christopher Tilley. *Re-Constructing Archaeology: Theory and Practice.* Cambridge: Cambridge Univ. Press, 1987.

———. *Social Theory and Archaeology.* Albuquerque: Univ. of New Mexico Press, 1987

Shillingsburg, Peter. "The Autonomous Author, the Sociology of Texts, and the Polemics of Textual Criticism." In Cohen, ed., *Devils and Angels,* pp. 22–43.

———. "An Inquiry into the Social Status of Texts and Modes of Textual Criticism." *Studies in Bibliography* 42 (1989): 55–79.

———. *Scholarly Editing in the Computer Age.* Athens: Univ. of Georgia Press, 1986.

———. "Text as Matter, Concept, and Action." *Studies in Bibliography* 44 (1991): 31–82.

Shonk, Timothy A. "A Study of the Auchinleck Manuscript: Bookmen and Bookmaking in the Early Fourteenth Century." *Speculum* 60 (1985): 71–91.

Spearing, A. C. "Central and Displaced Sovereignty in Three Medieval Poems." *Review of English Studies* n.s. 33 (1982): 247–61.

———. *Medieval to Renaissance in English Poetry.* Cambridge: Cambridge Univ. Press, 1985.

Speer, Mary B. "In Defense of Philology: Two New Guides to Textual Criticism." *Romance Philology* 32 (1979): 335–44.

———. "Textual Criticism Redivivus." *L'Esprit Créateur* 27 (1983): 38–48.

———. "Wrestling with Change: Old French Textual Criticism and *Mouvance.*" *Olifant* 7 (1980): 311–26.

Speght, Thomas, ed. *The Works of our Ancient and Learned English poet, Geoffrey Chaucer.* 2d ed. London: Adam Islip, 1602.

Stanley, E. G. "Unideal Principles of Editing Old English Verse." *Proceedings of the British Academy* 70 (1984): 231–73.

Stillinger, Jack. *Multiple Authorship and the Myth of the Solitary Genius.* Oxford: Oxford Univ. Press, 1991.

Sturges, Robert S. "Textual Scholarship: Ideologies of Literary Production." *Exemplaria* 3 (1991): 109–31.

Tanselle, G. Thomas. "Classical, Biblical, and Medieval Textual Criticism and Modern Editing." *Studies in Bibliography* 36 (1983): 21–68.

———. "The Editorial Problem of Final Authorial Intention." *Studies in Bibliography* 29 (1976): 167–211.

———. "Greg's Theory of Copy-Text and the Editing of American Literature." *Studies in Bibliography* 28 (1975): 167–229.

———. "Historicism and Critical Editing." *Studies in Bibliography* 39 (1986): 1–46.

———. *A Rationale of Textual Criticism.* Philadelphia: Univ. of Pennsylvania Press, 1989.

———. "Recent Editorial Discussion and the Central Questions of Editing." *Studies in Bibliography* 34 (1981): 22–65.

———. "Textual Criticism and Literary Sociology." *Studies in Bibliography* 44 (1991): 83–143.

Thomson, David, ed. *An Edition of the Middle English Grammatical Texts.* New York: Garland, 1984.

Thompson, Ann. *Shakespeare's Chaucer: A Study in Literary Origins.* New York: Barnes and Noble, 1978.

Thompson, Edward Maunde. *A Handbook of Greek and Latin Paleography.* 1901. Rpt. Chicago: Ares, 1966.

Thompson, John J. *Robert Thornton and the London Thornton Manuscript: British Library MS Additional 31042.* Cambridge: D. S. Brewer, 1987.

———. "Textual Instability and the Late Medieval Reputation of Some Middle English Religious Literature." *Text* 5 (1991): 175–94.

Thorpe, James. "The Aesthetics of Textual Criticism." In *Art and Error: Modern Textual Editing,* ed. Ronald Gottesman and Scott Bennett, pp. 62–101. Bloomington: Indiana Univ. Press, 1970.

———. *Principles of Textual Criticism.* San Marino: Huntington Library, 1972.

Thynne, William, ed. *The Workes of Geoffrey Chaucer Newly Printed.* London: Thomas Godfray, 1532.

Timpanaro, Sebastian. *Die Entstehung der Lachmannschen Methode.* 2d ed. Trans. Dieter Irmer. Hamburg: Helmut Buske Verlag, 1971.

———. *The Freudian Slip: Psychoanalysis and Textual Criticism.* Trans. Kate Soper. London: NLB, 1976.

Tolkien, J. R. R., ed. *Ancrene Wisse.* Intro. N. R. Ker. EETS o.s. 249. London: Oxford Univ. Press, 1962.

Trigg, Stephanie. "The Politics of Editing Medieval Texts: Knight's Quest and Love's Complaint." *Bibliographical Society of Australia and New Zealand Bulletin* 9 (1985): 15–22.

Trithemius, Johannes. *In Praise of Scribes: De Laude Scriptorum.* Ed. Klaus Arnold. Trans. Roland Behrendt. Lawrence, Kans.: Coronado Press, 1974.

Turville-Petre, Thorlac. "Editing *The Wars of Alexander.*" In Pearsall, ed., *Manuscripts and Texts,* pp. 143–60.

Uitti, Karl D., guest ed. "The Poetics of Textual Criticism: The Old French Example." *L'Esprit Créateur* 27 (1987).

Ullman, Berthold Louis. *The Humanism of Colluccio Salutati.* Padua: Editrice Antenore, 1963.

Urry, John, ed. *The Works of Geoffrey Chaucer.* London: Bernard Lintot, 1721.

Valla, Lorenzo. *Laurentii Valle antitodum in facium.* Ed. Mariangela Regoliosi. Padua: Editrice Antenore, 1981.

————. *Laurentii Valle Epistole.* Ed. Ottavio Besomi and Mariangela Regoliosi. Padua: Editrice Antenore, 1984.

————. *The Treatise of Lorenzo Valla on the Donation of Constantine.* Ed. and trans. Christopher B. Coleman. 1922. Rpt. New York: Russell and Russell, 1971.

Watson, Nicholas. *Richard Rolle and the Invention of Authority.* Cambridge: Cambridge Univ. Press, 1991.

Watt, Tessa. *Cheap Print and Popular Piety, 1550–1640.* Cambridge: Cambridge Univ. Press, 1991.

Wattenbach, W. *Das Schriftwesen im Mittelalter.* 3d ed. Leipzig: S. Hirzel, 1896.

Welleck, René, and Austin Warren. *Theory of Literature.* 3d ed. New York: Harcourt, Brace, Jovanovich, 1962.

West, Martin L. *Textual Criticism and Editorial Technique.* Stuttgart: Teubner, 1973.

White, Hayden. *Metahistory: The Historical Imagination in Nineteenth-Century Europe.* Baltimore: Johns Hopkins Univ. Press, 1973.

Whorf, Benjamin Lee. *Language, Thought, and Reality: Selected Writings of Benjamin Lee Whorf.* Ed. John B. Carroll. Boston: MIT Press, 1956.

Wilhelm, James J., ed. *Lyrics of the Middle Ages: An Anthology.* New York: Garland, 1990.

Williams, William Proctor, and Craig S. Abott. *An Introduction to Bibliographical and Textual Studies.* New York: MLA, 1985.

Wimsatt, W. K., and Monroe C. Beardsley. "The Intentional Fallacy." *Sewanee Review* 54 (1946): 468–88.

Wing, Donald. *Short-Title Catalogue of Books Printed in England, Scotland, Ireland, Wales, and British America and of English Books Printed in Other Countries, 1641–1700.* 2d ed. 3 vols. New York: MLA, 1972.

Witt, Ronald G. *Hercules at the Crossroads: The Life, Works, and Thought of Colluccio Salutati.* Durham: Duke Univ. Press, 1983.

Wolf, Friedrich August. *Prolegomena to Homer.* Trans. Anthony Grafton, Glenn W. Most, and James E. G. Zetzel. Princeton: Princeton Univ. Press, 1981.

Woods, Marjorie Curry. "Editing Medieval Commentaries: Problems and a Proposed Solution." *Text* 1 (1981): 133–45.

Woolf, Rosemary. *The English Religious Lyric in the Middle Ages.* Oxford: Clarendon Press, 1968.

Wright, C. E. "The Dispersal of the Monastic Libraries and the Beginnings of Anglo-Saxon Studies." *Transactions of the Cambridge Bibliographical Society* 1 (1949–53): 208–37.

Wright, Herbert C. *A Seventeenth-Century Modernisation of the First Three Books of Chaucer's "Troilus and Criseyde."* Bern: Francke Verlag, 1968.

Yeager, Robert F. "English, Latin, and the Text as 'Other': The Page as Sign in the Work of John Gower." *Text* 3 (1987): 251–67.

————, ed. *Fifteenth-Century Studies, Recent Essays.* Hamden, Conn.: Archon Books, 1984

Zeller, Hans. "A New Approach to the Critical Constitution of Literary Texts." *Studies in Bibliography* 28 (1975): 231–64.

Zumthor, Paul. *Essai de poétique médiévale.* Paris: Seuil, 1972.

INDEX

Index

Sellyng, Richard, 174
Shelley, Percy Bysshe, 77, 182
Shillingsburg, Peter, 6–7, 67–68
Shirley, John, 174
Sidnam, Jonathon, 41
Sir Beues of Hamtoun, 160, 165, 167
Sir Ferumbras, 167
Sir Gawain and the Green Knight, 50, 99
Sir Launfal, 103
Sir Orfeo, 99, 165, 167
Skelton, John, 133
Snorri Sturluson, 112, 150
Socialization of the text, 61, 66–69, 72, 74, 180, 184, 206; relation to Anglo-American editing, 74
Society for Early English and Norse Electronic Texts, 220
South English Legendary, 164
Spearing, A. C., 126, 212
Speer, Mary B., 199; *see also* Foulet, Alfred
Speght, Thomas, 41–44, 89–90
Statute of Pleading, 150–51
Stow, John, 88
Suetonius, 17

Tale of Beryn, 163
Tale of Jack and the Stepdame, 61
Tale of Jack Upland, 88
Tanselle, G. Thomas, 33, 35, 65–66, 68–69, 72, 204
Text, 6–7, 138; as commodity, 75–76; medieval conception of, 141–45, 153–57, 161–69, 174, 179–81; *see also* Authoritative text
Textual criticism: applied to non-English traditions, 1–2, 40, 48, 50, 201; discursive field of, 81–82, 84, 91–92, 162, 168–69, 178, 184, 193; ethical orientation, 15, 31–33, 60, 79; European development, 16; historical orientation of, 71–72, 193; history of, 14–38; ideology of, 16–18, 27, 31, 35, 184; institutional sanctions of, 17–18, 70–71, 79, 88–89, 134; of Old English, 1, 48, 205; relation of Middle English to, 6, 39–41, 52, 112, 167–68, 178–79, 204; relations to humanism, 14–19, 27, 31, 35, 79, 139, 177–78, 183; relations to literary interpretation, 32, 33, 53, 220; theoretical hierarchy of, 70–74, 77, 183; as tradition, 33–36, 38, 59–61; *see also* Anglo-American tradition of editing; Bible; Edited text; Editions of Middle English; Editorial theory of Middle English; Humanism; Philology
Textual transmission, 21, 59, 158–60, 168

Thomas, Timothy, 44
Thorpe, James, 67–68
Thynne, William: edition of the *Boece,* 158, 187, 217; edition of Chaucer's *Workes,* 88–89, 91, 203
Timpanaro, Sebastian, 21, 22
Tolkien, J. R. R., 50
Translation, 2, 72, 143–44
Trevet, Nicholas, 159–60
Trevisa, John, 148
Trithemius, Johannes, 170, 173–74
Tuke, Brian, 88–89
Tyrwhitt, Thomas, 42, 91

Urry, John, 44, 90–91
Usk, Thomas, 86, 109, 152, 163

Vafþrúðnismál, 1, 2
Valla, Lorenzo, 16, 21, 29, 34, 57; on *Donation of Constantine,* 28, 30, 31
Veltori, Pier, 28
Vergil, 96
Vernacular authorship, 57–58, 97–98, 118, 131–35, 179–80, 208; contest over, 113–31, 135, 179; self-definition of, 101–5, 147; stylistic negotiations of, 99–110, 132, 135; traditions of, 111–12, 201; *see also* Anonymity of Middle English works
Version, 6–7
Versioning, 180
Vidal, Sir Raimon, 150

Walton, John, 161, 162
The Waste Land, 94–95, 133–34
Wellek, René, and Austin Warren, 52, 53
White, Hayden, 80–83
Whitman, Walt, 7, 58
Whorf, Benjamin Lee, 37
William of Aragon, 159, 166, 187
William of Conche, 158–59
Williams, William, and Craig Abott, 2
Wilson, Thomas, 149
Wimsatt, W. K., and Monroe C. Beardsley, 54
Wolf, F. A., 20, 21, 29, 31, 178
Wordsworth, William, 7, 57, 58
Work, 6–7, 138; lexical ontology of, 12–13, 27–31, 43, 45, 47, 65–66, 68, 82, 168, 177–78, 186; materialist conception of, 66–67; medieval conception of, 141–45, 157–69, 174, 179–81, 184–86, 191
Wycliffite Bible, 97, 151–52
Wycliffite sermons, 5, 170

Zumthor, Paul, 199